WALKING IN THE LIGHT

A FOOT PILGRIMAGE FROM THE HAGUE TO JERUSALEM

JOHANNA VAN FESSEM

Walking in the Light

ISBN 978-0-9926086-0-6

Published by
Dancing Mountain, Glastonbury
email: dancingmountain@outlook.com

first published as 'Lopen in het licht'
(ISBN 90 6416 3863)
by DABAR-LUYTEN Heeswijk
The Netherlands
in 2002

Translated from the Dutch by the author.

Typesetting and layout by Red Dog Books
Printed and bound in Great Britain
by imprint*digital*.net

To the boy with the autumn crocuses

Acknowledgements

This book has been compiled from a selection of diary letters written to my friend Joke Visser. I especially thank my friend, who - by her unconditional love, support and way of listening and reading - has stimulated me to write down everything on the way that touched and moved me.

I thank Ales Vanek, who designed my happy website and kept it up to date while I was walking.

I thank my children for their unwavering support.

All sponsors I thank for the enthusiastic reactions on my plan and their financial and spiritual support. Many people have supported me at home and on the road with letters and positive thoughts. They have especially helped me, as have all those whom I met on the road and offered me their hospitality and protection.

November 2001

Ever since my move from The Hague to Glastonbury in England in 2008, my new English friends have been urging me to have 'Lopen in het licht' translated into 'Walking in the light.' Especially Ian Brodrick, chairman of the Confraternity of Pilgrims to Jerusalem and a walker himself, has been unrelentingly pushing me into undertaking this massive task. And although I was very reluctant to start on it, the result is now lying before you. I also thank my editor Sofia Hansrod in New Zealand for the diligent editing of the text and undoing it of many 'Dutchisms'.

Last but not least I thank my partner Steve Leighton for his patience and kindness while I was concentrating relentlessly on the translation.

March 2013
Johanna van Fessem

Contents

Introduction

Jerusalem, City of Peace, City of Conflict. I have always had a strong connection to Jerusalem. From the prophesies in the Bible, and, from political developments during the last decades, I knew that there an important key to world peace is to be found. Peace in Jerusalem will have such a strong effect in the world, that it might be the beginning of world peace. Jerusalem is the focal point of three important monotheistic religions, Judaism, Christianity and Islam, and political and religious convictions exist here in inseparable entanglement.

I visited Israel for the first time in 1987, before the first intifada. When I stepped out of the bus, arriving at Jerusalem bus station, the first thing I saw was a large poster with the words of Psalm 122:

'Pray for the Peace of Jerusalem
They shall prosper that love thee.
Peace be within thy walls
And prosperity within thy palaces.'

One year later, in 1988, as I am walking the South West Coast Path in England, I see the distant white cliffs of Lyme Regis which bring to mind the connection to Israel through the legends of Joseph of Arimathea and his coming to Glastonbury with the Grail.

A few days later I meet an unknown Glastonbury man in the Undercliff Wood, just west of Lyme Regis. He recites to me a song about Glastonbury being the New Jerusalem. I know I have to visit Glastonbury to make a connection from there to the Old Jerusalem.

It is on this day that I am inspired to walk to Jerusalem to pray for its peace. But I dismiss the idea immediately as being impossible - too dangerous and too irresponsible. I have two small children and no money whatsoever.

7

I visit Glastonbury, climb the Tor and have an unexpected experience of unearthly peace and innocence, of a different Christianity still at ease with creation, plants, animals and nature-spirits. I connect with the Temple Mount in Jerusalem, the Dome of the Rock, where, one year before, I had another experience of deep and overwhelming grace.

August 1999. Eleven years later I take the first step. I lay a ruler over the map of Europe from The Hague to Jerusalem. The straight line runs through Middle and Eastern Europe to Turkey. Later I learn that the line Netherlands – Jerusalem, and its parallel line, the line Lyme Regis – Paris – Gizeh – Mecca, are part of a terrestrial pattern and ley line structure called 'the Abraham Triangle'.

For me, the distance as the crow flies is 3,500 kilometres. So I estimate the walking distance to be 5,000 kilometres and the walking time one year. My children have left home, my working contract will finish next February. It is the year 2000, the year I always imagined I would walk, but still I have no money.

Then, around Christmas, my father gives each of his children a surprise gift. It is the equivalent of 3,600 Euro. I didn't know he had money to give, and, HE doesn't know that I am contemplating a walk to Jerusalem! As I estimate it, 3,600 Euro is not entirely enough, but I could start with that!

On Boxing Day I decide that I will go. It feels so good; it feels so utterly right.

Within a week after I have told my friends, all the money needed for the trip is brought together. I estimate the total cost to be about 5,400 Euros. I have been asking for loans, but I have also received gifts. Now I get really scared. I know I have to go for real! In Jerusalem and America there are preparations for important peace talks between Israeli Prime Minister Barak and Palestinian leader Arafat.

I leave my home on April 2, 2000, a solitary walker carrying my tent and sleeping bag in a backpack, camping out during most of the walk. Many good things have happened on my way to Jerusalem. Nobody and nothing has harmed me.

During my walk I call on churches, monasteries, convents, synagogues, mosques, earth power places, meditation centres, spiritual organisations and individual people, to ask them to pray with me for the peace of Jerusalem. I also collect written prayers on small slips of paper, carrying the good thoughts of the people in a physical way through the whole of Western Europe, to bring the good energy of the teachings that reached us from the Middle East in the past, back to its roots in Jerusalem, together with the green wisdom of our more temperate regions.

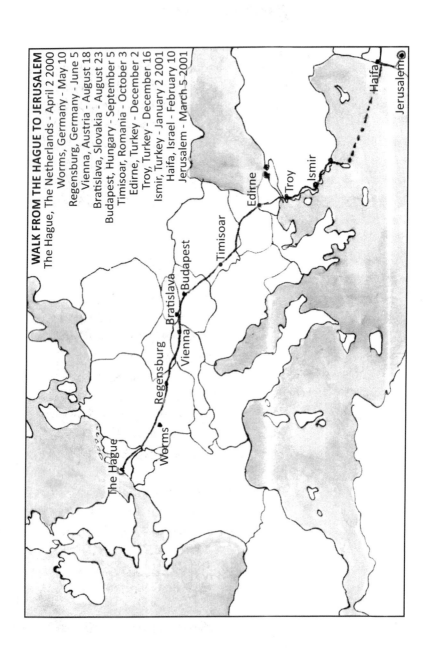

WALK FROM THE HAGUE TO JERUSALEM

The Hague, The Netherlands - April 2 2000
Worms, Germany - May 10
Regensburg, Germany - June 5
Vienna, Austria - August 18
Bratislava, Slovakia - August 23
Budapest, Hungary - September 5
Timisoar, Romania - October 3
Edirne, Turkey - December 2
Troy, Turkey - December 16
Ismir, Turkey - January 2 2001
Haifa, Israel - February 10
Jerusalem - March 5 2001

THE NETHERLANDS

Sunday April 2, 2000

This morning the weather is beautiful. I must rise early since I failed to finish packing last night. I am putting shampoo and night cream in little plastic containers instead of their heavy glass ones; I am cutting plasters to stick on any future blisters; making a Jerusalem sign to attach to the back of my rucksack and more of these trivialities. I am still not ready even after all this preparation in the months before. I check my rucksack, thirteen kilos without food and water. The tent and sleeping bag are well attached.

At 10.00 am some friends are coming to see me off. My children are already here. We go to my meditation spot in the little park-wood of Don Bosco, just behind my house. Thirteen years ago I laid an Indian medicine wheel there: a ceremonial circle of stones as a compass on the four directions. I walk round the wheel a few times and make a thorough connection with the North, East, South and West. To the south-east Jerusalem lies, far away behind three trees and a church spire; behind the horizon. Here in the forest spring is bursting. I embrace my beech tree. It is good to go, very, very good. I embrace my children, my friends and I leave them behind at the tree; they wave at me. I wave back and turn the first corner.

I am on my way.

I walk through familiar streets, pass familiar trees along familiar canals. I walk slowly and savour my mood; this trustfulness and balance. I am tuning in to the Dome of the Rock on Temple Mount in Jerusalem. I feel peaceful. I walk more than two hours wearing my new walking boots. Then, when the new boots are rubbing too much against my old feet, I change them for my old worn walking boots which dangle temporarily in a bag in front of my belly. I haven't had the time to break the new ones in.

I decide sixteen kilometres east to Zoetermeer is enough for the first day. I walk along the motorway on the bicycle path. I can't pee on the side of the road; too many people are passing, but at a tea kiosk there is a toilet. I drink a cup of tea, but I am not allowed to pay. A man with a golden ring in his ear, a black moustache, beer belly and two big dogs under the table pays for my tea and wants to know everything.

Coming nearer to Zoetermeer I walk through the Westerpark. A creepy man ogles me sideways. I take a different path, but another suspicious man is making dishonourable remarks. There are too many creepy men to avoid. I must face them! So I push on and continue to walk. My hip joints are hurting!

Under a white blossoming tree I write to my mother. Of course I said goodbye to her yesterday, but I haven't been able yet, with too many people around, to really tell her what is in my heart. I carry her Grail badge on my jacket. The Dutch Grail Movement, the great inspiration in her youth, was a movement for the emancipation of young Catholic women. On the badge the cup and the sword/cross are depicted in blue, red and golden enamel, pointing at the Quest for the Holy Grail. Jerusalem is the city where the Grail came from. My mother's courage and valour have always inspired me. Now she sits in desperation on the sofa. Will you not give me your blessing, my mother? Will you not be proud of me? Will you not love me with faith and with trust? And with your courage and your power?

In Zoetermeer a friend waits for me in her clean and peaceful home in a garden full of spring flowers. Marja has cooked an excellent organic meal. I may initiate her new guestroom. A little icon is perched on the bed stand: 'the Entrance of Jesus in Jerusalem'. A suitable subject! She pampers me as if I were a queen.

Monday, April 3
She is coming with me, the difficult second day. My muscles hurt and my feet are sore. We walk twenty one kilometres to Gouda over tarmac, along blossoming magnolias, little lambs in the meadow, green budding trees, daffodils everywhere; across quiet lanes where unexpected cars flash by. She carries my second pair of shoes in a bag, when they become too heavy for me.

It is a wonderful day, a heavy day with this untrained body.

Tuesday, April 4
I walk along the river IJssel to Haastrecht. After a little rain in the early morning the sun is radiating again and the magnolias are flowering, but I am like a hypochondriac fretting about my health. I worry about a lump on my foot, a stressed muscle in my left calf, a lost bone in my right knee.

When I see the church spire of Haastrecht I attach the Jerusalem sign to my rucksack. I want to ask the priest of the Salvator Church to write a prayer slip for Jerusalem. Also I long to be in front of the old pilgrim statue of St. Mary-on-the-Road to ask for her blessing, and light a candle for my loved ones.

My cousin Christine and I meet in front of the chapel. She is the next friend, who will walk a distance with me. There she is, waiting for me in her thick black overcoat. After calling at the chapel, the door is opened by a lady, who says the chapel is not open for prayer. Well, then I will do my 'Hail Marys' in the porch!

We walk along the little river of the Vlist. The orchards are not yet in bloom, but yellow explosions of marsh marigolds illuminate the waterside. Here and there are some early cuckoo flowers, celandines, red campions, daisies and dandelions. The willows have been carefully pollarded this year. It is a clean and orderly land with well-kept little farms, long, intensely green meadows and clear cut tarmac roads.

13

Nothing reminds me of the fact that I am walking through the Dutch Bible-belt, but only the name of this farm: *'Dwaalt Gij, wacht Ik'*: 'While you roam, I wait'.

The horizon is green and far and wide; a group of trees, a church spire. This land is all sky, air and wind. At Schoonhoven we arrive at the first one of three great Dutch rivers to be crossed in order to walk south: the Lek. A little passenger ferry will take us over. Low sunlight shines over the river; a freight boat steams by. Its name is *'Confidentia'* - Trust. "You must write that down," says my cousin.

After we cross the river, the sun is ready to set. It is getting cold. The wind is bleak and strong. It flails over the flat polder land between Nieuwpoort and Groot-Ammers. At a farm we ask permission to pitch the tent on the lee side of the house. It is half past nine; a moment of meditation and we go to sleep. It is my cousin's first camping night ever and it is cold. The kind woman of the farm has given us an extra duvet for the night and towards the morning we really need it.

Wednesday, April 5

Today the wind is even bleaker than yesterday and we cannot meditate outside, so we do it in the tent. The sun however shines beautifully and our path is leading us through the flat, deserted polder of the Alblasserwaard. It goes over dikes overgrown thickly with grass; the daisies and the celandines keep their flowers tightly closed today because of the cold strong wind. There aren't yet any cattle in the vivid green meadows extending beyond the eye. Rows of pollarded willows stand along the long ditches. Windmills raise themselves on the dikes along the wide quiet canals; bridges bend gracefully over their waters. Old farmsteads are scattered sparsely over the land. There is not a man, nor a beast in sight; high, wide, blue skies with wind-feather clouds above the ruler-straight endless horizon; light and thin copses here and there. The distant spire of a church tower is pointing towards the sky.

Walking over the grass, away from the long straight metalled roads, it is easy to pray the Our Father in this land of the Lord.

At the end of the day we rest on a bench. A rough graffiti on it says: 'The Lord is God!'

I haven't had much success with my mission as yet. In Groot-Ammers, while calling on the Reformed Centre, we walk by mistake into a gathering of Bible-reading women. I am allowed to talk about my trip and the prayer slips for peace in the Middle East, which I want to gather, but they are a bit overwhelmed by my sudden appearance. The same thing happens in Bleskensgraaf, in the Bible shop. At the churches and the parsonages where I call, nobody is at home.

Because a night frost has been forecast and it was already very cold last night, we want to go into a B&B. We hope to find one in Hardinxveld, but no, the people in the pub say there are no B&Bs in the village. In the pub we call every hotel in the neighbourhood. All are fully booked! None of the customers knows anything and they don't offer any help either. Without any results we walk out of the light and warmth of the pub into the darkening dusk. With stumbling feet, aching shoulders and stiff legs, we walk on in the frosty darkness. We'll have to camp. In the back of an allotment garden we find an illegal quiet place. We keep our clothes on as we shuffle into our sleeping bags. The stars are shining and radiating in peace over our heads.

Thursday, April 6
But we don't sleep. It is too cold. According to St. Francis the true joy is, when you have been refused a roof over your head five times in bad weather by one's fellow human beings that

you don't get angry and you don't get sad. I am not angry and I am not sad, but I feel cold, tired and homeless.

The next morning ice is breaking in sharp slivers from the inside canvas of our tent. When we open the front flap, we see a thick frost on the grass and the trees before us. The glory of the rising sun mirrors itself radiantly white and blue in the broad canal.

Monday, April 10

Yesterday we have crossed the last of the three wide rivers which divide the Netherlands into a northern and a southern part and after walking the first 150 kilometres from The Hague (we are very proud!), we arrived in 's-Hertogenbosch in the province of Brabant. The country south of the Great Rivers is Roman Catholic country. The northern austere, clear, clean, conscientious and strict atmosphere has changed into southern informal jolliness; people are laid-back and warm here and I enjoy it.

It is time for my cousin to go back to Amsterdam and I wave her off from the train platform. My hip joints are aching and I take a day of rest. I stay in a B&B with a hippie family. My room is unheated and it is cold, that is why I feel ill today. On top of that the children spat fresh chewing gum on my bedroom floor, paying a visit to my room while I was out taking a stroll. Coming back I step into it unawares so now it is stuck onto my brand new expensive walking socks for ever and ever.

Nice things are happening too, but again and again, with the slightest cause, a feeling of homelessness overcomes me. 'Foxes have dens and birds have nests, but the child of man doesn't have a stone to put her head on.' I know my home is in myself and must wait and persevere until the gloom will lift by itself. It always does.

Afternoon

At this very moment I am sitting in front of 'The Sweet Mother of Den Bosch' in the only cathedral of the Netherlands. It is a miracle working statue of The Virgin Mary, centre of a special devotion. She is a slim little figure, carved in wood, early Gothic 13th century. Over her carved clothes, she wears a red, velvet, gold stitched mantle, reaching far over her feet. She carries a minute infant on her left arm and both are crowned with golden crowns. She has a funny black nose and black dirty cheeks. What a petite, happy and almost mischievous little queen she is! She will not be discouraged by any sort of misery. She wipes off all the tears that are brought to her by the people with a smile. She doesn't give consolation in the ordinary way. She doesn't indulge in your sorrow. When I close my eyes I see behind her a spider's web full of tears. All those tears and the web are transformed by the sunlight into a glistening net full of little diamonds. And she? She is merry and laughs and teases: "Look, this is how your sorrow can become!"

This is a cheerful statue in a cheerful city. I have become cheerful myself.

Wednesday, April 12

Montfoort, 07.00 pm, twenty three effortless kilometres today! Although my hip joints are still bothering me, my mood is excellent. In a roadside chapel next to an old holy well there is space for one prayer chair only. I burn a candle and feel a wave of wondrous tenderness.

In Roermond I visit the Minster. The volunteers who are taking care of the church are very interested in my walk. I tell them about the prayer for Jerusalem and they fill in my first prayer slips with their personal prayer.

After having walked out of the city I ask permission to pitch my tent next to a farmhouse. It is cold. The high-voltage masts above my head are buzzing. I put my plastic cover over the tent, because a thunder storm has been forecast. The roof of my little tent can cope with ordinary rainfall, but not with a downpour.

Thursday, April 13
What a night! Not a drop of rain fell, not a single thunderbolt struck, but all the time the plastic on my tent was crackling and rustling with the smallest breath of wind and kept waking me up. In the end I went out into the moonlight to take it off.

This morning an ice cold breeze is blowing. I have been sleeping with all my clothes on again, so I don't need to dress and I only have to wash my face. I walk through the stifling wind across the plains of Montfoort. I put my gloves on and wrap a woollen scarf round my head. I enjoy everything. I sing how wonderful it is to be on the road. When I rest a moment under a stately oak tree, tenderness is flowing through me, not human tenderness but plant-tree-earth-wind tenderness. Through it the face of a woman is showing. My own face? The Great Mother's face?

At eleven in the morning I arrive at the abbey of Lilbosch; I know it well from former visits. I arrived much earlier than I thought. I am shown my familiar room, take a hot bath and savour the special smell of the abbey: floor wax with incense. I feel welcome, I feel at home. Outside it has started to rain. The rain lashes vehemently for hours against the stained-glass church windows. From inside I can see it stream down the panes. In white warm, woollen cloaks the monks are singing the praise of God. And I sing with them.

Saturday, April 15
I had an impressive good bye talk with Brother John of the abbey. For the first time I could feel in my heart something of the What or the Who that moves him. It came together with a

feeling of great remorse. I don't know what it was about, but it made a great opening to Christ and even though it was in an orthodox way, it was also deep and authentic. I realised that I had always rejected Divine love and that this had hurt Him.

Palm Sunday, April 16

Annemarie has joined me. She is the last of my Dutch chums to see me to the border. As usual she is a happy and trustworthy company. We walk through gullies of little streams, forests, quiet small hills and valleys. In the distance we see the mega-industrial cities of Geleen and Heerlen. The wayside flowers are opening; the forest floor and the fields are covered with anemones, celandines, purple and white dead nettle, cowslips, dandelions, daisies. The orchards begin to blossom, brooks are murmuring, the forest awakens.

Around 09.00 pm we find a place to camp on the edge of the forest, in the corner of a field. A sweet breeze is passing; it isn't cold. Two one-person tents stand next to each other.

We are peaceful.

GERMANY

Maundy Thursday, April 20

My friend has said goodbye in Aachen and now I am walking by myself deeper and deeper into Germany. It is quite an experience to find the E8, the long distance foot path running from Ireland to Bratislava. I connect to a greater complexity: the whole of Europe.

Last night I slept alone in a beech wood. A thick layer of brown leaves is crackling under my feet as I walk. The trees are without any new leaves yet. The colours of the forest are brown and beige. A lot of sunlight plays between the bare branches and there is hardly any shade. This morning I can wash myself in a little running brook for the first time this trip. It is so refreshing! What is more beautiful than washing in a brook in the early morning light, while the sun is filtering through the bare branches and the birds are singing? I dry myself with a rough towel, put on all my warm pullovers again and am ready to face the whole world.

One thing is bad. Today I walked through beautiful forests, but the complete path seems to be tarmacked. Only once in a while there is a short un-tarmacked piece of path to help me keep courage. Tarmac is tiring me so! Mother Earth is forced to harden her face, not only on main roads but also on her sweet byways, where there is no necessity at all. My own heart is hardening because of it.

The hills here in the Eifel are fairly high. I pick up a strong stick to help me on the steep bits. It is pleasant to walk with a stick. Walking sticks are like extended front paws. Our bodies are really distorted when you compare them to the body of a cat or a dog. Look at our weak and shrunken front paws attached to the clumsy erected spine resting on a strange voluptuous rear end with proportionally very long hind paws.

And it occurs to me how strange it is for a mammal to walk on two legs only!

Everything in this little part of Germany is glowing with dedicated perfection; the houses, the farms, the forests. I walk through well-cared-for, well-organised forests where in measured and fenced plots of ground 'Nature may go its own way'. Where there might be rabies, the foxes are not shot, but pieces of meat with vaccine are laid. Signs have been erected with friendly but urgent requests not to frighten and chase away the wildlife by for example waving or crinkling pieces of white paper. And 'Stay on the path'.

In the Dutch part of Limburg you don't find just road crosses, but also little chapels in which Our Lady is standing. She also adorns the facade of many a farm. The atmosphere there is sweet and light, but here in the Eifel I don't find any St. Mary figurines and on the road crosses you can read edifying rhymes and admonitions. I feel more the quality of discipline than the quality of indulgence and yielding. Passing through a village I even see a sign at a parking lot: 'Forbidden to play'.

Then, in a bend of the forest road, just before I arrive at the highest point of a hill, five slim white wind turbines arise. They are very tall and planted in a perfectly curving green hillside. Their long wings turn and turn gracefully against a deep blue sky. It is almost like a vision, angels descending from heaven to bring energy from above to the people on earth. A large part of the village of Schmidt is powered by the electricity of these wind turbines.

At seven o'clock at night Maundy Thursday Mass is celebrated in Schmidt. It runs perfect and smooth, like everything here. The mass takes a long time, until quarter to nine. It is too dark now to find a camping spot. I am invited by a member of the congregation to stay at his house; a warm bed, a hot shower, warm people, who give the guest room a big cleaning before I can go in. I am not allowed to do anything. They are strict Catholics, no meat on Friday, to mass every Sunday, active in the parish in confirmation classes. But they also pour herbal tea at breakfast, cut good bread, only eat organic free range meat and separate rubbish in organic and inorganic. They tell me that in Heimbach, further en route, is a pilgrimage place of St. Mary at the monastery of Mariawald. I hope that I may be a guest for the Easter days there.

Good Friday

I sit on top of a hill called Hubertusheight. Beneath me I see a wide blue lake, a reservoir. It is 11.00 am. A heavy, good silence lies like a veil over the land; there is no activity anywhere. Everything is closed on Good Friday in Germany. I walk on. More and more walkers appear. It is warm. For the first time ever I take off my woollen jumper. I walk together for a while with a family of three generations.

Granny, happy, light blue T-shirt over leggings, a walking stick in her hand, tells me that for several generations now her family makes a walking pilgrimage to the Abbey of Mariawald (Mary's Forest) on Good Friday to pray at the Stations of the Cross there. Every year — she tells me — it is her last time. It becomes more and more difficult for her to kneel down at every station, but every year she is still there. Because of the devotion, the spring, the special loaf she bakes for on the road and because of the joy. "We are of farmers' descent," she says and points to a tall man with a baseball cap, wild black hair, metallic sunglasses and T-shirt with skull. He pushes a buggy with a baby. The older grandchildren are playing around and logging thick branches to shove them in the lake to make them drift. Two young mothers are chatting while walking and peeling oranges for their offspring. When they arrive at the abbey, they will all will join following in prayer the Stations of the Cross.

And all of us walk through this divine forest, along the reservoir with the wooded high rising hills behind it. Parts of the hillside are green with firs and pines. Among them, in very bright green the larches are showing off their new needles. Other bits are still brown and dry. In a week they will be full of foliage too. Halfway on the hillside small currant and wild cherry trees have started to blossom. The willows are showing and the birches too with their elegant haze of green, almost invisible buds. I sit beneath an old oak; I cannot discern anything yet of him, apart from fat red buds.

I think about something that my hostess said to me this morning when I told her about the objective of my walk: to pray for peace in the Middle East. She thought that the Jewish people would be persecuted for ever. She didn't believe in peace there. I often hear that. But I don't believe that. No way. Because my gut feeling says, that EVERYTHING SHALL BE ALRIGHT; completely and wholly.

I always become very peaceful when I formulate my arguments: I know it *will* be OK. I don't hope it. I know it. That's why I'm going. And that anti-Semitic argument about being persecuted for all times, that is simple nonsense. That is not necessary anymore, if it ever was. And then I adorn that nicely with some biblical prophesies and a few thoughts of my own. Well, there you go. Perhaps my guts don't always speak the truth!

I walk on. '*Floret, floret, floret, silvas undique*'. The forest flowers everywhere. I am so happy today. Today I find Germany and the Eifel perfect.

In Heimbach I arrive exactly on time to go the service at 02.30pm in the Pilgrims' church. However my heart has closed somehow. I look at the 'miraculous' *pietà*: she is an upset older woman with a peasant face; in her lap she holds a shrunken, stiffened corpse. I feel nothing, nothing at all. The church is modern; it has a large black vault. It is dark on my eyes. Stone walls, stone floor there is not one ornament, not one candle today. The service is well put together, well timed, oiled texts, oiled answers from the congregation. Sterile; I don't feel connected. I don't listen to the texts anymore. Beneath those texts something is moving in dark hollow emptiness. It is Good Friday after all. At exactly three o'clock the sun disappears behind rain clouds. Darkness enters the church.

I walk on from Heimbach to Mariawald. Not just the Good Friday darkness, but also the tarmac is now slowly entering my soul. In the Abbey there is no space for me. The guestrooms are all taken. I had expected that. But I am not even allowed to pitch my tent near the Abbey. All the land around it is 'clausuur': shut off from the public for the monks, taboo even for guests.

As strict as the rules are, as gentle is the monk who has to tell me this. He is a bit worried about what I am going to do now. I will walk on, direction Gemünd, but before I take a round of the abbey shop and the abbey cafe.

With my pilgrim's staff and my The Hague – Jerusalem sign, I have been noticed by a few café customers. They accost me and we speak together. They are sensible people (they are not immediately falling in adoration at my feet because of my project) and they confront me with my own doubts about passing the Balkan Peninsula on my own. They formulate exactly, that which has been bothering me in the back of my head: 'You are putting God to the test.' I explain how I see it, and that I am not sure how to cross the Balkan myself. I love it so much to be on my own. I even don't want to think about having the company of a stranger or even an acquaintance. I don't want to live together so closely for at least three months.

The conversation does something to me, as if a balloon has been deflated. I throw my pilgrim's staff away. People make so called jokes about it from which it is apparent that they think I want to beat them with it. What on earth makes them think that?! I had picked it up as support for my walking, but secretly it also gave me pilgrim's status. It was too conspicuous. I walk on. I conscientiously follow the markings of the E8, while I think: I don't feel well. What am I going to do?

1. Put God to the test? I don't want that. What I do want is:
2. Learn how to trust Him/Her/Existence more and more.

There is a subtle difference; I feel it, but cannot formulate it.

Suddenly I notice, that I am walking west instead of east. I've been following the wrong road already for two kilometres. I understand I must change something. I have to bow my stubborn head and admit that I am doing 1 and not 2.

It is Good Friday. I am standing in front of one of the many Way crosses. I do *teshuwa* - turn around: 'conversion'. The tarmac around my heart is breaking. Tears flow; for two kilometres on the way back my tears are flowing. I shall need company in the Balkan, in Romania, Bulgaria or Yugoslavia and even in Turkey. And I don't want it; I hate it. Because I will lose my freedom; I will have to fight for my own space. I shall have to give in where I don't want to. I shall have to make compromises. I shall have to connect for real to another person. I shall have to accept the guardian angel that life sends me.

I know that in my life making real connections is a central theme. It makes sense. To go to Jerusalem is to throw off everything superfluous and that goes much deeper than 'Johanna has done it all on her own'. I already feel my ego inflating.

I surrender. I submit, my Lord/Lady, it is alright. I have understood. It makes sense. I promise I will look for company to cross the Balkan Peninsula. I will search via internet and friends.

At this moment I arrive at the point where I went wrong. Now I go for the right way.

I camp near Wolfgarten and take off the 'The Hague – Jerusalem' sign from my rucksack. It provoked a lot of discussion and that was fine and my intention, but it was also disguised bragging. I knew that, and it is not terrible, but it doesn't suit this moment. I must turn completely inwards and afterwards we'll see. Now I'm at peace again.

Easter Saturday, April 22

But the next morning I wake up with a feeling of hangover. I cannot meditate. I cannot pray. I feel disconnected again. It sounds childish, but it seems as if I'm doing something wrong and that is why I don't dare to pray and go closer to God. I seem to have a bad conscience, only I don't know what about. It is as if something very old is emerging: I am not allowed to exist. I am evil. Sitting on a roadside bench I start researching what it is and find that it is connected with the feeling deep inside me, that I have abandoned my mother. She is old and sad and I am her favourite daughter. I feel guilty, but I also get angry. I'm HER child, she is not MY child! I don't need to be her mother. And: 'Who is MY mother then?' I've been my own mother all my life. I shout angrily: "Go to your husband (my father) when you are sad. Let him give you consolation. Or go to Mother Mary. Why did you stop praying? I don't want to be your mother anymore. I've been your mother all my life. Always you have come to me with your complaints and your worries, and I don't want it anymore. Find your own solution!"

I know that she can't do it and I know my father wouldn't listen to her. A bad conscience, anger, compassion and understanding are fighting for prevalence. I pick a twig from the ground, it is a Y-shape and furiously I break off one of the ends. I say: "I'm going my own way, and you have to do that too!"

For a moment I am breathless at the fact that I dare to say this to my mother, even although she doesn't hear this. After that I feel relief and liberation and have I come back into balance. And of course my mother is not only sad and old, because she also is honest, loving, caring and selfless.

Thinking back on the whole matter I suspect also that these feelings of guilt are not just my issue with my mother. I wonder whether it has something to do with the buffer country that the Eifel is. It is between France and Germany and in 1945 there were terrible battles here which cost 65.000 people their life. Also I feel a sort of tortured twisted energy; matter which has been under great pressure. The Eifel consists of old volcanic mountains. It was the bottom of the sea in old times and — according to the theory — has been pushed up as mountains in a very short time.

Good things are happening again. Somebody shows me the health food shop in Gemund. I didn't even ask for it. Another shows me the only B&B in the whole region, also unsolicited. I want to sleep inside for two nights, because I want to go to the Easter Vigil and the High Mass. I cannot make an Easter table with a flower arrangement and painted eggs while walking, so I need extra organ music.

The Inn in Vollem is one kilometre from a 17th century church with old grave stones in an untidy little village. (Oi, this is the first untidy village that I pass in the Eifel!) The Inn is also a little untidy, just like the service. What a relief!

The priest is conducting the impressive liturgy of Easter night. He hardly gets any response from the congregation, which is hesitatingly singing half known songs. He is reading the Easter Gospel in the middle of the dark night. His heart is completely open. I enjoy it. He is doing it all on his own. He is pulling off this church completely on his own.

I softly sing the old German song: *"Christ ist erstanden, von den Martyr alle. Des wollen wir alle froh sein. Christ wird unser Trost sein. Halleluja."* Christ has risen from his torture. So we all rejoice. Christ is our consolation. Halleluja.

April 24, Easter Monday, Eichenscheid

It is 06.20 pm. This afternoon I visited the ruins of an old Roman temple at Pesch. Originally it was a tree sanctuary. Here 'the Three Women' were venerated that the Romans took over from the Celts. The altar stone with the image of the three women in bas-relief is still there. They are sitting with their baskets full of fruits of the earth on their lap. I give them each a posy of periwinkle and would have done a small ritual, but it was too busy with people. The upside of that was having interesting talks with people about the Female Trinity. It was almost as if I was sitting there under the protection of the Triple Goddess. Their energy is very different from Mother Mary. It is more rounded and feisty, and strong.

Tuesday, April 25

I have stopped being annoyed about all the tarmacked forest paths, because it doesn't help and it only makes me miserable. I shall put up with it. I mean: I will accept it with love. And lo! Suddenly there are real leafy earth paths under my feet and, as an extra treat: grass paths! Those are most lovely to walk on and slowly I start to open up again to nature.

Last night I had a camping place near the edge of a wood. I had to go into the sleeping bag fully clothed as it is still very cold at night, which means: leggings, thick socks, vest, T-shirt, woollen pullover, woollen headscarf and gloves. But then suddenly today I walk in a sleeveless top in the hot sunshine. Do you know that you can wash yourself with the heavy dew on the tent and the condensation in it? Just lap it up with your flannel!

Right now, 04.00 pm, I sit high over Altenahr in the valley of the river Ahr on a cafe terrace and drink 'Kolsch', a lager-like local beer. I have just arrived up here with the chairlift (I just love chairlifts! Is that a responsible spending of the Jerusalem money?) and am enjoying the view. I take off my shoes and socks to give my feet a rest. Deep beneath me the meandering Ahr flows in the deep trench which it has worn out in the mountains. Next to it are little houses and castles on promontories in the river. I can see exactly where I came from and where I will go: steep wooded mountains about 1.500 feet high. In a moment I will sail down again.

Wednesday, April 26, Oberbreisig
Yesterday evening I sat high on a wooded ridge above the Ahr in my tent. I heard a sort of light snore next to it, but I thought it was some bird. This morning the grass near the tent appeared to have been rooted about by wild boar! I'm glad I didn't realize it at the time!

Thursday, April 27, 01.15 pm
It was HOT tonight. Strange contrasts!

I have arrived at the river Rhine and enjoy wide views from the West bank. I am constantly climbing and descending hills. And that with the load on my back and this heat! It feels like 30ºC. I drink a lot and don't pee.

This afternoon I arrived unsuspectingly over a narrow path at an old Jewish cemetery. Strict and sober stand the slabs in a forest light green with the leaves of spring. Everywhere on the stones I can see little pebbles. They are prayer stones of visitors. I add mine on the grave of a Cohen, a priest, which is apparent from the two blessing hands depicted on the stone. I pray for safe arrival in Jerusalem, and that my walk may contribute to the Great Peace, in whatever form. Then I sing the first line of the Kaddish, a prayer for the deceased. I don't know more than that. It feels like nobody has been here for centuries. Sunlight is filtering through the soft green of the beech leaves. The grass is growing abundantly on the graves. They have been here so long and unseen. I sit down to paint a watercolour in peace and quiet.

Friday, April 28, Andernach

The blossoms are already losing their petals and the fields of dandelions have transformed into fields of their lamp-like seed heads. Along the road I see purple and yellow archangel, blue violets, cheeky daisies, gypsophila, clear blue 'honour and praise', big purple ground ivy. The wild strawberries are already flowering. The blueberry shrubs, which eight days ago near Aachen were still bare and wispy, are full of leaves and dangle their pink little flowers.

Oh how I long to wash my hair! I had to buy a baseball cap to protect my head against the sun. It said NY on the front. But I'm not going to New York, so I picked the N off. I like the Y, the forked cross. With some fantasy it now says 'Yerushalaim'. The forked cross is a mystic symbol for two to become one (or the unity which becomes two - see yesterday).

Along the roadside I see primitive stone road crosses; hewn from one piece by the local stonemason of four centuries ago. The name of the donor is written on it in large unruly Latin characters.

I walk a lot today and towards the evening I take a wrong turn in the extensive orchards west of Koblenz. It is beautiful intimate landscape, but everything is privately owned. It is getting dark. I am sorry I have to pitch my tent in one of the private orchards; I have no choice.

All day long the weather was hot and damp, and I am hot and damp in my sleeping bag. There is a thunderstorm approaching, but it just keeps hanging over the land without unleashing. I look forward to a quiet night in such romantic surroundings with the blossoming apple trees above my head and go to bed at 10.00 pm. At midnight I wake up by a well-known dom-dom-dom sound. Are they driving around with noisy cars? No, people are having a house party in the old shed just on the other side of the orchard. The racket keeps me

30

awake until six o'clock in the morning. Then I am allowed another hour of sleep.

This morning I feel weak and trembling. And finally the thunderstorm breaks loose above my head. How lovely I could pack my tent up dry. My poncho serves its purpose. For the cloud-burst I take shelter in the supermarket in the next village.

Koblenz, April 30, Queensday, Walpurgisnight, Beltane

My tent is on the campsite at *'Deutsches Eck'* at the confluence of Rhine and Mosel. On the northern part of the peninsula protruding in the water, stands an enormous equestrian statue of William the Great —the 19th century German emperor. He is much larger than life and is accompanied by a winged Nike, goddess of victory, carrying his imperial crown on a cushion with enormous bronze tassels.

Previously I only used to see the pomp and pride of such a statue, the literal and figurative inflation of what is an ordinary human being. But today I also see something of the ideal behind it. I try to appreciate the grandeur of it all and then it impresses me, even touches me: this unquenchable desire to be a perfect noble human being in a perfect and noble Fatherland that serves the community of all people with its talents.

That ideal became distorted in the time of the Nazis, but the essence of it is good. The difference between right and wrong is in the contrast Serve/Rule. And that is where the confusion was.

Beneath the statue, on the enormous pedestal, I can see the German coat of arms: a fierce, warlike eagle, who — to my surprise — is working itself up from a clue of writhing adders. Germany's sign of the zodiac is Scorpio. In astrology Scorpio is also depicted as the serpent becoming an eagle; the noble nature, which rises above its own poisonous inclinations and can elevate itself highest of all star signs. Two powerful animals touch the earth with their bellies and hide under stones. In other words, the scorpion and the serpent are two totem animals which connect with the element earth, with the ultimate form. But who have the potential to transform into ultimate light: the eagle which dissolves into the sunlight.

In other words: the famous German term '*Grundlichkeit*', which means 'groundliness': solidity or thoroughness, is a commitment to manifest ideas into the perfect material and spiritual form. This can get stuck into rigidity, in immovability of the emotional life that gets stuck under stones, when the vision of the eagle isn't used.

In Göttingen, mid-Germany, in 1933, German/Jewish scientists discovered the secret of atomic fission which is matter transformed into light. It is the same image. Maybe it wasn't a coincidence that this was discovered in Germany.

Tonight is Walpurgis Night, Beltane, and tomorrow it is 'Queen's day' in the Netherlands, when the Queen celebrates her birthday. And today here in Koblenz I see dozens of little queens and pages (children doing their first Communion) walking to church with their families. The boys aren't very conspicuous. They look very neat, of course, with their new suits, ties and shining shoes, but the girls are glowing in their long white silk and satin frocks, a small veil on their heads, gloves, purse with a new prayer book and a little gold cross on their necklace. A combination of vanity and sanctity hangs around them. They are beautiful, the girls, and they know it but they have also been very well prepared from the religious point of view and many will know what it is all about: the welcoming of Jesus in their heart.

It is about 02.00 pm and after the festive lunch, a little First Communicant is playing next to the fountain on the small square, near the terrace where I am drinking apple juice. She wears a trouser suit made of white lace, has white flowers in her hair and she is romping around with cousins of her own age. All of them are at their Sunday best, visiting their celebrated family member, but after all the solemnities in the church and at home they now need to play football and run around. She is — in her spotless trouser suit — the centre of attention, enjoying it greatly.

One hour ago, far back in the Eifel Mountains at the sanctuary in Pesch, a women's ceremony will have started to honour the Triple Goddess. And in church, after Mass, the communicants have decorated the Statue of the Virgin with many flowers, because, She is also the Queen of May.

This way the Goddess of Spring is gathering her powers to receive and give many blessings these first true days of spring. Maiden/Mother Earth opens herself in her flowers towards the sun. It is time for the sacred marriage.

At the campsite a nice man honours me with his attention. Tomorrow I will walk on.

Tuesday, May 2, Boppard

I don't understand why I can walk 24 kilometres very well one day, and the next day not at all. Yesterday it was supposed to be easy. Just walk along the Rhine from Koblenz to Boppard. The weather was great. Not too warm neither too cold. There were hardly any hills to ascend or descend. But — please let me complain for a moment — my knee hurts, my hip joints hurt and there is something new too! My feet are in excellent condition, but above the seams of my walking boots my legs are swelling strangely. The skin is getting sensitive and strange red spots are appearing. Now what is that?

Sankt Goar, 08.15 pm, Rock of the Lorelei, a campsite on the Rhine

This is the third day I am walking along the Rhine. I have been taking it easy today. Only 16 kilometres and still I am exhausted! It is so hot! In the morning I start with difficulty.

I am tired, sweaty and shaky. It is better in the evening. At this moment I sit on the bank of the Rhine and look at the setting sun shining on the famous rock of the Lorelei, for this is the time of day she combs her golden hair. The river is flowing very fast here and the ships have to round this sharp promontory very quickly and dexterously if they don't want to crash into it. The Lorelei, who sits here according to tradition, is a beautiful siren, distracting the skippers with her antics in order to sink them and their boats to the bottom of the river.

From the west I can see a thunderstorm coming. I have to be very quick in putting the plastic over the tent if I want to keep myself waterproof. I'm in the tent now, hearing the rain battering on the plastic.

Thursday, May 4, 12.45 pm

In the Eifel I met many older widows, who told me about their life and loss. Here in the Rhine valley I meet for the third time men without a partner. I am quite in demand in spite of my 52 years. And, different from the past, when I was young and juicy, I am wooed in a pleasant and respectful way, which, in return, makes these men more attractive. One stopped me on the tow-path; a long, thin man of 53 on his bike. He was so charmed with my solitary walk, that he felt encouraged to finally go on this long cycle holiday of which he had dreamt for years. The last one, yesterday, was a warm and kind, short, stout man. He had bought fresh buns and made coffee to lure me into his yellow camper van. He succeeded. The men speak about loneliness, the runaway wives, the unfit partners. They have difficulty being alone. The women speak about the never-ending pain of loss.

And I? I am single. Not of free choice, but I am at peace with that. However on this walk I am definitely single because I want it! Solitary travel empowers and liberates. The nice thing about meeting these men is, that my erotic interest, which had fallen to point zero, has regained its normal level. It is lovely to have physical desires, even if you don't put them to use.

Friday May 5, Roxheim, near Bad Kreuznach

I am sitting here in a hunter's seat high above the ground and look at the sun setting behind the mountain ridge of the Soonwald, the Forest of Soon. I can see three villages from here. I will wait until after sunset to put up my tent. Tomorrow it will catch the full sunrise from the other side. Oh bother, a jogger has just run past. He was looking hard the other way, trying not to see me, but now I have to find another place, because I don't like it when people know where I camp. The grass is getting higher and has grown up to my waist. Why haven't the people started mowing when they knew I was coming! It is awful having to press it down; all those lovely flowers, flop, tent smashing down on them. And all those poor insects; I have put off my cap for just one moment, and immediately a little spider starts to weave her web in it.

Saturday, May 6

And all the damp and the dew that this long hay is producing! The tent, the sleeping bag, rucksack, my hair, everything is soaking wet in the morning.

When I arrive in Bad Münster am Stein, I am too late to buy food for the weekend. All the shops are closing at 02.00 pm. So I eat in a restaurant. The owner is from Pakistan. He tells me that some people from Pakistan do the Hadj to Mecca on foot and partially by boat. His prayer for Jerusalem is that everybody shall have free access to the Holy City and the Mosques. The Dome of the Rock is the oldest Islamic religious edifice especially built for worship in the 7th century. It was built by Muslims on the razed remains of the old Jewish Temple, which was torched and destroyed by the Romans in 70 AD to break the insurgence of the Jewish people. When this

35

holy place came into possession of the Christians a few centuries later, they desecrated it even more and turned it into a tip. Only after the Muslims took Jerusalem they cleaned the place where once the Temple stood, allowed Jews to enter there again and even gave them work. They reconsecrated the place and respected it as a place of God. Those were the good deeds the Muslims did.

Sunday, May 7, Alsenz am Alsenz

In spite of having lost connection to my mission for the moment, I have gone to church in a Lutheran little chapel built in 1690. Hochstätten is a Lutheran enclave in Roman Catholic surroundings. It has been built as a protestant prayer house and is decorated with just enough gilded baroque ornaments to stay beautiful and simple. The walls have been painted clear blue in marble pattern. I sit in a very high, white church pew with only my head sticking out. Sunlight is entering the windows in slanting rays and shines on grey and blonde heads. It is Good Shepherd Sunday and many texts have been chosen on this theme: 'Miracles exist and do trust in the new ways that God will show you.' A young parson delivers a well-wrought sermon. That is why I only understand half of it. I've no trouble with those Roman Catholic little sermons. A child can understand those, but today I really have to pay attention in order to be edified.

After the service the parson, shaking hands at the door, asks where I am going. I tell him and he is very interested. He asks me to linger, for first he has to continue shaking hands. When he finishes, he wants extensive information and suddenly I have to cry when I quote the verses from Isaiah about 'the veil which covers the nations' and that I hope that this year something can be torn from that veil, and that I want to ask everybody's prayer for that.

"What a pity I didn't know that, it would have fitted beautifully in the service." He is really listening; I'm not releasing tears for nothing. He takes my card and promises to speak about it in the congregation.

Later I sit beneath the village's linden tree and talk about this and other things with three members of the congregation: an elderly couple and an older woman. They pour out stories about the Second World War. So many people from the village were killed. How great was the enthusiasm for the new fresh spirit of the Nazis and how great the bewilderment and the disappointment when the dark sides of their business came to light. The Army was rounding up men of the village to take service. The father of the younger woman wanted to refuse, but his friends said: "Don't you refuse; they'll put you against the wall!" So he came with them. Two weeks later her mother heard that he was missing. And he never came back.

1938: *Kristall Nacht* — Night of the Broken Glass. Not many Jews lived here in the village, but there were enough to play very nasty games with. I don't dare asking what games. Instead I tell that my acquaintance with Judaism and Talmud has enriched me tremendously.

I haven't had breakfast yet and I ask if there is a restaurant here or a bakery which is open on Sunday. I haven't finished my request and already I am given two thick slices of fresh bread with pickled pork and a piece of cheesecake. I eat everything. Pickled pork from somebody's heart is by no means to be sneezed at. Not even by vegetarians.

People eat a lot of meat here; usually from their own home-reared pigs. The sturdy house wives speak of home slaughter and a lot of work to cure the ham, make the sausages and the pickles. "Tomorrow we will do it together, with three friends. It is a lot of work, and we also have to work the vegetable garden." Deep sigh. "But it is nice too. Next Sunday there is a confirmation here and we will have many guests. My legs are already hurting when I think of it." Another deep sigh. The older woman under the linden tree says: "Until my 40th I have worked like a dog, until my 65th I will just work hard and after that I will do what I like."

And now I am here: in Alsenz, on a little terrace covered by a marquee against the coming thunder. I have already eaten salad, ice cream, strawberry cake and I had a beer. A group of 'nature ramblers' are having their drinks at the table next to me. After hearing that I'm from The Hague, an older gentleman, enthusiastic orchid specialist, has the audacity to tell me: "I was there too in 1944, when I was seventeen. That was a wonderful time."

"But it was not for us; it was horrible!" I say indignantly. He waves my protest away with the easy remark, that at seventeen you don't understand anything much yet. A fellow nature rambler, hearing our conversation, looks very uneasy.

I am really angry about his outrageous insensitivity. How can he be an orchid specialist with such ideas?

When I was in Germany for the first time in 1961, being thirteen years old, there were a lot of war veterans, men without arms, without legs, blind etc. Often even from the First World War. Some of them apologized for the horrible things that happened in the last war; apologized to a Dutch thirteen year old girl. You don't see these old soldiers anymore. They must all have died by now.

So much more I could write about: the vineyards with the sprouting vines; the heat between the rows; the difficulty to find proper camping spots; the leprechaun in the oak tree; uncountable flowers and herbs; my struggle to remain soft-hearted in this solid, sound country; the friendly Rhinelanders. Sudden instructions of my intuition: "Don't go onto this path!" I have obeyed, but don't know why. Now there is a thunderstorm looming. I am on this terrace. It is 05.30 pm. I want to continue, but I'm not fool enough to venture into the rain. I will paint the thunderstorm instead. And that the earth is red here I haven't mentioned either yet.

Monday, May 8, Donnersberg

Towards the evening I arrive at the 'Donnersberg', Thunder Mountain. It is about 2.000 feet high, and formed like the shell of a snail. It rises steeply from the surrounding plain, the Rheinebene. I have seen it grow higher and higher on the horizon for days already and I felt that it was a powerful place. I looked forward to it, but was also apprehensive. The days before I had been able to avoid unpleasant names on the map, like 'Gallow's Mountain' and 'Gallow's Wood', where I didn't want to pitch my tent (to spend the night on a former Gallow's Field!). But now I have to face it. Because, look what I am reading on the map: I have to pass the Murder Brook, the Murder Room. There is a big Celtic Oppidum (Iron Age hill fort) on top of the mountain and a high rock called the 'King's Chair'.

It is getting dark. I'd rather stay in the lovely little village of Mariënthal, Mary's Valley, which lies at the foot of Thunder Mountain. There is a B&B there, which costs more than 50 Deutschmark, which, for my standards, is very expensive, and no, the weather is much too beautiful to sleep inside. And I spend too much money anyway.

It is half past eight at night when I start to climb the mountain. I have to climb it in order to continue on the way. There is no way to get round it. In the twilight I think of evil spirits and trapped souls which might be here on the mountain. I know the old Celts weren't always such nice people. They were head hunters, first of the real ones and later of stone heads, which they charged with magical power. And at the King's Chair the Nazis probably held their black magical rituals. This could be a horrible place and I feel scared, but I can't stay in Marienthal or here along the main road and it is no option to take a long detour either. I surely shouldn't make a detour because of my own horror fantasies. So, I decide: up on to the mountain! And there I go! The paths are turning as if they follow the turnings of the snail's shell. I think: obviously I HAVE to be here. I have no other reasonable choice, ergo, I don't need to be afraid. Ergo, I am strong enough to face anything popping up, visible or invisible. It is a VISION QUEST. In a vision quest people will climb an initiation mountain on their own to confront their deepest fears and highest hopes.

I pass Murder Room, but I hear myself say: "How beautiful it is here, how sweet!" On the hollow path some beech trees are standing in the high verge. One of them has formed with its roots a little cup in which it can save water for dry times. It is such an inviting little bowl, that I have to pick some flowers to put into it as an offering. Another beech tree stretches her pure and serene Cinderella foot towards me. Is it a piece of trunk or is it already a root? It is a slim beech tree with a skin like satin without any unevenness and she has a foot, not a root. The bow of this foot just begs to be touched. I caress this graceful foot again and again. It gives me so much energy that it is difficult to stop, but I must continue my ascent. What a nice, sweet forest this is! When it is almost dark I find a level place to put my tent. There is no dew this night. The moon is a thin crescent. It is warm. There are no mosquitoes.

In the morning I wake up early because of loud birdsong all around me. On the forest floor everything has remained dry and so has the tent. In front of it lies a stone with an inviting little depression in it, just right for an offering. I form a little medicine wheel around it with stones lying about. Towards the south-east is Jerusalem. I meditate and while I burn a little fluff of tobacco in honour of God, in the Native American way, suddenly the first rays of the rising sun are shining on my hands, and I feel that I have been seen and blessed.

While the birds are singing all around me in the trees, I take a walk in the early morning to the Iron Age hill fort and from there to the rock on top called The King's Chair. From there I can see all the land through which I have been walking for the past three days, a distance of about 60 kilometres. There, far from behind the misty horizon in the north-west, that is where I travelled from; I really walked it step by step.

And here I sit on the King's Chair, how light and playful am I sitting on this throne, and how serene and lovely is this mountain top. I breakfast, enjoying the panorama.

What do I hear now? A class of noisy schoolchildren are climbing to the top. It is only quarter past eight, they are early! They are just as playful as I am. They have come to clear the rubbish and wave happily but seriously with big rubbish bags in which they put every little cigarette end they can find, putting their noses close to the ground not to let any iniquity escape. This morning everything is perfect.

I feel serene and light when I start to descend. I have the address of a convent which lies at the foot of Thunder Mountain, 'Kloster Getsemani'. The E8 long distance path goes straight past.

I still have to gather up courage to step up to people with my story and my request to pray for Jerusalem, but this time it is rather easy, because a sister is just leaving the building, shining a radiant smile to me as a welcome. I respond automatically with a smile just as bright. As I am led to the reception room I can feel that the atmosphere in the convent is just as light and serene as the mountain.

I tell my story to Sister Martina; she is in charge of the guests. I can speak Dutch to her for she is from Sittard. She brings me fresh coffee, two pieces of fruitcake, chocolate biscuits. I can't eat it all.

My story gets a good and interested reception. The abbess also comes to listen. I am invited for the noon service in the chapel.

This is a simple space in the former children's home. There is an altar; around it are meditation stools like those in Findhorn or Taize, and some higher chairs for the older sisters to sit and to kneel. There are six sisters in nuns' habits. One is a novice in white, and one is a postulant in grey. The choral song of the women is different from that of the men in the monastery in Limburg. It is much lighter, more melodious, sometimes a little hesitant, but my meditation can go very deep here. I am sorry to notice it has already finished.

In the guest reception room the table has been laid for my hot lunch! With a lot of freshly cooked spinach! What rapture! I've not eaten freshly cooked vegetables for a very long time. I eat everything. The sisters come to take their leave. Sister Martina gives me a prayer slip for Jerusalem and tells me they will pray for my intention in their services and privately, but also for me. I leave the convent thoroughly happy, the deep meditation in my heart, the delicious spinach in my belly, the prayer slips in my little homemade cotton case and the loving and interested welcome of the sisters in my memory.

Wednesday, May 10, 04.45 pm, Monsheim near Worms

In this heat, this full, green, blossoming, sweltering heat I have to rest every hour at least 20 minutes. This is level country, the Rhein-Ebene, the Rhine plain. It is densely populated, but there are always earth and grass paths to walk on and a little river called the Pfrimm to follow. I hear for the first time in my life the song of the Golden Oriole, which according to an old Dutch song sounds like 'Dudeljo', for that is what I hear. I find pheasant feathers and put them in my hair. In the afternoon I call on the Lutheran community in Monsheim. My story is so enthusiastically received by Sigrid, who is the secretary of the church parish that she asks me to hold a lecture for the women's group. Then she invites me to stay with her and her husband. And in the evening during the lecture, I receive a lot of response and even financial support from the women, which is lovely for me and for my undertaking. All of them will pray for my intention and for me. And that they can pray I did notice! I am also happily surprised by the high level of ecological consciousness of these people: energy saving light bulbs, separated rubbish, selective use of the car; water saving shower head, leftish political and social consciousness, but not so interested in the spiritual side of ecology.

In the morning I find my muddy walking boots cleaned, polished and shining like mirrors in front of the door of my bedroom. How sweet!

Thursday, May 11, Worms, West Rhine bank

I am spending a few days in Worms and am lodged in the 'Friends of Nature House', cheap, clean, and wonderfully situated on the Rhine. The first thing I did today is going to the post office to collect my letters. Six wonderful letters are waiting for me and ten more messages on email and on the website. Even unknown people are starting to write.

Worms gives me an unexpected feeling of coming home. Perhaps that is because of the letters from home, the support and the love they convey. But I feel it is more than that. It intrigues me that I feel touched looking at the strange and special Dom (cathedral) in Romanesque style. The Church of Our Lady, why does it arouse emotions in me? Worms was very famous in mediaeval times. In the Dom the emperors of the Holy Roman Empire were crowned. It is the city where St. Martin of Tours was kept as a prisoner and that other Martin, Martin Luther, said: "Here I stand, I cannot do otherwise." Near to Worms Hildegard von Bingen, the mystic abbess was born and it is the city where the 'Nibelungenlied', the song of the Nibelungen' was written. This is a mediaeval epic describing the enmity between Hagen and Siegfried, between Brunhilde and Kriemhilde and the tragedy which consequently unfolded.

Although written down in the 12th century, the story was much older; it might even have been pagan and must have dated from the 5th or 6th century as Attilla the Hun also figures in it. I read that story when I was fourteen years old and was under its gloom for days, mourning the fate of all the protagonists.

The story is too long to tell here completely but it comes down to that the male protagonists, Siegfried, King Gunther, Hagen and consorts by machinations, pride and jealousy wounded deeply their female counterparts Kriemhilde and Brunhilde, who could have been friends but now were forced into becoming enemies. The women had no defence against the intrigues of their men and instead of confronting the men, they started to rage between the two of them, resulting in the complete destruction of the family. The knight Hagen, vassal of King Gunther, threw the treasure of the Nibelungen, property of Kriemhilde, in the Rhine at Worms, where it is still supposed to be. Metaphorically speaking it is the sinking of radiant feminine qualities back into unconsciousness, under the water level, where nobody is aware of them anymore. Brunhilde was deceived, and robbed by her husband King Günther and by Siegfried, whom she loved. Kriemhilde, Siegfried's wife, was hurt by his unfaithfulness and revenged herself on Brunhilde and thus started to roll the wheel of destruction. Knight Hagen was a Loki, a Hermes-like figure, who stole and destroyed everything which was valuable for Kriemhilde, her love, her treasure.

The epic was written in the 12th century. Exactly the time that the last remnants of Matriarchy disappeared and the cult of another, less dangerous female figure - the Virgin Mary - became popular. That epic oppresses me. These women choose their dishonest husbands, instead of integrity because they need them, because they think that they can find with them that connection and consolation without which they feel their life is empty, instead of choosing for truth and justice. It describes women undone from their power by strategy, selfishness and pride of men. What a horrible figure this Siegfried is. He was gifted with all sorts of heavenly powers; still greed and pride brought him down. Siegfried was an example for Germanic superiority in the Nazi era. Well, they really have not understood the story.

That is what I'm thinking about after another sweltering hot day. I am sitting in the darkness on the bank of the Rhine. In the distance a thunderstorm comes closer and closer. I am still moved by the old story; by its impossibility of creating a real connection between men and women. The last sentence of the epic is: "*Dies war der Nibelungen Not.*" (This was the anguish of the Nibelungen.)

Then the thunderstorm breaks loose with thunderbolts I can see a long way over the Rhine. The rain pours down on me while I'm running inside and I cannot tell the difference between the raindrops and my own tears when I see that constantly a connection is made here between heaven and earth, a furious violent connection. The lightning strikes the water like the light of Kriemhilde's treasure thrown anew in the river. It happens all evening, all night until the rage is over. The window of my bedroom remains open until there is harmony again and heaven rests on the earth like a man on his woman.

Friday, May 12
While I am visiting Worms Cathedral and walk along her dark aisles I have an unexpected meeting with the Triple Goddess. As I admire the ancient baptismal font, they are suddenly standing behind me, in high relief against the wall. The three women at Jesus' grave are depicted in much the same way as those on their heathen altar stone in Pesch. This is an eye opener! The archetype of the female Trinity will of course

suffuse into Christianity too: three women at the grave, at the mouth of birth, life, death and rebirth. They tell me kindly but strictly to continue walking and praying. I'm doing fine. They stand behind me!

I visit the synagogue. It is the oldest one of Europe and built in Romanesque style in the 11th century. It was destroyed by crusaders a few years later. It was rebuilt and then and destroyed again in the 14th century because Jews were blamed of spreading the plague. Again it was destroyed in the 17th century, together with the whole city. Again it was rebuilt. Again it was destroyed; this time in the Night of the broken Glass in 1938. And again it was rebuilt. I know of a beautiful pre-war picture where the sunlight shines through the high windows reaching in between the pillars. Raschi, the great Jewish teacher, studied here in the world renowned Talmud School in the 11th century. At home I have very special music from the 14th century composed in 'Die Heilige Gemeinde Worms' (the Sacred Community of Worms). It is incomparable with other music from that time. It was written in this synagogue.

The building is open to visitors. In Worms there are not enough Jews to form a *minjan* (the prescribed minimum of ten Jewish men to be able to have an official service), but Jews often come from elsewhere to celebrate Shabbat; the presence of prayer is evident. I stand in the middle of the renewed synagogue and see the sunlight stream between the pillars. Suddenly - like a sweet sunray - a sense of homecoming pierces my heart. I have come home to Worms in general, but especially here, where this light is and where that beautiful music originates. Something of that light enlightens the dark cathedral and reconciles me with the tragic epic of the Nibelungen.

I have a chat with the keeper of the Synagogue. He was raised as a Catholic, but has great interest in Judaism. I play for him on my recorder the music from the '*Heilige Gemeinde Worms.*' I stand among the pillars in the sunlight. I stand in front of the Holy Ark, where the rolls of the Torah are kept and play the sweet high notes of the Wormser hymn 'Jerusalem'.

Monday, May 15, Odenwald, Auerbach-Bensheim
I've just enjoyed eating an enormous piece of Black Forest cherry pie! It did me a world of good.

I am very happy this morning and enjoy everything. Adding to that I just bought a very good map, which, according to the Wormser bookshop where I tried to buy one yesterday, didn't exist. And now I can shortcut the many detours of the E8, because I love walking, but I don't want to make the path longer than necessary. Everywhere around me yellow and red roses explode into bloom. The elder tree is budding and early cherries dangle among the leaves. (But it was only last week I saw them blossom!?). Stinging mosquitoes are here in the night but not in the morning. The moon is almost full. Roses bloom next to my tent; I see them in the moonlight. I live in fullness. O how grand this sounds! But it is greater still.

Tuesday, May 16, Luidenfels
For the first time this journey I have received threats; from an old lady. She started rather nice with: "Aren't you afraid all on your own?" But when I said: "Usually not; most people are nice", she started to wave her finger in front of my nose and said in a really nasty tone that last week two women in the graveyard had been sexually assaulted. I got the feeling that she hoped it would happen to me too and serve me right!

I have seen the first mowed hayfields today. The tufted vetch is flowering fully; the sycamore trees are crammed with their butterfly seeds; the air is full of pollen and small insects dancing and buzzing. For the first time in my life I have a little hay fever. I walk through beautiful villages where elderly gentlemen, washing their cars, will kindly fill my water bottle with tap water. Life is good and good and good. A sweet old lady in front of the church wants to give me six Deutschmark and asks me to pray for her in Jerusalem. When I refuse the money she says: "Take it my dear! The monasteries and churches are already getting plenty; go and eat an ice cream!"

Wednesday, May 17, Michelstadt
What a cute German townlet this is, with all its Saxon style timber-framed houses and the energy of a fairy tale. To find a contrast I step into a Turkish shop and ask if I could visit the mosque and the imam. After I have changed into more appropriate clothes (I was wearing a top which left my arms bare and shorts doing the same with my legs), two Turkish men give me a lift to the mosque. I am a little apprehensive at first, but they are politeness itself. They ask if I have permission from my family and if I didn't have something better to do. When I told them my family was proud of me, they shook their wise heads. The imam wasn't at the mosque and not at his house. So I walked on.

Friday, May 19, Walldürn, Odenwald
This morning I visited the pilgrim church of the Holy Blood in Walldurn. It is a disgustingly boastful, overloaded high baroque church. In the 14th century during Mass, a priest spilled some wine during the consecration. That didn't become a wine stain, but a bloodstain in the form of a cross on the little altar cloth. The priest was so frightened that he hid it and told nobody until his dying day. They found the altar cloth. The pilgrimage started. I never know what I am to do with that sort of story. When I sat in front of the altar where the cloth is being kept I felt anger and disgust. And it hadn't to do with just me, but also with the story just told and this setting. The church is cluttered with exuberant and twisted exhibitionist crucifixes.

I think: "Here's another crucifix and another one, and another one. Now, Jesus, come down from it immediately! I want to throw stones at them. They display false emotions and are purported to make an effect. Everything shows the outside, nothing from the inside. But there is more to it. Underneath all this I feel: Something has been soiled and desecrated here. Here something good has completely disappeared beneath a layer of filth. I catch myself looking away from the altar like Judas from the Last Supper. Suddenly I become furious about that 2,000 years sustained hanging on the cross. Jesus suffered physically only from nine o'clock in the morning until three o'clock in the afternoon. Other people have suffered longer and worse! Jesus has forgotten it by now, but the church has extended his relatively short suffering for almost 2,000 years. Don't they remember? He is Risen! The cross is empty! And so is the grave! Time to rejoice!

Yesterday I was asking the wildlife: "Please, don't always be so frightened and run away from me when you see me! I find it mortifying that you are so scared of me! I love you; I'm a vegetarian and I don't want to hunt and to harm you!" Of course that was rather childish, but I also meant it.

Today I walk a little path. To the left and right hares bolt off in front of me, but one remains. He sits there on the side of the path while I come closer step by step. I keep tight to my walking rhythm so he knows what's happening. He doesn't run! He presses himself against the ground; his back turned towards me, and looks at me sideways with one large dark melancholy eye. I pass him at less than two feet distance. My boot steps must drone in his long, gracious ears. But he stays!

And there is a roe deer, eating peacefully without seeing me. I stand still and don't move. Every now and again she looks in the direction of the strange tree - I wear my forest green pullover and brown jeans - which wasn't there before and continues nibbling. In the end she becomes a little suspicious and warily trots off.

Ten metres in front of me I see two roe deer chasing each other in circles through forest and meadow. They didn't even see me during their play! Finally they disappear through a green wheat field diving and emerging like dolphins in a waving sea.

This morning I have been vaccinated against the virus variety of the dangerous nerve disease called Lyme or tick disease. I plucked two from my body this morning. I get a tick at least every other day. You can't avoid it on a camping trip through nature. You can guard against the bacterial variety by paying very good attention, remove them within 24 hours and stay wary to see if an infection or red ring around the bite develops. And then take antibiotics immediately. Against the virus variety the only thing that helps is vaccination, although there is a slight risk of getting meningitis. Farmers and foresters usually get vaccinated. In a week I have to have another one and two weeks later the last one. Every morning and evening I check myself for ticks with a mirror, but I can't see my back. This evening I pitch the tent early. I need to lie down. I am a bit feverish. Is this the vaccination?

Saturday, May 20, Gissigheim, 03.00 pm
It is cold today, 10° C. I am almost sorry that I left my warm red coat in a second hand clothes container. I rise with a headache and feel feverish. It must be yesterday's vaccination. I take it easy today, but I'm out of balance. I stumble over a branch in the forest and fall on my back between the ferns. Luckily my rucksack breaks my fall. And this morning I almost slithered - even wearing my high profile boots - from the slippery stone steps, leading to the brook below my camping place.

A little dazed I walk through the landscape. I take wrong paths; my joints are hurting again because of the cold and damp weather. For the first time I think: 'How far yet to go!'

I dreamt something beautiful: I stuck a beautiful round healthy German loaf in the little bag where I keep my 'meditation kit'. Then I saw that there were white lilies in the bag instead of a loaf. Interpretation: bread is sustenance, support, daily needed. In other words, I meditate with daily regularity. In return I receive spiritual energy: white lilies.

This morning I had an interesting talk with a woman with a little dog which was nervously barking at my rucksack. People suffered in the war. She tells me the story how as a child she fled into the forest from the advancing frontline. She lost her father and mother, who had also fled and was alone for days on end. Sigrid, with whom I stayed in Monsheim to speak for the women's group, told me about her flight from Poland as an 8-year-old child. The Germans who had lived for generations in what is now Poland, were driven out after all the Polish suffering under German Nazi rule. Her mother and her five siblings were on the run for days. She counted her children time and time again. After two days she only had to count to five. The baby had died on the road.

I am sharing the stories about the war which I heard from my parents and grandparents: the hiding away of young men and Jews; the betrayals; the fear of the marching soldier boots in the middle of the night; the thumping on the doors; the house searches. The arrests; the torture; the black market; the famine in the last very severe winter of war; the razzias; the hunt for Jews; the liquidation of traitors by the resistance. Other stories, other traumas. It is a good word, trauma. Instead of 'breach' you could translate it as *'Traum'*, dream. After 55 years people are still dreaming on a daily basis about the traumatic events which happened to them in their childhood.

I feel more and more feverish this afternoon. I take a room in 'The Angel Inn' to take it very easy today. The room has a balcony and the setting sun is shining on it. I can dry my sleeping bag, tent and mattress. I clean my boots and now I am sitting here painting pictures. I want to make one on the subject 'connection'. By mistake I make the sky a deep purple, looking like a thundercloud. I still have some red left, I want to use that up and paint the windows of the church red. Then I see it is on fire and I only need to paint a thunderbolt to make the picture complete. I do. And then I become scared. A wave of fear spills over me. Am I that church? Am I on fire? Have I been struck mad by the Living God? Do I meditate too much?

But maybe I shouldn't worry; it is probably only me getting a little bit of lethal meningitis because of the vaccination.

That night I dream: I am in The Hague on the beach. On the other side of the sea is England; in my dream it is very close. A man in a rowing boat is coming towards me. He is short and stout, has a neat beard and very good and loving eyes. He reminds me of that nice photographer in the film 'Secrets and Lies'. He steps on land and tells me that he loves me and I know I can love him too. He says: 'Last year, when you and P. split up, I was already there, but you didn't see me. I was nobody.' And that is true. In the dream I remember him sitting on the couch with a little vague companion by his side, but I never paid him any attention. Now he takes my hands to make a 'connection'. He tells me he is from Hastings (William the Conqueror?) on the coast. For him it is 'the New Jerusalem' where he always wants to live. He drinks too much on occasions, so he is not perfect, but that doesn't matter. We are in his boat together and suddenly high waves are coming up and I almost fall overboard. I shout: "We have to sit in front to shift the centre of gravity towards the right spot," but he says: "No, hold on to the line!" A thin thread has been stretched from port to starboard. End of dream.

I wake up with a happy feeling, but when I think more about it, it fades away. A dream lover has no body. I quote: 'I was no body!' It is someone contacting me from England (in Dutch: Angel-land). What is he? Is he my guardian angel?

The next morning I ask the landlady why the Inn is called 'The Angel'. She says: "The chapel across the road is dedicated to the holy guardian angels." That is worth thinking about.

I cannot have a real lover with a body at the moment. But I have been given a wonderful guardian angel from Angel-land.

Sunday, May 21
At mass this morning I listen to a fantastic sermon of a very remarkable priest. He is physically disabled — because of a stroke? On his head there are loose bits of white and black hair. He has tics around his eyes. With his distorted mouth he says the most consistent things and he blesses the congregation with a magnificent golden monstrance beset with rubies. He has to pull it over the altar cloth to get a grip on it before making a crooked sign of the cross. His sermon is about 'being in the heart of God'. "We are always in the heart of God, but most time we don't notice. We can start noticing by praying and meditating more." He gives an example of a priest who was in a concentration camp in the Second World War and had to do forced labour. The knowing and feeling that he was in the Heart of God and the jolly thought *"Ich bin doch nur zur Erholung da!"* (I am only here for convalescence!) got him through it. "And," he says, "It helps me through it too".

He stumbles over his chasuble and shoves the big prayer book almost over the edge of the altar. The congregation laughs and so does he; they are used to him. During

53

intercession he reads out my intention. After mass we talk about the walk. With his sharp eyes he sees everything, he is joking and serious at the same time. He prays from his heart for blessing on my journey, weighs my rucksack on his hand and takes his leave with a very un-celibate caress over my cheek.

Today I see a very special depiction of the Trinity. The traditional elements are all there: the archetype of the Father, sitting on a throne. He holds the horizontal beam of the cross, which is in his lap, with his son hanging from it. But the Holy Spirit doesn't hover above the Father's head as usual; it comes flying straight out of his Heart!

Like most people, I have difficulty with the concept of the Trinity. I feel it as an invention, not a mystery. But this has suddenly changed by this eye opener. I feel a shift in consciousness.

I now see a new image of the Trinity in my mind's eye:

The Mother of God is sitting in the lap of the Father, she is crowned by the Dove of the Spirit flying from his heart. Both He and She hold the horizontal beam of the cross where their Son is hanging. Is Mary, mother of God, the incarnation of Spirit on Earth?

Monday, May 22, Sachsenflur

I walk through a dark fir forest. It is just like the Mirkwood in The Hobbit; uncanny, deep, dead, dark, dry and dim. The narrow path is like a tunnel in the night, high fir trees growing over it take away the day; only at the end there is a suggestion of green light. On a fork in the path lays a huge stone, exactly in the middle, and I know: 'you must do a ceremony here'. But I don't feel like it. I am in a good walking rhythm and I want to be past a certain village before dusk. A ceremony will cost me at least half an hour, and I don't feel like it. And it is a nasty place as well.

But it asks for it. I hesitate. I don't have to do it, but for what other reason am I doing a pilgrimage? It is an official journey, to serve. Is it that important to walk past that village before darkness?

I don't mind doing it, but then I want to feel it inside and not because I have to. The next moment I notice that I have swayed off my rucksack and delved up my 'meditation kit'. While I prepare and light a little wax candle, I feel a dark transparent presence behind me. It is still, it doesn't do anything; it is no threat, but it is dark and it looks at me. I am not getting scared; I take no notice and finish my little ceremony with a Hail Mary and an Our Father. When I pray the Our Father I notice that the dark presence dissolves into nothing.

Wednesday, May 24

The night has been cold and wet, and I have to pack my tent and sleeping bag all being soaked through. It is cold during the day and I have to keep moving to remain warm without an opportunity to dry the tent. It would be impossible to sleep in the soaking thing. At the *'Evangelische Diakonie'* in Rothenburg I asked for prayer for Jerusalem as usual, but they didn't trust me. Then, as I sat in their public canteen (warm and dry) to drink a cup of coffee, I asked if I could dry my tent there in an unobtrusive corner. They got very angry and I was chased away as a pickpocket or tramp.

I know this is all part of the deal, but still I was upset about it. Crying helps better than telling myself that this is how life is! True as it may be, it doesn't work. So I sat in the cold on a low stone wall and cried. Only after I had finished and felt relieved I noticed that, for the last ten minutes I had been staring at the air conditioning outlet at the back of a sauna/tanning studio. Divine coincidence and care! So I got my dripping tent out, and my damp sleeping bag and sat in the lovely warm air stream myself too. Within fifteen minutes everything was dry. I am so well cared for!

Thursday, May 25
Today I pass the 1,000 kilometre mark. It is half the distance of the E8. I hope to be in Bratislava in six weeks.

Saturday, May 27, Weihenzell
Things which draw my attention on the way: the Bavarians are surlier than the Rhinelanders. The landscape and the houses are less tidy than in the Eifel and there are more earth paths, thank God. The cemeteries are being cared for with much love. In the villages you recognize the hand of one stonemason in the tombstones. The result is cemeteries in one consistent style.

My mouth is watering when I pass the shops where the local traditional dresses are sold: stylish 'Dirndls'. Supposedly only very conservative people would wear them, but I love them. It is very good quality stuff, well cut, natural materials, linen, cotton, wool, cambric in traditional models, tight bodice, wide skirt in many variations and lovely colours.

Yesterday I got my second vaccination against the tick disease. Again I have a headache and feel dazed. Last night I slept in a gypsy caravan near a pond. The nice hippie couple in the house next door said I could take a bath and have a meal together with them and their three dogs, cat and daughter. They keep horses. In the pond the frogs are giving an all night concert, the carps are jumping and the fire salamanders are sneaking. Round the pond the alder trees stand dreaming with their roots in the water.

I have seen my first real Bavarian. He was a fat man with a double chin, sitting on a bench. He wore a large '*Lederhose*', a Tirolean hat and had a jolly look in his eyes.

People greet you with a '*Grüß Gott*' instead of '*Gutentag*'. It sounds like 'cuckoo'. Sometimes I say 'cuckoo' instead of '*Grüß Gott*'. Nobody has noticed yet.

June 1, Ascension Day, Altdorf

It is 11.00 am. The bells of the baroque church are ringing. The church has just gone out. I had such a beautiful experience. I joined a '*Flurumgang*'; an old Christianized tradition, still much alive here.

After Mass the priest in gold brocade chasuble walks with the Sacrament in procession through the village, along the fields, the meadows, through the woods to bless nature and to pray for the people. We faithful folk follow behind and sing and pray the standard prayer, Our Fathers but more so Hail Marys; time and time again, in rising cadence in honour of the Great Mother, whose effigy is also carried in the procession. It seems as if we walk through the folds of her mantle, along the houses of the village, a hollow path, a beech tree, a bit of pine forest, between undulating hills covered in grass, a field with green barley; Hail Mary, full of grace, the Lord is with you, thou are blessed amongst all women. Time and time again. For a fleeting moment her face, as large as a giantess becomes visible above the procession. Men and women walk and pray separately. Intercessions are prayed by a few and responses by all. Strong, tough old peasant women with sharp eyes and hard hands keep at it. During the week I see them with head scarves against the sun, cardigans and flowered aprons working in their vegetable gardens. Today they wear solid, square lady suits and support the prayer whenever it seems to dwindle.

My hostesses of last night, Hildegard and Elisabeth are neighbours, who take care of their husbands and children in spotlessly clean houses. Yesterday evening I rang at Hildegard's door to ask for my 'evening water' (my washing water for the next morning) and, after my pilgrimage story was invited to pitch the tent in her back garden, and to have a shower, and breakfast the next morning. They washed and dried all my muddy and dirty clothes (no launderettes on the way) and today I was with them on the Feast of the Ascension.

I see less and less timber-framed houses and more and more baroque village churches. I receive a lot of invitations to hitch a ride. Of course I reject them all. At little corner shops in the villages signs next to the fresh apples mention conscientiously: 'with artificial polish'. Sausages: with additives. But they have organic sauerkraut, even in such a small shop. Bavaria, which has a right wing political tendency, is all the same very ecologically conscious. In several villages I have seen those natural sewer cleaners: halophyte filters, the system where the sewage is processed by a lot of plants and clean water remains. A village of five houses and a barn still has an environmental organisation.

Friday, June 2, Riedenburg
Today it is very warm again and I take it easy. I just had a refreshing swim in the river Altmühl. Life is good, even with just a lump of bread in my bag, which I bought from a restaurant, for there are no shops anywhere. However the land is teeming with *'Gaststätten zum Weiszen, Roten oder Schwarzen Rossl'* (Inns called 'the white, red or black horse'). I feel like a *'Lustige Witwe'* (the merry widow) who walks singing and sounding through the forest.

Sunday, June 4
I sit here just above Regensburg with a view towards the valley of the Danube. In a few hours I will meet the Great Mother

River, which shall accompany me a long way through the Balkans. I notice I come closer to Bohemia. I encounter the same baroque-ish building style. Houses are painted in warm pastels; they have red-scaled roofs with little half-round attic windows, which look like the half-closed, loving eyes of a friendly housemother. All of a sudden it seems as if that house is a living being.

Walking through the land with its long stretches of grain fields and little copses in between, I see on the horizon, on a slight raise, an enormous lime tree. When I come closer I see at its foot a small standing stone in honour of Saint Isidorus, dated 1703. A very faded painting of a kneeling angel in armour is still visible. Next to it grows a sycamore. The linden tree is enormous with leaves as large as sheets of A4 and never before have I seen such a girth.

That little commemorative stone is almost invisible. When I tried to connect to the energy of the tree, I only felt him making confused little jokes. "Little daughter, little daughter," he said to me in a good-natured but absent way, as if things were not quite in the right place with him. I thought that was unlikely really, with such a healthy powerful tree. There he stands on his own, viewing the land for kilometres around; King Lear without his daughters. When I close my eyes, it is as if the belly of an enormous egg hangs in his crown. He is like Atlas, carrying the canopy of stars.

I hold a little medicine wheel ceremony with small stones. Perhaps it will help this confused energy. But it doesn't. Nothing changes, but when I stand up and shoulder my rucksack suddenly the sun appears from among the grey clouds and shines until sunset.

Monday, June 5

I can't deny it any longer. I am fit enough and very keen to walk at least 30 kilometres per day, but my right foot is protesting. The ligaments of my ankle are hurting and there is a strange red bump on my foot sole on the place where the bladder meridian ends. Do I drink too much or not enough? Have I stepped into something without noticing? My whole foot is stiff and painful and I am afraid that I need rest instead of being able to go for it, the last 200 kilometres to Jeleni Vrychy in the South of the Bohemian Forest. And the heat of 32ºC isn't helping either.

Something strange happened to me yesterday. On the footpath next to the Danube, a quickly flowing brown mud river, I am overtaken by a frail, angelic young man. He is dressed in white, has blonde curly hair, blue eyes and a red rucksack. His age is about 22. He asks me if I am also going to Jerusalem and as I look at him incredulously, he fishes a diary from his pack, with stamps of vicarages, manses and churches where he spent the night, plus all the good wishes which accompany him and the date of the start of his walk. Fifteen minutes past midnight on New Year's night. While we continue to walk he tells me his shocking life story and his motive to go to Jerusalem. He has started with only one Deutschmark (half a Euro) and trusts that everything shall be alright. I admire this boy, half saint, half eccentric. What will happen to him? There is a true wisdom in him. He struggles to forgive his mother and his unknown father and is far from stupid. I have been treated by others so much, so now I offer him to have dinner together in a little restaurant. He seems pleased and then wants to order starters and the most expensive platter on the menu. I am just in time to stop him. He is welcome to eat at my expense, but there is no need for exaggeration. Yes, a strange figure he is. Will he succeed? Not only in arriving at Jerusalem, but in his own life?

In front of the campsite we say goodbye. I have thought for a moment whether he was the guardian angel to accompany me through the Balkan. He really looks like an angel, but I tell God that this one is too tiresome, with too many connections in homeless and drugs circles. I think he would like to come with me. I have the feeling that he needs a lot of motherly energy before he can properly incarnate in his body and I am not at all inclined to give that to him.

What I can do from my heart is to take his two hands with so much warmth as I can muster, plus the admiration that he dares to touch the bottom of existence. I couldn't do that.

There he goes, to an unknown place, cigarette in hand, under the protection of an unknown god. Perhaps we will meet again.

Faithful to my mission I ring the bell at the little convent in the inner city of Regensburg to ask for prayer for peace. A very old nun opens the door, but she has such a youthful face, that I forget all about her age. With interest she listens to my story and when I tell her how much peace is needed in the Middle East, in Jerusalem, I can see true compassion in her eyes while she says sadly: "But the Jews are so stubborn!"

Like a slap in the face the old prejudice hits me, especially coming from such a serene source, and brought forward so innocently too, without any judgement. Perhaps that is the worst of all. I have to catch my breath before starting with the usual counteroffensive: the letter from Paul to the Romans, my acquaintance with the Talmud, the faulty interpretation of Bible texts, the unfamiliarity with what Judaism really is. She listens kindly and with attention, but I am not sure she takes it on board.

When I have finished talking she tells me something about the 19th century Russian pilgrim, who learnt the Jesus prayer. This is a short prayer which you can say with every footstep. That is a good tip. Only this morning I tried to think of a short prayer which I could say while walking.

When I take my leave, she looks me in the eyes with a clear, even-tempered glance and says: "I hope you have learnt something from our conversation". I am too much of a coward to say the same to her.

I sit down on a bench in a little square with shady trees next to an old woman with a sulky face. Of course you exchange a few words; I only tell her that I am on a pilgrimage, and immediately the whole beautiful tragic story of her life comes out. Her mother bore a child every year and had to bury one most years as well. Four children remained of the eighteen. She died when she was 36. This old woman, when she was a little girl, had read somewhere about a blessing which mothers gave to their daughters. And so she had asked her mother for that blessing. She tells how her mother blessed her then, with hands on her head and shoulders.

Then, just before leaving, she draws her purse and I know what is going to come, but I don't want that anymore. I don't want to wheedle money from old women. But she looks radiantly into my eyes with a five mark coin in her hand and says that she has loved this talk so much and please will I pray for her in Jerusalem. Of course I will pray for her, but not for money. But she wants so much that I accept it. "Pray, give this pleasure to me. Go and drink coffee with cake and think of me!" Now what can I do? I've accepted it again; have written her name on the slowly growing list of people to be prayed for in Jerusalem. What if I never arrive in Jerusalem? Quickly I visit the famous little Mary chapel just around the corner to mention her name there. You can feel that women pray a lot here. There are four of them here right now and in the time that I sit there to enjoy the soft atmosphere of goodwill, many more are coming and going.

Each wall is covered with portraits of the Great Mother, and ordinary human mothers. There are expressions of gratitude, notes with intentions, embroidered pictures and sketched portraits. On the altar Mary is standing like a long calm beauty, as large as life and dressed in white satin. Her nickname is: 'the beautiful Mary'. Here I can pray passionately for peace in the Middle East. This is different from my meditation. Meditation is connection, being receptive. This is urging, convincing, asking without ceasing. After I leave and being back on the road I say it in the rhythm of my footsteps. It turns into a tight cadence. It starts to feel like a battering ram: "Give it, give it, now give it; speak to the heart of Jerusalem, that her suffering has ended, that she has paid double penitence for all her sins (Isaiah. 40,2).

But I am not used to pray with such a drive, from the will. Is this alright? Deep in my heart I find it primitive. Shouldn't I be past this sort of praying? Although Jesus recommends it! Then, who am I? And if it helps! What does it matter, primitive or not! I feel something is released, liberated. I feel tears, anger and frustration: 'It is time, the misery has taken long enough. Give it now and give it forever. Give it for Jerusalem and with it for the whole world; you promised, now go for it. I want it all and I want it now!' With every footstep it becomes more still and more intense. It reminds me of the Kelheim pilgrimage with its loudspeakers and storm of intercessions and responses.

It doesn't exactly make me responsive, but there is a sort of surrender to the flow of the will, which I don't recognize. Is it pushy, or pulling, or begging? No, not begging. It is too powerful and autonomous. It is new for me.

Tuesday, June 6, Wiesent, near Wörth on the Danube

Today I was blessed again, walking through the glorious landscape, the glorious forest, the glorious temperature. How grateful I am that I can do this, and still for such a long time if everything goes right. I am walking through the valley of the Danube. South of the river are the outstretched flat lands. On the northern side the Bavarian Forest begins immediately. On its highest point it meets the border and the Bohemian Forest. Only ten days, and I will arrive at my Czech friend in his forester's home on Deer Mountain. Between him and me there is extensive woodland with parcels of primeval forest. Ever since Aachen near the Dutch border I have been walking through the forest, and how much have I enjoyed it! How much it evokes gratitude and stillness. It has been such a good friend.

Just before Wörth on the Danube, where I have to buy a new map, a beautiful lady of my own age speaks to me in the street and invites me into her home. My instinct says yes and a minute later I step into her house. It is a renovated old watermill on a quickly flowing brook. They generate their own electricity. A wonderful chat develops. She is a teacher at a school for children with learning difficulties and she is married and has four children. We are the same age and immediately exchange experiences about relationships, how you can be more loving for yourself, group work, in short: there is a click. We also talk about pilgrimage. As I had already noticed there is a strong tradition of pilgrimage in Bavaria. People walk to power places, where now there are churches, or places where there has been a lot of prayer traditionally. When during my walk I meet people and tell them about my pilgrimage, the faces brighten and each person gives me her or his story of faith and those of the pilgrimages from which they have returned with so much insight and peace. Don't get me wrong. They mean walking pilgrimages of one to four days, not bus, train or airplane pilgrimages. Sometimes they walk 80 kilometres a day. Well, I find that a bit too much of a good thing. If this isn't mediaeval masochism! Why so many kilometres? To feel properly what suffering is? Alas, most people know what suffering is anyway.

Pilgrimage. Bavaria is full of it. Also the well-educated go. Also my hostess, who knows of chakras, energy work and the power of the land.

At night Renate takes me with her to friends. It is a barbecue party, and she has especially bought some cheeses for her vegetarian guest. There is a gathering in an old wooden hunting lodge in the middle of the woods, which are owned by the Prince of Thurn and Taxis. Two foresters are there too. Very simple people, who immediately understand my love for the forest and the intention with which I walk. When I ask for stories and songs from the region, they start to sing authentic 'yodelling' songs. I never realized that their rhythms are so dashed complicated! I have to relinquish all my prejudices about *Lederhosen* and yodel girls to hear with how much pleasure and pride they sing. Then follow stories, in the almost incomprehensible Bavarian accent, which is translated by Renate, about the Prince of Thurn and Taxis. When the Prince came to visit and inspect his forests and enjoy his favourite prospect, the mother of one of the present foresters took great pride in sweeping the forest road, so that not a pine needle or tree leaf could be found and not a grain of sand would be in the wrong place.

Wednesday, June 7, Wiesent on the Danube

This morning an earthquake has turned over my life. My right foot has been painful for over a week now. I was wondering which acupuncture point was blocked. Are my kidneys OK? Perhaps I don't drink enough. The rest of my body is flourishing, healthy, strong and happy. What is the matter? In

Wiesent, the next village, I pay the doctor a visit, but after consulting him I am in complete confusion and shock.

1. I need a 6-week rest to give my inflamed Achilles tendon a chance to heal.
2. I need to have orthopaedic soles made for my shoes.
3. I must give up the walk to Jerusalem. I won't get very far with my flat feet.

So the lump under my right foot wasn't something complicated with meridians and acupressure points, but quite simply the result of a lot of walking and a heavy pack. I have fallen through my foot! But up till now in my life, my feet have never bothered me at all!

After the consultation I sit on the village green and cry out of pure disappointment. All the joy has vanished and this apparently was into the bargain from the beginning, because I have always had flat feet. And walking agrees with me so; I enjoy it so much. It was going so well the last few weeks and I had become so happy! It was pure heaven! This is so difficult to digest; what a disappointment...

But I also know that going to Jerusalem is symbolical for dying. In other words when you go to Jerusalem, you have to be prepared to give up every personal wish. Perhaps my ego has to die by NOT being able to go there. And then I will have reached my Jerusalem as well.

Just try to let go, Johanna, because this is all attachment and ego. Remember, that you are not going to Jerusalem for yourself. If you are not needed there then just accept it and surrender to your poor feet which cannot cope. Those sweet dear feet, which have carried you already for 1200 kilometres.

For the time being I will take a long rest and then try again, and, if walking is impossible, continue by bicycle. But the gleam over the journey has faded. Or so it seems now. I decide to call my Czech friend, who lives not far away from here on the other side of the border in the Bohemian Forest. I want to ask him if I can stay in his house to rest for some weeks. He gives his immediate consent, the treasure.

At that very moment my eye catches a text, carved on the village fountain just in front of me: *'Fiele jemand vom Himmel, er muszte in Wiesent fallen'* — 'If somebody would fall from heaven, he must fall in Wiesent'.

Seven weeks later
Monday, 24 July 2000
After all the resting, upset stomachs, flues and fevers, having special orthopaedic soles made and the fear and doubts whether I can walk to Jerusalem or not, I finally return to Wiesent to say hello to Renate and connect to my last real pilgrim steps to continue on my walk.

Today it is time for walking again. Carefully, slowly, don't force yourself, you have been weakened; you still have a slight temperature and a slight headache.

To my surprise it goes well, and it is getting better with every step. First I walk on the main road from Wiesent to Worth and then the path turns left into the woods, the Bavarian Forest.

I am amazed how fast I am catching up between the trees, how I am getting into shape again. It is strange to be travelling again. I have travelled such different directions, that my head and heart have become confused. But here, in the forest it is good. I slowly start to believe that I am on my way again; on my way to Jerusalem.

Do you know what really boosted me today? Raspberries. The raspberries are ripe. I have never seen so many raspberries together in my life. They are growing as profusely as blackberries. So refreshing! I also sleep for two hours in a little clearing between the trees. I wake up invigorated and happy.

In the evening I pitch my tent near a farm at Pilgrim's Mountain.

The people there invite me for a shower, breakfast and protection. My tent is in the chicken patch; I hadn't realized that there would be such a lot of chicken poo.

Wednesday, July 26
Rain, thunder, rain, sunshine, rain. My feet hurt because of the new orthopaedic soles. I will go without today. I feel a bit grumpy. No idea why.

Thursday, July 27, Schonau, east of Viechtach on the Regen
Today I dawdled. There are holes in my socks and in my precious elegant red T-shirt and I lost a flannel today in the woods. So I have shopped in Viechtach. Easy enough to get flannels and socks, but where do I get a T-shirt which is just as nice as the one I have worn threadbare? I've had it for fifteen years. In the end I had to buy an ordinary red T-shirt, with one of those tight high necks, which I will cut and sow into a V-neck in order to look nice and not to suffocate.

I arrive in the region of the country where during the winter months it used to be very cold (-30ºC). When somebody died he couldn't be buried, because the ground was frozen. The corpse was therefore laid out in the attic (it was just as cold as outside) on a special *Leichenbrett* or *Ruhebrett* (corpse board). After the funeral in spring, those corpse boards were painted beautifully with name and dates and were placed in the ground next to the house or near road crosses or chapels. I see a lot of them here. My first acquaintance with them was in a dark road chapel with only one tiny window. In the semi-darkness I see the 'resting boards' hanging on the wall, anno 1785, 1810, 1865. Then suddenly I notice on the ground in front of the altar a stretched-out half naked corpse. After recovering from the shock I realize it is a life-size statue of the laid-out Christ in his grave. But that is not all. Above the altar a colony of hornets has been building a large paper nest and they are flying on and off by the dozens. It is a lugubrious place indeed.

In the north east I can see the mountain ridge rising, the border between Germany and the Czech Republic, the former Iron Curtain. I guess one more day, and then I will be back in the Bohemian Forest.

Friday, July 28, Bodenmais

Oh, everything is horrible at this moment, please, can I moan and meow and blubber against your shoulder a little? Everything was OK until last night half past nine. I had tapped my 'evening water' and found in the very sloping forest on the mountainside a nice neat little level place near a big stone. There were no mosquitoes, the tent was pitched to perfection and I was as pleased as Punch. Half an hour after going to bed it starts to drizzle. No problem, I close the tent. But it rains harder and harder and more and more. Still no problem. But I start to be a bit anxious. I stretch out my hand to feel my trousers, which are lying on the rucksack next to me. Its foam plastic carrier straps and hip band are fully soaked in water. I feel the place where the tent is leaking. Outside it is pouring. I am too late to put my storm plastic on the roof. I dab the pool of water with my towel, put it outside the tent to wring it. Inside there is a new puddle. I keep dabbing and wringing one and a half hour long. Not dabbing, bailing! Luckily I cannot drown, I think, and I'm glad it isn't cold, but I get tired, so tired, and I have to go on. I have wet arms, wet hair, mopping and wringing while the tap is running. I must. On my knees on the sleeping bag, which is far from dry and the first town is eight kilometres away; eight kilometres of forest in the pouring rain, which is continuing and continuing, and I am so tired and in the end I burst out crying. Thank God, what a relief is that and the words from psalm 139 come into my mind: '...and I praise you Lord, because I am wonderfully made...' Only I change it into: 'That all this is wonderfully made...' O, how I love nature! But it is really true; I feel a sort of love for the whole miserable business. It is all coming out of the hand of God. I also think: 'You might change your tune if you had been cold and hungry.'

I decide upon a desperate act. I will undress completely and will go outside to put my plastic over the tent. The forest is pitch-dark. I happen to see the white tent guy lines and know exactly where the poles are. Immediately the rain is plonking and splashing away on the plastic; I hurry back into the tent, shivering with cold. I put my damp T-shirt back on, and start dabbing again. Whatever is in my rucksack will be soaking wet. Oh my dry set of change! I can just about save my underwear, the rest is lost. Still there is water entering. The rain continues. After another bailing session my towel has become strangely long and thin. I am so exhausted (it is three o'clock in the morning) that I slide into the sleeping bag. It is still warm. I lay my soaking hair on the pillow. I will wait for the disasters to come, but I won't lift a finger anymore. I sleep. I wake up at half past six. It is still raining. Under my mattress there is a puddle, but weirdly enough I am dry and warm.

I have a small piece of bread for breakfast; I have drinking water. I put on my wet trousers. I don't need to wash — I had a shower in the night — and make an inventory of the damage. All is wet. I remain in the tent for another 45 minutes. I play my recorder, but the true joy will not come. The rain is pounding on the tent roof.

Suddenly I've had enough. I'm going out now; roll up the plastic, roll up the tent containing litres of water, shoulder rucksack, ooh, soaked carrier straps; T-shirt wet too now, wet trousers, keep moving, keep moving to keep warm. Better put on my poncho, better than nothing, and walk. The rain seems to diminish. For half an hour it is almost dry.

Then it starts again.

Wide muddy brooks are flowing over the path. The town where I am going to is only eight kilometres away, but I have to take shelter often; I cannot walk through this cloud-burst. I arrive only at two o'clock in the afternoon, shaking with hunger. I look for a B&B; there is one, it feels good. How much is a room? A very ugly, nasty, tyrannical woman comes to the door. She mentions an outrageous price. "You must stay at least two nights," she says. I walk on; even my intuition doesn't work anymore.

Sunday, July 30

The weather has cleared up. Not outside, but inside. I intended to do a lot more complaining, but I don't need it anymore. Friday I did find a good little B&B where the lady made me a wonderful welcome and helped me to spread and dry all my wet stuff. And she only wanted me to pay half price.

Bodenmais is about 20 kilometres from the Czech border. The timber-framed houses have completely disappeared in this region. Instead I now see large chalets, with splendid woodcarvings in dark brown on long balconies on every floor. From the balconies hang flower caskets with all sorts of geraniums, petunias and unfamiliar garden flowers in challenging bright colour combinations. Everything is perfectly cared for, very large and very rich. I don't see any small houses. The people are proud of their 'Bayern' Bavaria, their former kingdom and are a bit rebellious against the rest of Germany. They are proud of their low level of crime, of their old customs, which they keep in good repair. Many of them wear regional dress, but will happily change this into jeans and T-shirts when necessary. There are many obese people here too. Perhaps they have too much '*Schweinefleisch*' on the menu.

A vegetarian recommendation: '*Semmelknödel mit Pfifferling soße*'; a large, tasty, boiled dumpling in a deep plate full of brown mushroom ragout. Doesn't it sound attractive? But it is really very nice, and nourishing.

On the opposite side of my B&B there is a Lutheran church. It is round with a wooden vault. Towards the southeast there is a stained-glass window in blue and red. In front of it stands the table for the Lord's Supper. I am busy singing negro-spirituals in German (aaargh) with the others when I notice that the stained-glass window depicts the New Jerusalem from Revelations: the twelve gates, the four directions of the compass, the flowing waters; a triangle depicting the Trinity living amongst us. I pray that the New, heavenly Jerusalem will begin to penetrate the Earthly Jerusalem. That that Gordian devil's knot which is there in the mundane life, will start to loosen up and that between the cords a little light will start wringing and stinging. That light, which is the wonderful atmosphere of Jerusalem, but which doesn't penetrate the daily practice of political and religious contradictions. Because that is what we want: oppositions which harm each other transform into beneficial contrasts. Barak, the prime minister is trying hard and so does Yasser Arafat at the moment.

Jerusalem, come down from Heaven! God, come live with us between us people. On Temple Mount the New Jerusalem touches the Earth. Many people are receiving visions. Some become quite mad and think they are the Messiah, or Mohammed, or they see Jesus. There is a special Jerusalem clinic for 'the Jerusalem syndrome', to take care of all those pilgrims gone out of their mind.

There on Temple Mount, the *Haram al-Sharif*, that most sacred of places, the navel of the earth, the heart of the world, is also the most inflammable situation of the current conflict. The oldest mosque of the world, the exquisite Dome of the

Rock, an edifice of great beauty and piety, stands on the spot where once the Jewish temple was built.

A small group of ultra-orthodox Jews have already rebred the red, spotless sacrificial bull. The great *menorah* is a fact; the architectural designs for the third temple are ready. With impatience they wait for the time that a new temple can be built. And the old, primitive and barbaric sacrificial ritual will be re-installed. The altar covered in blood, the ceremonial clothes of the high priest sprayed with blood, the soil soaked in the blood of innocent animals: a primitive half magic ritual from the past.

And the Palestinians? They know it. They know that an eye is focused on the oldest mosque in the world and it makes them white-hot with suspicion.

Why should there be a new temple? For Christians it is Christ and the temple of their own body. For Judaism it could be the 'Palace of Interpretations' (from 'Paleis van Betekenissen' by Tamar Benima) It is the body of Midrashim, Mishna, Talmud, Kabbala and Zohar, the comments of the great Jewish teachers. It took 2,000 years to build. In the beginning it was the compensation for the destroyed Jerusalem temple and its rituals, but more and more it became a value in itself. It developed in a higher level of consciousness of Judaism, that in spite of, or thanks to the destruction of the temple in 70 CE and the dispersion, could fully develop into what it is now. It was an internalizing of the outer building, exactly how it is stated in the Bible. I quote by heart in the vein of one of the biblical prophets (for I cannot find the exact place): *'And in those times there will be no temple built by men in places on the earth. But I the Lord God will have built my temple in the heart of my people and I will stay there forever.*

When I ask the parson for his intercession for Jerusalem's peace, he is very gratified that I have noticed that the stained-glass window points exactly south-east to the real Jerusalem.

He says daily prayers for peace and he studied there for a year. He is happy to meet yet another Dutch pilgrim to Jerusalem. A few months ago there was another one going there on foot; a Dutchman. "A Dutch tradition, isn't it?" He would love to come with me, but he has his responsibilities here in Bodenmais.

CZECH REPUBLIC

Monday, July 31

Yesterday I walked the last bit of Germany: from Bodenmais to Zelezna Ruda on the Czech border and well known to me from my first walk through the Bohemian Forest a few years ago. And to my great joy, I am here again; walked all the way from The Hague. I shouldn't be so proud of this, since this is a pilgrimage and self-adulation is not a part of it, but I can't deny a feeling of satisfaction. I walked more than two months through the forest and I can't get enough of it. I love it just as much as on the first day. The Bohemian Primeval Forests are Europe's green lungs. Nowhere else have I seen such giants of the forest, digging with their roots in and around large rocky boulders; they are now of enormous girth and several hundreds of years old. At their feet grow decorative moss, mushrooms, ferns and wood sorrel all radiating a most perfect harmony.

Near Cesky Krumlov

I walk through silent and serene woods and fields. The great forest lies behind me, but this is beautiful too. So still. I come through quiet, untidy, Slavic villages with a little square and a little church and two or three houses in folksy baroque, which is the imitation of the high baroque of the cities by local craftsmen and which is so much nicer and simpler.

It is harvest time; small ancient combines are reaping the wheat and the grain is shed into old and dented iron containers, standing in the field. Afterwards it is poured into bags of the size which can be lifted and carried by an adult man. A boy in a blue blouse is standing on the stepladder against the container and wades through all that grain with his arms. His father approaches slowly with a pile of hessian bags and a shovel. When he is binding the first bag it seems as if

I see again something of the joy and respect which many Czech people have for their food.

In the forest I see figures bending down between the trees. People return from the woods with large baskets full of enormous mushrooms. It is a good mushroom year and looking for mushrooms is a national sport in the Czech Republic. Every family knows a few sorts of which they know they are edible. It is being passed on from (grand)parent to child. Just like with fishermen and fish, stories about enormous mushrooms go round, and how long the family could be nourished by them.

Thursday, August 3, Nove Hrady
This morning something unpleasant happened. I had camped next to a brook and sat looking at a little sick alder tree. The few leaves it had though were illuminated by the sun. Among them a little spider had just finished her web; it might have been her first one. It was a delicate, shining round little web and she sat proudly in the middle like a little diamond. I thought it looked just like a lens, with the sunrays peering through on the sick tree. I wanted to do something for the tree as well and I made a nice arrangement of leaves, alder catkins and grass blades and laid it at her feet. Now to my great dismay apparently I broke a main thread of the little web, because it suddenly hung broken, torn and vandalized between the twigs, hardly anything left. I felt mortified. It was so beautiful, and then I had to DO something also with my big well-meaning ego. I should have stayed put and just looked at the spider in the web and the sunlight shining through it on the tree. That would have been more than plenty and would have been healing for all three of us. No, of course I had to meddle with it and now that little spider has to start all over again and she really didn't deserve that. I am full of remorse. Later however, after I pack everything and take a last look at the place of my

overnight stay, I feel that everything is OK. It is all in the bargain that I make mistakes. Everything is love.

As if I haven't learned enough that morning I order my lunch in a cafe from the menu: '*Fleischlose Gerichte*' (meatless meals'). A spaghetti Carbonara. Gosh, I'm curious what sort of vegetarian dish they have made of the Carbonara! The spaghetti arrives: a plate full of pieces of ham among the pasta. I am flabbergasted and point to the menu and the vegetarian list.

"The spaghetti Carbonara is with ham," says the waitress.

"But I am a vegetarian and I wanted something without meat," I say while I point at the Carbonara on the list 'meatless meals'.

"But spaghetti Carbonara is always with ham," she says.

Furiously I take the menu and cross out the word 'meatless meals' under her eyes.

She gets angry too, takes the menu, throws it behind the bar on a little table and abandons me.

I'm not eating it. I eat the salad, don't touch the spaghetti, drink my beer and get the bill. The bill is inclusive of the Carbonara. I'm not paying it. It is their fault.

We are all getting quite heated. I tell them to call the police as far as I am concerned, but I'm not paying.

The solution comes when the big boss of the restaurant gives me my way. And the mystery is solved when the waitress says that ham, sausage etc. is not considered meat in Czech. It is processed meat, which is not meat??!! Anyway, apparently this is a language matter! In German and Dutch everything edible of an animal is meat, but not so in Czech.

Everybody is upset by my anger. Look what harm you are causing! I make a mistake this morning and am immediately forgiven, and they make a little mistake and are getting a good bawling out of me. I am exactly like the unjust steward from the Bible. I disappear with my rucksack through the door and am remorseful again. Last week I got into a temper as well; I gave a snarl to a boy who ran into me without looking. Yes, I was soaked through and unhappy, cold and hungry, but still, do you remember the expression on the little face?

For an hour I have remorse and for an hour I apparently follow the wrong way, but fortunately I can return easily to the right path. As a reward for my sins somebody gives me a new map, exactly at the stage where I needed it; it had not been for sale in the shops. I am allowed to sleep in a beautiful monastery with a free evening meal and breakfast, while outside there is a thunderstorm and buckets of rain. There you see. God lets it rain on the just and the unjust.

With one of the monks I talk about the Israel/Palestine political issue. I am pleasantly surprised with the open-mindedness of many a monk or nun. Where did I get the idea that they were narrow-minded?

The baroque refectory has been renovated in a simple way by painting all the elaborate stucco work white. An older man asks permission to touch my arm; to touch somebody who is walking to Jerusalem must certainly be beneficial. I stand confused while he does so. I am given a medal, a little device to wear on your person, of Svaty Peregrin Laziosi, a pilgrim monk, who has become the patron of pilgrims and sufferers of foot ailments and who is specifically connected to this monastery.

AUSTRIA

Sunday, August 4

I walk to the Czech/Austrian border. I spend my last crowns. I am sorry to leave the Slavs. I am homesick for them already. I have a special connection to this untidy, friendly land with its withdrawn shy people. But here comes Austria. I expect something like Bavaria and just over the border I notice the well-swept, park-like landscape; undulating fields, trimmed forest edges and copses. On a road cross I read the following wise rhymes:

Wer das Kreuz fasst, tragt halbe Last ('Who takes on the cross, half of its weight is lost').

And another one:

Lieber Gott, Bitte Schutze die Natur, das Wald, die Tiere und die Flur. Amen

('Dear God, please protect Nature, the forest, the animals and the field. Amen').

As I am peering at my map having lost my way a little, a small window of a nearby house opens. "Do you need help?" A moment later two elderly ladies and a dog walk a five kilometre stretch with me on a lovely forest path bordered with lots of wild mushrooms. One of the ladies tells me, that, as a 15-year-old, she had to take care of her younger siblings after her mother died. On top of that she had to help with the work in the fields. And she worked so hard, she couldn't sleep at night anymore. The people in the village said, if she continued like this she would die. She didn't grow, didn't put on weight. When she was nineteen she was allowed to go to an aunt, a teacher of domestic science. She was in the kitchen from seven o'clock in the morning until eight at night, grew seven centimetres in half a year and put on eight kilos. For her this was *'Erholung',* recuperation. She tells me that as a child she was fond of reading, and that there were no books and no libraries. She read every snippet of newspaper, all user manuals, every thatch with letters on. She was given a book with two fairy tales, and she stills knows them by heart. The reading hunger is only stilled in the present day. "I am 66 years old, and don't need so much sleep anymore." She reads religious and philosophical books, geography and geology and - says the other lady - she is a well-known herbal and mushroom specialist. They duly note that I walk to Jerusalem on my own, but don't find it something special. They promise to pray with me for peace in Jerusalem and while saying goodbye the first lady says: "Don't be afraid. It is not necessary. You are in the hand of God. I'm never afraid either."

In the evening I repair the leaking places in my tent. It is sure to rain and I will be able to test the repairs.

Sunday, August 6

This is a mystical still landscape. Groups of overgrown, erect rocks stand in very tidy fields. I had to walk without a map today. I thought that the people would be able to show me the little distance from Weitra to Zwettl, but I am walking already for five hours. People don't know a lot about roads and distances.

Monday, August 7, near Zwettl

I didn't make it. I was so tired of those blind detours, that five kilometres before Zwettl I sank down in the rain and was in bed already at 09.00 pm.

The theatrical, baroque style, awful Mother Marys in the road chapels are enough to turn my stomach at the moment. They are so ugly and so abundant that they start to stand between me and God.

During the night there were thunderstorms and downpours (I was OK with my plastic cover), but this morning the weather is reasonable apart from the big drops falling from the trees. I am in a pine wood next to the river Zwettl. After last night it is extremely swollen and speeds along, the water muddy brown and wild, carrying broken off branches and torn off trees.

I have no breakfast. Yesterday evening I begged a little piece of bread from a farmer for supper, since I can't find any shops.

There seem to be a lot of old Celtic ruins here in the neighbourhood: an initiation pyramid, dolmen, special rock formations. I have run past all of them without knowing it.

These sorts of things are constantly happening the last few days. All Anti-gifts. I skim straight along all sorts of beautiful possibilities without knowing it. Am I doing something wrong? The shop, which closes just before I arrive, the library which is closed exactly on the day I pass etc.

I feel I am stuck as far as spirituality is concerned. I am faithfully meditating at fixed times, but nothing really happens. All crosses, chapels and baroque ornaments are against the grain. When I think of Jerusalem I feel a great nothing. I just have to keep going. I'm not depressed, but more grumpy and dissatisfied. I don't like being like that. I'd rather be loving and joyful, but I behave better now and keep to myself when something or somebody annoys me. And that rain; will it go on forever?

Wednesday, August 9

I'm sitting in the large inner court of the enormous abbey near Zwettl. I went to Mass this morning and received communion and felt the usual healing of the atmosphere often present in monasteries. I talked with one of the monks about my feelings of emptiness and grumpiness and being stuck, but he said it was absolutely normal. It happens to everybody who is praying a lot and it is just part of the process. It happens to him and every other monk and I was doing nothing wrong. So at least I know I don't need to worry.

Last night I was given a room with breakfast in an uninhabited wing of the abbey. The room gave a view on the great still cloister garden with its cypresses, a high beech tree in front of a soft yellow wall. On the right the entrance of the church can be seen. Originally it was gothic, but was baroquised in the 18th century. There is a large statue of St. Michael over the gate. He pierces the dragon with such a loving and compassionate look on his face that he lifts up my spirit.

On the felt slippers which the monastery gives to its guests, I glide through the long deserted corridors on shimmering polished but old parquet floors. The high doors which open up to the rooms behind them are of polished cherry wood. I look behind every open door. Behind it are large empty rooms with half crumbling and half renovated murals. In the kitchen next to my room there are some chipboard kitchen cabinets, a stainless steel sink and an old crystal chandelier like in a ballroom. In the top corners near the ceiling there are paintings of garlands and wreaths. At the end of the long wide corridor there is a niche. In it a gilded mitred bishop stands, lifting his eyes to heaven. Where are the monks? They are invisible.

Peace is palpable in the inner court. It is a large square, painted in creamy colours with only a few ornaments. On the abbey's roof the storks are nesting. Flights of swallows swerve chirping through the blue sky, but also the deafening fighter jets of the military basis close by. There is a fountain in the middle of the square.

This morning I feel a harmony again. I pack and walk on through the wooded valley of the Zwettl. I see a sign with a remarkable announcement: *'Bundesheer Achtung!'* 'Army, Attention please: here begin the forest roads owned by the monastery of Zwettl. To drive and to walk here is only permitted with written permission of the monastery. You cannot appeal to an order of your superiors. It shall not be considered. Abbey of Zwettl.'

Just like in the Eifel Mountains there is a lot of tarmac, but there are also many organic farms, shops, even in the villages. And the offer of the Tourist Information Offices has a high New Age level:

"Mystic Waldviertel. Visit the secret places of the Celts. Every Saturday departure at 12.00 from the Town Hall. Costs DM 4,50."

In spite of all my unhappy detours I have - after all - visited the Celtic initiation pyramid lying deeply concealed in the forest. It reminds me of the Tower of Babel and is an edifice built from loose rocks rising in a spiral from a broad base to end high up in a tiny platform. It depicts the path of humanity seemingly going around in circles, so coming back to the same predicaments every time, but still and almost unnoticeably ascending.

I had hoped to be alone there, but two workmen were renovating the pyramid. It looked beautiful and I asked permission to walk around it. It was a big shock to discover that at the back the pyramid had completely collapsed. According to the men this had happened two years ago under the pressure of the number of visitors. I think secretly to myself: "Those are the hordes of New-Agers coming to initiate themselves (just like me?)". On my way up through the forest I had already noticed Germanic runes on a big rock.

There are places here with names such as: 'Heidnische Opferplatz', Pagan Sacrificial place; an amount of large rolling stones from which round forms have been hacked. It looked more as if the Neolithic inhabitants needed some millstones. I got that information from the signs placed there by the town council. To my happy surprise the term: 'energetically powerful place' was used. Here at the town council they know what an 'energetically powerful place' is and they are not afraid of not being taken serious.

Another ancient place is: '*Heimliches Gericht*', Secret Judgement; a deep ravine for throwing criminals in and used by the inhabitants of the three local villages. It had a beautiful panorama and was very peaceful now.

In this region I walk today over a mountain ridge full of strangely formed rocks, among which and on top of which all sorts of trees are growing. I see a plant which I have never seen growing in the wild, only in pictures: dwale or Belladonna; a very poisonous nightshade. It is one of the ingredients for the witches' ointment, supposedly used on the night of the First of May to rub their bodies to invoke a collective hallucination: flying on broomsticks to the 'Blocksberg' to dance with the devil. To eat one berry will cause your death! The plant looks powerful and a little threatening. Another power plant that I saw today is flowering in pots in front of kitchen windows: the datura plant or thorn apple, another nightshade, a famous American hallucinogen that is mentioned in the 'Lessons of Don Juan' and also ingredient to the witches' ointment. How that could be I don't know, for the Americas were only discovered in 1492, and supposedly the recipe for witches' ointment is much older than that. The plant is of a decadent refinement, reminding me of the morbid *Jugendstil* drawings of Aubrey Beardsley. But I haven't only seen dwale and datura, but also wild cyclamen. On the footpath! They are just like in the shop, only smaller. And all those different types of mint; many of them I never saw before. I also saw two big snakes. A dice snake and another one with long stripes, whose path I crossed and who hissed vehemently at me.

Harvest has started here too. The sun is shining fiercely after all the rain and the combines are growling, doing their work in the fields. Today I see many women serving the tractors. They have pointed faces with clear brown eyes and they don't wear scarves against the sun. They are of a disarming kindness when they greet me; real nice smiles. How terrible this must be; sitting on these roaring beast-machines all day long. The work is going fast, but won't this deafening noise undermine your system?

In a little village I ring the bell at the vicarage and am invited into the untidy kitchen. The vicar brews tea for me; the housekeeper is on holiday and he tells me he is from Poland and doing relief work for his German colleague. He shall make intercessions for peace in Jerusalem in the three churches he is servicing. He is an elderly corpulent man, asking me many questions about my private situation and the motivation for this walk. When I leave he gives me an official blessing and his address in Poland. He promises that his churches shall pray for me. "For peace I hope?" I say startled. He stares at me doubtfully. "We will always have original sin to deal with."

I should have reacted there and then, that this is an unchristian point of view that boils down to: 'You cannot really improve this earth'. But when I had come to that conclusion I was walking again through the woods with two bulging pockets full of apples, which he gave to me.

Friday, August 11, Ober Meisling-Krems
The wheat is ripe. The blackberries taste better and better. Yesterday I walked on too long, because I couldn't find a good camping spot on the steep hillside. In the end - it was dark already - I had to lie down in the overgrown cart track, without tent, just the sleeping bag. I lay under the holy awning, stars shining, a crescent moon disappearing early behind the hill and Earth passing through the shower of meteors, as usual around August 9. I saw three shooting stars with long tails. In the morning the sleeping bag was soaking wet with dew, but it had been warm during the night. And waking up in daylight I discovered I was laying between the ripe blackberries.

Breakfast! Nothing compares with sleeping under the stars, but it is too wet at this latitude. It is not really possible.

Saturday, August 12, Krems

My Achilles tendon is really hurting again! I have to rest for a day! In a health food shop I ask whether they know an alternative practitioner, because I don't want to be prescribed another six weeks of rest by an ordinary GP. Perhaps something else can be done. I am given three addresses of Reiki people. The last one is home when I call him from a telephone booth. What a nice man he is! He immediately starts to treat me by phone. And when I have run out of coins we meet each other in the park near the fountain to continue the treatment. F.L. is a very gentle and sensitive person and the effect of his treatment on my system is immediately perceptible: my heart is opening and my intuition works again. He interprets the things which are happening and my spiritual block in a very clear way: by my constant physical exercise, which is not habitual, I have activated my right side. Follows: I am slightly out of balance, I want to DO too much and I cannot be receptive. By the constant exercise of my will I have relapsed in my 'ego'. Now I have to find the right balance between dream and action. My Achilles tendon says that I have to rest. But I'm not doing enough at all! And I want to walk! Yes, exactly! That's what it is all about.

He feels blockages at my ankles and my shoulders, which are in correlation. "As far as the ankles go, there you want to do too much, and your shoulders are carrying the guilt when you feel that you are not doing enough."

He doesn't want to be paid for his extensive session and gives me instead a picture of Sri Mataji, an Indian female guru, whom I find unsympathetic. "That's alright," he says. "Just feel your dislike!" Also he invites me to have a meditation together at his family's home; maybe tomorrow, but when he sees I hesitate he doesn't push on to give me his address.

My foot feels much better, light and free, but towards the evening it deteriorates again. He said: "You must do it yourself". But how?

Today I have put the tent on an official camp site on the Danube and I don't do anything. I already feel how grumpy that makes me. I suppose that's the stuff that needs sticking out.

In the evening the full moon shines over the wide Danube. The water is flowing at great speed over my ankles. In the darkness I stand on the lowest step of a '*Treppl*' a little stone staircase descending into the water. Far away on the other side, floodlights are illuminating a beautiful monastery on a wooded hill. Everything is so magnificent and I am so unhappy.

Sunday, August 13

After a damp hot night I go for the sound of church bells ringing in the distance. I need organ music, singing and a few good words. The sound lures me from the camp site, makes me cross a busy traffic road into an alleyway on to the high street of Stein, a suburb of Krems. Mediaeval and renaissance houses follow each other up in a long row, each different. There are wall paintings, graffito, crenellated walls and baroque curls; wine tasting establishments in every other building, and it is a bit untidy too. I rather like that. At the end of the street I see the church where the bells are ringing for the nine o'clock service. The organ is playing. I take a hymnbook, because I long to sing. But the congregation sings only one verse of every song, and that is not enough for me to learn the melody. In between they sing many other songs, all by heart, and I cannot join in! There may be many good words spoken from the pulpit, but the Austrian accent is just as incomprehensible for me as Chinese. All that I had hoped for here is denied me. And it makes me grumpy and angry.

Actually I am furious! And also I know that this fury is completely unjustified. I am so unhappy with my annoyances. If I'm sitting here being furious, what am I doing here, in a church of all places? So instead I choose to have a good cry, out of disappointment. That is better, it does me good and nobody harm. Everything is over-activated on the right side.

When Mass is over I step outside and start walking home on the left side of the street. On the front door of the first house I see - o miracle - the nameplate of the man whom I met yesterday in the park. O glorious synchronicity! He invited me yesterday for a meditation at his home! Shall I dare to ring the bell?

He opens up, still wearing his pyjamas. In the background I hear a woman's voice and noisy children. He is very pleased to see me, and invites me inside, in pyjamas, without a bogus sense of shame, leading me through his untidy office with spare computer parts and papers lying on the floor into his meditation room with a softly coloured pink altar for the elephant God Ganesha and Sri Mataji, his guru. We talk for an hour, and meditate. He treats me with camphor and burning candles. While passing a candle behind my head, a few hairs are set alight for a split second. "That is a good sign," he says. "Fire behind the head is the burning of past ballast.' I have to laugh about his wonderful New Agey solution of what others would interpret as a health and safety moment.

He tells me that Jesus has opened the chakra between the eyes and that all people could benefit from it if they wanted, which is translated in old fashioned Christian terms as: He has opened for all people the gate to Heaven. In the human body the chakra between the eyes is the gate to the crown chakra, where the soul is in union with God, is in Heaven.

We sit in front of his little altar and I look at the wild, powerful face of Sri Mataji. F.L. is convinced that she is an Avatar: an incarnation of the Divine. And as an extra gift this morning, I get a powerful intuition. Not just Mary, but EACH woman is - in principle - the embodiment of the Holy Spirit on earth and partakes - in that way - of the Divine.

I am peaceful and balanced when I thank him and take leave of him. He refuses to be paid. He says: "I got it for nothing and I give it for nothing". My fury and irritation are gone.

I arrive just in time at the campsite to pack up my tent and walk on along the Danube, direction Vienna. I walk for a few hours and now I am sitting on a bench in a little park, to write this letter.

Two passing Turkish women look at me curiously and then come shyly forward to invite me for a meal at their home. I am pleasantly surprised. What a lovely family, and how they do everything to please me and make something nice for me. They speak better German than the Austrians and they cook chicken legs for me I'm afraid. I can stay to sleep, they say, but the house is rather overcrowded. I am sure I would have to sleep in the best bed, robbing someone else of it. And I also prefer to sleep outside. Two men and the children show me a safe place in the grass along the Danube. The next morning they come to find out whether nothing bad has happened to me. It hasn't.

Tuesday, August 15
Today is Mary's Ascension Day. According to the archetypical dogma of 1950 of the Roman Catholic Church, she was taken up soul AND body into the celestial realm. The perishable and finite is finally recognized as divine. The female body is acknowledged as sacred and gets the honour which it deserves. No longer are we a sack of bones and offal, as one early church father tried to depict our bodies in an attempt to overcome his own lust.

Dogmas are not just a nuisance to aggravate intelligent people. They are petrified expressions of a deeply felt divine truth. But they are petrified and not flexible; that's what can make a past truth a present lie.

Wednesday, August 16, between Tull and Vienna, 02.30 pm, 30° C in the shade
I am in one of the little water sport cafes on the south bank of the Danube. One after another people are helped on the water skis to learn how to keep standing while the speedboat is leaping forward. The speedboat is steered by a glamour boy with his glamour girlfriend sitting next to him. Beautiful face and body, a bit superficial and external perhaps, but they have a lot of good fun too, these water skiers, and a lot of water sport skills and discipline.

Just ten minutes ago I had my afternoon dip in the Danube; it has refreshed me after walking on the tarmacked bicycle path, running along the top of the dike in the direction of Vienna. The path lies in the burning sun, without shade. I would immediately have accepted an offer of a lift from one of the many speedboat captains, who pass here on their wild water bulls.

But it was lovely under my willow tree too, on the last step of the '*Treppl*' descending in the water of the river. Mother duck with two adolescent children are waiting patiently for a morsel of bread. Every now and then she quacks in order to remind me not to forget her.

I have not been able to buy the correct maps this week, so I must take my lead from the Danube, which flows here through level country and fans out widely in all kinds of creeks and brooks. In between there are marshy bits, which need circumnavigating and also large power plants, softly buzzing factories in the silence of the countryside. On the extensive yards around them there is no man visible but the gatekeeper. Did you know that nuclear stations are prohibited by law in Austria?

Away from the river the apple trees along the road are bending heavily under the weight of their fruit. Broken off branches are lying beside them. Their apples are still sour and I have to think about the folk tale where a lazy girl walks past an apple tree just as heavily laden. The apple tree calls out to her, begging her to help relieve it from its burden, but she refuses. I feel guilty; there are so many apple trees; it is impossible to help them all.

The benches on the road have a wide seat of four sitting planks just like in Germany instead of three like in the stingy Netherlands. Lovely to have a real rest and my rucksack doesn't fall off either.

Yesterday I had a special encounter. I hear someone calling behind me: "*Shalom!*" I turn round and see a small delicate Indian, dressed completely in white, sitting on a heavily loaded bicycle. It carries an enamel board with the text: '*World cycle tour for love and peace*'. His name is Rajpalsingh; he is Hindu. He started in India with his wife and 8-year-old daughter. From Japan he flew over to America. His family members returned home to India, and now he hopes to cycle via Russia, Ukraine etc. back home. On the go he leads discussions about economic injustice and the bad distribution of wealth in the world. He shares an apple with me while we walk together for several kilometres. When I tell him about my walk to the Holy City he seems to feel an immediate connection. He is silent, something opens up within him. After crossing some cornfields on the footpath he climbs on his bike again and waves goodbye.

I camped off the dike of the Danube this night. It is lovely to be able to have an immediate dip in the morning with this hot damp weather.

A woman with two dogs passes. One of them, a young Alsatian, is very afraid of my tent. We help him to get used to it. Her thin husband is coming along jogging barefoot on the grassy verge. When I tell them about my walk he can't stop enthusing about it and starts to tell me in his incomprehensible Austrian accent about the esoteric significance of Israel and its place in the Divine Plan. He is connected with the Christian Embassy in Jerusalem, a fundamentalist organisation financed by evangelical Christians. A good thing is that they dealt with all anti-Semitism in Christianity, but they have been propelled with the same momentum into the opposite. Now Israel cannot be at fault whatsoever. He can't stop telling me about his insights and visions. His wife, who has a more down-to-earth view, is embarrassed and right in front of me they start to quarrel. Now how do I practise 'peace' in this case? I'm not saying anything anymore. Now I see with my own eyes how futile it is to try to convey something from passion. Such a nice man, and so blinded by all sorts of ideas, which are, as a matter of fact, not even far away from mine. It is the way we want to deal with it which makes us stand opposite each other. I don't know why, but he says goodbye to me in a delighted way, being very happy I want to do something like this pilgrimage, and he gives me an unexpected 'gift'. He tells me that the Hindu greeting 'Namaste' with hands joined in front of heart or forehead means: 'I am greeting the Light in you!'

Kritzendorf
Arriving on a big square in Kritzendorf I ask a lady if a footpath exists to Klosterneuburg, a village close to Vienna with a campsite. I would like to put my tent there for two nights in order to go sightseeing in Vienna. The lady happens to be Dutch and 35 years old. She lives here and is work mediator for disabled people. She is also devotee of an English enlightened master. She invites me for the night. Her house is

furnished in a simple way with only the most necessary: a woollen rug in vibrant colours, a remarkable candlestick, an old settee, a large picture of a long-haired laughing Briton. In the bookcase I notice well-known titles like: *'The knee of listening'* by Da Free John, *'Running with wolves', 'Cosmic Light'* and author names like Marianne Fredriksson, Hugo Claus, Connie Palmen and Henry Miller, and even the book *'Inner guidance'* by my own teacher Hans Korteweg.

Last Sunday, while I had this impressive session with F.L. under the scrutinising eyes of Ganesha and Sri Mataji, she had been reading an introduction to the work of Sri Mataji. Good synchronicity. Thank you, Divine! And when I tell her that I look for a friend to walk with me through the Balkan countries she says: "O, I will call Ganesha, I'm sure he would love to!"

Ganesha is a 54-year-old friend who has cycled the pilgrimage way to Santiago de Compostella. He has a special connection with Jerusalem. Ganesha would love to come, but he doubts whether he can manage with his ischias. "I could cycle, but I can't walk."

What a pity, but he does give me a contact address in Budapest and one in Tel Aviv. When we talk together about Jerusalem I say that I have a strong feeling that it will be alright in the end. At least, that is what I feel! He says that he has the feeling it will become worse and worse. I think about that. I know I have the habit always to see the light side, not so much to deny the shadow side, but just not think about it.

A strong image remains with me from the autobiography of Carl Gustav Jung (famous psychiatrist, and pupil of Sigmund Freud). One of his clients dreamt that she stood on a mountain near Jerusalem while the black shadow of Satan descended on the city and made it pitch dark. But when she had a better look, she could see that that shadow was at the same time a slip of the mantle of God.

Of course that woman had her own personal connection to the dream, but Jung tended to interpret it more in general as well.

It is a strong image and has come back in my own dreams, also in connection with Israel. Ganesha reminded me of it: an enormous threat, which after all lies in the open hand of a loving God. Yes, it is possible that things have to become worse and worse, but it can never take away the final truth: that 'sin behoveth and all shall be well' in the end.

After that I lie in my sleeping bag on her balcony and look at the stars and the full moon shining down on this inner court planted with trees. And I enjoy this harmonious house, the new adventure and the spontaneous cordiality and love which are given to me by my sincere host. She sleeps inside and I sleep outside.

In the morning, before she has to leave for her work we drink a cup of herbal tea together and afterwards I enjoy the silence and the time and stretch myself on the settee to read *'Men are from Mars and Women from Venus'*.

Then I finish off her muesli, close the door behind me and walk, direction Vienna.

Thursday, 17 August, Klosterneuburg

In the afternoon I pitch my tent on a campsite at Klosterneuburg. This is an exception. I generally don't like campsites. My minute tent stands there among all the giant ones. I have to pay the same amount of money for a tent ten times as small! But I did manage to pitch beneath a shady tree. It is so hot! 30ºC in the shade. Today I want to rest to spare my feet and tomorrow I want to go sightseeing in Vienna without a backpack, so I'll leave the tent and the backpack here and make this my temporary home. There is still space in the shade next to me, but not very much. If I moved my tent towards that dusty, bare, uncomfortable bit, it would give more space for another tent. But I don't want to move. I like space myself and I like grass to pitch on and my tent is only small and I was here first.

A young couple on bicycles want to put their tent next to mine. Do they secretly want me to move my tent? They have to put their tent elsewhere, in the burning sun, and leave me with my bad conscience. But I don't want to move to that dirty spot, my little tent is small enough as it is and I was here first and if I'd had a bigger tent, there wouldn't have been space anyway.......

Is that a good state of mind for a pilgrim? Actually I feel quite horrible because of it. Shall I tell them, that I am prepared to move my tent? They are already pitched with a big silver tent. I have been selfish. Shall I go over and talk to them about it? But on the other hand, that might be overdoing it a bit.

I am rewarded for my asocial behaviour with the following: because I want to swim in the Danube in the afternoon I am looking for a place with access to the river. I look for the 'Strandbad', the bathing beach. I am grumbling because the way has not been signposted correctly and I take the wrong path several times. I get even more annoyed and irritated when the 'Strandbad' turns out to be a luxury open air Danube swimming place with restaurants, toilets, easy chairs, sunning meadows and so on, completely crowded, and I have to pay an equivalent of eight pounds to get into it. But I only want to take a quick dive in and out of the Danube like I've been used to the days before, for free and I don't need all that stuff and I don't want to pay for things I don't really want.

I ask an elderly lady, who is just passing through the gate, where I can get into the Danube for free. She answers that it isn't possible. The main Danube is miles further and this side arm is completely built up with boathouses and villas, but - and now she looks rather mischievous - "You can come with me.

I'll introduce you as my guest, and you can take your dip; I have a season ticket." And so it happens. I swim and she watches over my money and passport. With my big city experience of always having to watch my belongings I find it very difficult to leave that to her. Johanna, you have received so much trust, especially here in Austria. Give it back for once now.

When I return from my dip, refreshed and energized, we chat. She is about 60 years old and representative for the pharmaceutical industry, selling medicines to general practitioners. Of course I know from publications, how objectionable this business often is including bribes as a reward for buying a particular product. Should I venture to tackle this subject? I only say that I am greatly in favour of natural medicine and rarely or never use allopathics. "O I will give you some herbal ointment for your feet and Achilles tendon and something against rheumatism for your hip. Those have no side-effects." She offers me one kindness after the other. She is well-read and knows a lot about the history of Klosterneuburg. Long ago, in mediaeval times, a Duke and Duchess lived here. They were conversing on the pinnacles of a tower of their castle, when a sudden gust of wind snatched the costly veil off the head of the Duchess and blew it away to the forest on the horizon. She felt so duped and humiliated by the accident that the duke sent out men to look for the veil. He promised to build a church if it was found. The men looked for days, but without any result. Ten years later, during a hunting party, the duke sees something flapping high up in a tree. It is the veil of his wife. Full of awe he falls on his knees. The church is built, the monastery founded (Klosterneuburg means the new monastery on the mountain) and a part of the veil has been kept there until this day. Hertha has seen it. It is very fine light blue material stitched with roses of gold thread.

She wants to show me the monastery and a few nice little streets. She has difficulty walking, so we go there by car. In that big car it is a mess. It is full of pharmaceutical samples, brochures, groceries, old newspapers and magazines, slippers, a bottle of dishwashing liquid, telephone directories, baskets of cat food, another three bags of brochures, a plaid, several pairs of sunglasses, an aerosol against mosquitoes, holiday folders on the floor plus a large amount of pens and broken pencils. There is no place for me!

"Yes, there is!" she says. "You have to help me to clear the front seat."

And that is what I do. There are a few recycling containers very close.

"I don't mind helping you to tidy your car," I offer, while pointing at the containers.

But she is very quick to turn this offer down. Finally I sit next to her in the car, with stuff under the seat and behind us, under and on the back seat. The only things I am sitting on are a little pillow, half a bottle of shampoo and three pens.

I see that she has glued half a transparent screen on each car window. "Yes," she grumbles, "people don't have to see what the inside of my car looks like."

She shows me around town and we end up on a little terrace of a 'Heuriger' cafe. ('Heuriger' means the last harvest of the wine of the previous year.) We drink wine, eat salad and share stories about our love life. Politics, Mr Haider (FPÖ-extreme right) and racism are also a subject. It is not the first time the subject pops up in conversations. You can see signs of controversy in the streets: the fury of 'autonomous left' against 'the beast Haider' and the aggrieved and nasty reactions of conservative 'Spieszburger' who want to step out of the EU. Most people who bring up the subject with me feel unreasonably rejected by the EU. They are simple and cordial, the Austrians, and they mean well and the FPÖ isn't Austria. But what about the racism of many FPÖ-ers? They look at you with vague eyes when you say that and it seems of secondary importance.

"Austrians are no beasts! Not a single assault on foreigners has happened here in Austria. Look at Germany or Portugal instead!"

"But that is not institutionalised," I say.

"Well, what is better? Nasty assaults ending in death and attackers who cannot be found? We Austrians are really nice, and we will keep an eye on the extremes."

And that is true. I like the Austrians I have met. They are nice, ordinary, without pretensions, cordial and a little shy, social people, who are happy when you are nice too.

I try one last time: "And the FPÖ party crying about 'Jewish pigs in the government', and waving with medals received from Hitler?" (I just read that on a poster in a street window.)

"Those are all lies from the extreme left!"

I don't know. As the discussion has come into the phase of Yes/No I will keep my mouth shut. And then we drink another beer together. I will never be good at confrontation.

Friday, August 18, Vienna

Today I have been sightseeing in the beautiful city of Vienna. Vienna is like a stately empress dowager, dressed in silks and satins, but yet young and playful, with plump wrists, a little attractive double chin and a gorgeous décolleté surrounded by a cloud of rich lace. She loves Viennese patisserie with cream, chocolate and poppy seeds. Thus does the spirit of the city strike me while looking at her superb mediaeval, baroque and neo-classical buildings, wide squares and avenues and many others of her delights. I walk around all of the morning and the afternoon.

In the internet cafe there is a message of a certain Magdalena from Belgium on the email. She wants to accompany me for three months through the Balkan countries.

So she is the answer to my search for a companion. I hadn't counted on company anymore; I must confess having got used to the idea of going it alone.

Towards the evening, when the oppressive heat of the day changes into a more mellow temperature, I enter into a meditative mood. Before returning to the campsite I intend to relish an open air concert in front of the Gothic Town Hall. On the large, tree planted square an enormous screen has been erected. Hundreds of chairs are placed in front of it. Because of the 'Summer weeks', recordings of two concerts of Herbert von Karajan are going to be performed on the screen. The composers are Dvorak and Mussorgsky. Towards 08.00 pm the sun goes down in a baroque setting of red glowing clouds, from behind which any moment playful cherubs could show their rosy cheeks and plump baby bodies. The lights in the towers of the Town Hall are extinguished. The screen lights up.

The opening chords of Dvorak's 'New World Symphony' are filling the square. The audience has quietened down. Around the square I still hear a few traffic noises, but they soon die away. In the distance the lightning of a faraway thunderstorm flashes on the horizon. I sink into the music. Mild evening, Vienna, violins, trumpets. The Empress is rocking me in her lap.

Suddenly the synthetic doodle of a mobile phone sounds behind me. A young man reaches into his breast pocket and answers it. He finishes the call very quickly, but then dials himself. And he keeps speaking and speaking. There my anger is rising again: "Could you please hang up? We are listening to the music!" But he will not stop speaking. I flare out: "Are you out of your mind? Hang up! You are a disturbing us dreadfully!" On these words he rises and steps out of the row, not looking at me and still speaking. And me? I feel miserable. The door is closed for the music now. Von Karajan is directing his orchestra, but not for me. I cannot concentrate anymore. Now I've lost my self-control again! Did I have to say it this way?

I could have done it in another way I'm sure! He's just unthinking; he is not mean! This is what I really say to him: "You are evil, because you have bad manners!" Nobody likes to be called evil!

When I return to the campsite, the distant thunderstorm I saw during the concert has discharged itself on my tent. It has collapsed miserably beneath the fury of the rain. Everything in it is wet. However it is still so warm, that I can fall asleep comfortably on my wet mattress in my damp sleeping bag.

At about two o'clock in the night I am awoken by the loud merry voices of a group of young people, who have just arrived and are pitching their tent on the last empty space of the campsite. They make a lot of fun and shout in the darkness, as if they are alone in the world and there I rant and rave again: "Shut up! You have woken us up, we want to sleep!" A deadly silence descends on the campsite. And I am sorry again. I just can't correct people politely and without judgement anymore. I frightened them, but they didn't mean any harm, and I am a sour and intolerant bitch.

In the moonlight something hops into my tent, plop, straight onto my white sleeping bag liner. A huge black creepy crawler! Quickly I give my white sheet a push so that it is outside again and then I try to close the tent quickly, but it is too fast for me. There it is inside again; now in a less visible place. It is more than ten centimetres long, has a long black body with six large crawly legs. A gruesome great insect, jumping in every direction, because when I try to manoeuvre it outside, it jumps into the darkness of the tent and I don't know between which folds of the sleeping bag it is now hiding. I sit up straight for half an hour, feeling miserable. I don't dare to lie down, because it might jump on my face, also I might crush it by mistake, and have to find its yellow insect blood and crushed wing shell, its revolting mortal remains, tomorrow in my sleeping bag. Where is it for Pete's sake! After half an hour I see it slowly creeping towards the ridge of the tent. Just above my pillow. Shall I quickly get it in my towel and throw it outside? But I don't dare that. It is much too fast and not for all the gold in the world must it jump inside again. I must try something else. Is it possible that I could love it and not be afraid of it anymore? Is it a metaphor for my irritation and anger? Is it my punishment for being so aggressive? It doesn't work. After sitting straight for another three quarters of an hour I get so exhausted, that I gather all my courage, looking hard at its long dangling body. Then, shuddering, I manoeuvre it quickly out of the tent with an empty margarine container. Close tent, deep sigh, sleep! Oblivion at last.

Saturday, August 19, Vienna

I walk through Vienna and arrive at the Prater, a large public park. At the end of the Prater I leave the city and link up with the Danube. Just before I step on the little ferry which will bring me to the north bank I see, much to my surprise, a white pagoda in the distance. Is this a 19th century oriental folly or is it a real pagoda? I step back from the ferry and walk towards it. The evening breeze brings me a waft of fragrant incense. It is a real pagoda! As I walk around it I see burning incense sticks in a bowl of sand at the foot of a staircase leading up to a golden Buddha statue sitting in peace in a niche on the east side of the pagoda. On the last step of the staircase sits a black cat which looks hard at me.

Next to it is a simple house from which a pounding noise is coming. What's that? It sounds like a steam engine. Is this a steam pump house, like we know in Holland, hauling superfluous water from the polder into the Danube? I walk up to the house, stand on tiptoe and peer into one of the high windows. I do not see an engine hall but a beautiful space adorned in red and gold, a red carpet on the floor. A monk clad in yellow sits in front of a great drum and beats it as if his life depends on it. I hear him sing. Behind him a Western man is sitting. He sings too and beats a little hand drum. I quickly withdraw. It is a Buddhist temple. How I would like to join in their prayer, but I don't dare to disturb them.

I sit down next to the stupa and eat my bread and cheese. I will wait until the drum stops. I want to ask permission to put up my tent next to the pagoda for the night, and ask them if they will pray with me for the peace of Jerusalem. When the drum has stopped, I walk up to the door and knock. The monk opens the door. His face lights up when he sees me. "We saw you when you peered through the window just now, and we hoped you would come in, but you didn't. But you're here now. Come in and have some tea with us" In the kitchen are more people. Karl, the man I just saw, Masunaga, the Japanese monk, and two ladies from Sri Lanka. Over a cup of tea I explain my visit. Masunaga is delighted. He won't hear of me sleeping in the tent. Only this morning he painted and prepared the new guestroom. Now he knows why he did it today and not tomorrow as he intended. He explains that he is a member of an autonomous Japanese Buddhist order specially ordained to build peace pagodas all over the world and to support and initiate peace walks. He has built the white pagoda with his own hands and he himself has walked, all singing and drumming for peace from Vancouver to Washington DC in the past. We all delight in the beautiful coincidence, which has brought me here.

The ladies from Sri Lanka take their leave. To my surprise and dismay they kneel down in front of the monk and bow deeply to him, their heads in their upturned palms resting on the floor. I am shocked about two human beings humiliating themselves in front of another human being.

Masunaga tells the story how thirty years ago he came to Europe for the first time to raise funds to build his pagoda. He was in Finland, in winter. Sometimes the sun didn't even rise. All people were so tall and so red in the face. And they looked all alike. He couldn't tell one from the other. He earned money by washing up in a restaurant. He was washing up all the time, although the restaurant owner told him he could have a break every now and again, but if he did, the plates piled up quickly over his head and he wouldn't get finished in all his living days. The only friend he had was the restaurant pianist, who often played the melody of Dr. Zhivago. For him darkness and loneliness is connected for ever with the song of Dr. Zhivago. Eighteen years he lives here now, by this peace pagoda built with his own hands from his own earnings and the money he raised. He is not lonely anymore. There are many people around him who help him. "But they are not Japanese," I say. He points at his heart: "As long as this is alright." And laughs.

I listen - shocked and gratified - to this spontaneous laughter, which sounds so exotic to me, so different from a European spontaneous laughter. It is very high, has a different rhythm, and finishes suddenly and abrupt and is completely and totally natural, spontaneous, but so different to what I'm used to.

I laugh with him. In the evening he takes me out to a Dutch acquaintance in the neighbourhood to introduce me, so that I can speak some Dutch and she as well. How fast is he walking; I can only keep up with him when I break into a trot, which provokes in him another of his miraculous laughters, however without slowing down his step.

At five o'clock the drum will wake me, Masunaga promises and he hopes that I will join the morning service. I am going to sleep in my luxurious bed in a spotless room, with the window wide open just behind my head. It is still suffocating warm.

I wake up by a spluttering sound just outside the window. It is two o'clock in the morning; Masunaga is watering the plants in the pots beneath the windowsill. I lie on my back staring with wide baffled eyes into the darkness! He is still at his chores then!

At ten past five - it is still dark - I sit behind him on cushions in the temple with a drum in my hand and I sing with him: '*Na mu myo horen ge kyo*'. A quarter of an hour later two ladies appear, violin teachers from Vienna. Masunaga is dressed in his white and yellow robe and beats the big drum; the ladies help him in turn. A whole hour we sing and drum. He sings and we answer and a peace is entering me, different from the peace I'm used to while in meditation. I notice my thoughts are changing, not my feelings. Suddenly it seems possible, that I do walk through the Balkan countries on my own. Yes, even that this would be good and suitable. Should I? Don't I have to have a companion to go through these 'wilds'?

At six o'clock the monk sits down next to a large singing bowl and finishes the inside service with sounding beats. I see that he is quite exhausted with singing and drumming, but he is trying to hide it. We leave the temple and go to the pagoda. Dawn is approaching. We walk around the pagoda singing and drumming. At the large Buddha statue to the east we bow down deeply three times and so we do at all of the four directions. On the north-east the priest stands still. He changes the mantra to a higher pitch and sings and drums. Then he stops. We wait in silence, facing the north-east. Then, very slowly the first radiant spark, pouring the first sunrays of the day over us, appears from behind the low trees on the other side of the Danube.

Again the mantra and the drum are sounding. It so seems that the sun is allured from its hiding place, as if it is listening to our music. Again deep deep silence... The sun is climbing a little higher and then, at full drumming and singing, it looks as if it is leaping free from the trees and shows itself completely and vulnerably and as such is starting its way on the bow of

Heaven. We stand in awe while watching. An early bumblebee passes us with its loud buzz. Then slowly we start to move. We bow three times deeply for the Buddha and I greet the sun with a 'Namaste' and we go back to the temple to finish the service in the rich and quiet morning.

Although I have slept so little, after this ceremony I am as fresh as a daisy. After the communal breakfast I have to say farewell and be on my way. Masunaga blesses me in the temple. Unexpectedly he kneels down for me in one of those very deep bows, which I had been so judgmental about the day before. His forehead is resting in his cupped hands on the floor and I look down on his humility. It startles me and I am ashamed about my proud thoughts of yesterday and immediately I find myself kneeling as well, and bowing down to him, if possible even deeper. And I feel grateful for the new balance being struck and the silent lesson given to me. He also gives me an envelope with a postcard of the pagoda. I wave and am on my way, happy with what life has been giving to me. In the envelope I not only find a postcard but also some banknotes. I look back to thank him. Masunaga has disappeared. The white pagoda radiates against the blue sky. A great peace emanates from it. The first pink sunbeams glide over the golden Buddha, who looks in still meditation towards the east. That is my direction.

Tuesday, August 22, Eckartsau, between Vienna and Bratislava

I'm trekking through the National Park 'Donau-Auen'. It is River land at its best with marshes, forests, meadows full of strange birds, special plants, small creeks, wind, tributaries of the Danube, her arms between which I lose my way. Mother Danube takes me in her arms. It is still 33°C and on the shade-less dikes it is certainly hotter. I bathe a lot. Yesterday I came across river beaches where all the people were naked, so I can leave off my old bikini with a clear conscience; it is pleasant and practical. I begin to feel a connection to the river. I see large, untidy, peeling Russian ships on their way to the Black Sea, oil tankers, white tourist cruise ships, the small boats of the water police. The largest waves however are made by the smallest speedboats. In the night the ships pass, illuminated like Christmas trees. I can see them approach, lying in my tent beneath the dike. The moon is clear. On the meadow the frogs are leaping right and left when I approach. In the morning I see the first autumn crocuses (*Colchicum autumnale*). I become melancholy. The autumn, the winter is coming.

It is very nice walking on the mantra of Masunaga. Yesterday during sunset, I bathed in the Danube, tent already pitched, evening sandwich prepared, bed spread. Peace, quiet and the gentle waves of the water. The sun sets already at half past seven.

In Eckartsau, I ring at the parsonage with my request and I get a most enthusiastic reception. The priest finds it a wonderful idea. He is a Dutchman from 's-Hertogenbosch and has just retired. Together we look in his big atlas to find a route towards Bulgaria. Medjugorje, the famous place, where Mary is supposed to appear every day, is too far from my route. He insists on contributing to my walk and gives me banknotes to the enormous value of 1,000 Schilling (about 100 Euros) He will put my prayer for the intercessions in seven churches around this region. He is interested and positive about the peace process in Israel/Palestine. I am a bit flabbergasted when I say goodbye. What is happening this week? One thing I am sure of; in the next village I will buy a very large ice cream! (He said I could finish all the money!)

August 23, Hainburg, bordertown Austria, Slovakia and Hungary

Through the meadows on the Danube I walk on to Hainburg. The first three mountains of the Carpathians rise suddenly from the plain. The silhouette of Hainburg, with its walled town and rococo church tower lies strangely in between. Behind the town I see the blue sky. I will go 'into the blue' and leave the countries where the well-known German is spoken. I will enter Slovakia and Hungary, other countries, unknown languages, a new adventure.

In Hainburg's Rococo church an evening service begins. I join the praying of the rosary in honour of Mary of Amsterdam; she is supposed to have appeared in the fifties and called herself 'Mother of all peoples, who once was Mary'.

After the service the priest allows me to pitch my tent in the garden of the parsonage and have breakfast with him in the morning. He has been to Israel eleven times; he loves Jerusalem and will certainly pray for its peace.

What a strange little border town is Hainburg. It has heavy fortifications and high grey city gates. I enter through the 'Blood Gate' where many citizens were slaughtered in the 18th century, when the Turks invaded the town. I climb towards the town centre via the Blood Alley, where the blood of the innocent flowed through the gate into the Danube. I can see the Turks, with their scimitars and shamberlooks, their red waistcoats, high fezzes and shoes with upturned toes. Very different from the Turks we know these days. One way or the other, the town has a bit of an oriental touch. The baroque house fronts contrast with the colourful gypsy women in town. Or are they Turkish? I go to see the happy rococo Mary column in the marketplace. How now? I like this one in spite of the abundant ornaments! Am I getting used to all the baroque knick knacks?

I am looking for the synagogue. According to my old E8 long distance path booklet there should be one, but it is not mentioned in the tourist brochures. At the town hall however, they know. It is close to the Viennese Gate, which is a Turkish gate reminding me of Istanbul, but a large mounted cross on it makes it Christian again. I pass through a garage to the parking lot behind some houses. I see peeling doors, empty crates from an adjoining supermarket and a concrete fence. Behind it I find a ramshackle building. It is a long house with very small windows, a few only, and there, in front, a round red brick tower with a spire, the plaster peeling off. Two small square windows stare from it like eyes. I look through an open door and see cross vaults and a lot of dumped rubbish. Is this *'the place where you stand is holy ground?'*

From the synagogue, but especially from the tower, emanates a ghastly energy. It is as if I hear poor souls in hell screaming and wailing, as if there are a lot of trapped souls there. It feels as if there is a curse on the tower and I get the image of a black round disc, like an old 'vinyl' record, which rests on the tower, to prevent the souls ascending to Heaven. It is like a 'rat board' round the hawser of a ship to prevent rats from coming on board. Can I help? When I think of restoration of the synagogue and re-inauguration by a rabbi I become very peaceful. That will bring light and rest. And there should be a lot of music too.

The owner is supposed to live somewhere here. The neighbours know of his existence, but nobody knows his door or letterbox. In the courtyard there are a few shabby-looking doors open, leading to a dark vaulted portal. Is that his house? He is on holiday in Kärnten, they say. For a while I sit on the fence at the parking lot and play on my recorder the beautiful synagogue music from Worms, which is as always, opening my heart. Do I now hear the damned souls sob and weep? When I finish playing, a well-dressed elderly gentleman steps from the dark portal. *"Kennen Sie vielleicht Herr B.?"* I ask: *"Jawohl,"* he says, and points at himself. He has arrived here not half a minute ago; his car engine is still running. He is very willing to show me the synagogue. It is probably the oldest synagogue in Austria, built in the 12th century. He says something about the Jewish ghetto which was out of bounds. The citizens didn't want them in the town because "they were unpleasant". I start my monologue about discrimination and suppression. He is the proprietor of the synagogue because it is such a special old building; it deserves to be kept for posterity. He didn't allow the local Turkish community to make a mosque out of it. He respects the fact that the building has been here for such a long time and will be long after he has died. He has no connection to Judaism and thinks there will never be peace in the Middle East. He congratulates me for my optimism.

I sound him carefully to see if he would be open to what I just felt.

He says: "Go ahead, during the war I have been through such horrors, nothing will surprise me."

I tell him about the tower. He admits he doesn't like it there, especially during a thunderstorm and even at dusk he never goes there. "A curse by the Nazis?" No he doesn't believe that the Nazis did such things. "They left the synagogue be instead of destroying it."

He tells me something about the terrible time in the war. He was lying in a bomb crater between corpses, dying and wounded people. It was night and he thought: "I can't survive this; this abhorrence." Then an overwhelming rest and peace came over him, a Help, which was there in all the following moments of horror. He is an educated man. He must have been an officer in the war. Today he preserves old Jewish heritage for the future.

I tell him that I hope that the synagogue can be restored and reinstated. We say goodbye and for a moment I feel as if a shadow is walking behind me. I pray the Our Father.

SLOVAKIA

Thursday, August 24, Bratislava

Having left Hainburg I follow the river in the direction of the Slovakian border. I am stopped by Austrian soldiers.

"There is no passing point along the river."

"But I can see the towpath! And a few hundred meters further the border."

I have to go back a long way and walk via the motorway to the border passing point and from there to Bratislava. Three hours I walk along the roaring traffic, between the crash barrier and the edge of grass. To pitch a tent so near the border I find a little risky. Perhaps there are illegal border jumpers hidden in the brushwood. I only arrive in Bratislava at 10.00 pm. It is very late. The first Slovakians I meet are some beautiful prostitutes along the road. Do they know a place to sleep? Yes, I can pitch my tent in their garden for an outrageous amount of money. In the darkness I plod on along industrial estates, finally a few houses and the bridge over the Danube. On the other side there is an illuminated castle on a mountain. I feel better, but my feet feel like lead. The hotels I enter are luxurious and cost 200 Euros per night. The porter of one of them will look for a cheap hotel or B&B while I stand in the posh reception hall with my dusty walking boots, backpack and sweaty top on the Persian carpet beneath the crystal chandelier. He is really very helpful, the treasure. I need to take the tramway to a suburb. Hotel Druzba.

When I arrive there the price is reasonable. Only 20 euros per night, but... I should have booked. There are no vacancies. I am exhausted. I just can't walk another step. Where do I go to? The faces behind the counter are hardening; they feel guilty. A woman who is just arriving knows a hotel in the neighbourhood. I make a phone call, yes, there is a room for

150 euros. I don't know anything anymore, and I can't do anything anymore.

A little Asian man, who is sitting in the reception hall, comes towards me. He says that I look tired. He wants to have a chat. I tell him what is wrong. He offers I can sleep clandestinely on the floor in his room. A good solution, but what does he mean exactly? I am saying in all frankness that I am a little anxious to accept it. He reacts offended and says he knows lots of lovely Slovakian girls which he can get, and where did I get the idea that he wanted something with me?

Relieved I walk with him to his room. Will he put a package of drugs in my rucksack and do I smuggle that unawares across the border? Will he kill me during the night? Prejudice, prejudice. For the service he renders me I have to pay. I pay his room for this night, but OK; I can't lie on a bench in the middle of the night between shops and houses. He is from Cambodia and has lived in Paris for 25 years. His mother is Buddhist. What a marvellous Far East chain I have followed ever since I met F.L., the yogi who has Sri Mataji as a guru. Then came Rajpalsing, then the man who taught me the significance of the Namaste greeting; the Japanese Buddhist peace pagoda and now the son of a Buddhist is helping me.

At seven o'clock this morning I leave the large hotel in all silence and go to collect my Poste Restante mail. From a shop window in the thoroughfare an enlarged photo of Sri Mataji is smiling at me.

I expected a lot of mail, but everything has been returned to their sender apart from the last two letters. How I cried. Poste Restante doesn't work. Although I had written to the post office asking to keep my letters until September, they haven't complied. They have kept the letters for only two weeks. Bratislava has a modernized post office, with the sort of gift-shop-type-well-meant rubbish for sale, just like in the Netherlands, to 'better serve their honoured clientele', but real service? Forget about it. But the remaining two letters are a comfort. Also there is a lot of email on the internet. I ask Magdalena in Belgium to walk with me for one month, possibly for three months. She seems a very nice woman, but I still hesitate; I hope she can accept this compromise. I am curious to meet her now. I put my idea to walk everything on my own in the rubbish bin.

When I rise from my chair in the internet cafe my place is taken by a man, who curiously asks the meaning of my text 'The Hague - Jerusalem' on my rucksack. He is a Palestinian who has lived in the US since 1967, the Six-Day War. He hasn't been to Jerusalem ever since. He could go now, as an American citizen, but he hesitates. He is afraid so much has changed. He is very positive about the peace process.

"At least they are talking. Who would have thought it five years ago! It cannot be stopped now. We have to have peace."

The Yugoslavian Embassy tells me how to get a visa for its country. I have to return to the Netherlands and get one from the Embassy in The Hague. Of course this is no case for consideration. So now I have to go via the country about which the nastiest stories are going round. Romania. On this walk I always get exactly on my plate everything I wanted to avoid. OK Johanna, go for it. If Magdalena comes with me, I won't be afraid.

Friday, August 25
The Danube has three arms on this track. The original meandering river, the wide Danube canal and, on the Slovakian north side another narrow canal.

I found a large white feather: a swan's feather. Usually I stick the feathers I find on my hat or in my hair, like antennas, but this one was too big to stick into my hair. At night I pitch my tent for the first time at the canal on the north side. Three swans are swimming towards me, in between them seven young cygnets. They are waiting. Do you want bread? Just a moment, you will get it presently. When I am ready to bring them bread they suddenly have lost interest. They are haughtily preening their feathers and turn away from me. Well, I will eat the bread myself then, I am rather hungry. But when I am finished eating they come towards me again. A fourth swan has joined them, but he keeps a little aside. You want something, but it isn't bread. I am looking at the large swan's feather. I shall keep my evening meditation in their honour! I place it in the ground in front of me. I close my eyes. Here is the fourth swan. Left of him a black abyss, as strict and dark as a swan's eye can be. The dark eye of wild Sri Mataji is shimmering through it. At his right I see a radiating light. The swan moves from left to right. I say humbly: "Yes master swan; I know about the light and the dark."

The next image: I see a long path of loam in the sunshine without shade, to the right is a loam wall, on the left the river. This is the Path. I am not allowed to look behind the wall, where the black shadow is. It is enough that I know it is there. I protest gently; it looks very hot. Immediately I see a few trees throwing shade. The sunlight is mixing with the shadow. There in the dappled shade I can take shelter when it is too hot.

Third image: the swan has a blade of straw in his beak. He rinses it in water, moves it to and fro in the water. It reminds me of the thin thread stretched from larboard to starboard in my dream about the guardian angel.

To clutch to a straw hasn't got a positive meaning, although a few blades of straw can give you just that support to keep you standing on a slippery path.

The swan wants to give it to me as a gift: something that seems to be fragile and worthless, but which he treats with great care. 'Hold on to your thin thread! Hold on to your blade of straw.'

In the morning the swans are still there.

Sunday, August 27, small village on the Danube, 30 kilometres SE of Bratislava

The weather is cooler these days. I enjoy the excellent walking weather, but today is Sunday/resting day and I want to write and paint pictures. I have walked 1,836 kilometres.

I walk on the narrow canal on the north side of the river, between two high dikes on an earth path with a little tree here and there. On the large dike runs the cycle path to Budapest. The view is much better from there, but tarmac hurts my hip joints and I am very happy with this cart track. The water in the canal is clean and clear. I can see the bottom of it with all sorts of water plants, small and large fishes. I swim every morning and evening in this aquarium. Herons stand motionless between the reeds; ducks and a solitary dog are swimming with me. Every evening the sun sets behind the winter dike, every morning it rises from behind the sleeper dike. I sing Masunaga's mantra: '*Na mu mjo horen ge kyo.*' He didn't want to tell me what it meant. But I do want to know it.

Sometimes I climb to the crest of the winter dike, to look at the view or I climb the sleeper dike to get some provisions from the Slovakian villages behind it. Or, like right now, to have a meal. I sit at a long wooden table in front of a little restaurant. At another table men are playing cards and drinking beer. This really feels like Eastern Europe now. It has a different smell; there is wood smoke in the air. In contrast with Bohemia the little chapels are often open. I visit one. It is small and simple. A little altar in the naive style of farmer's baroque is beautiful to look at. Everything in the little church is polished and clean and taken care of. Loving hands have starched and ironed the spotless altar linen, put fresh flowers everywhere, mopped the floor, polished lamps, censer and candlesticks, dusted the windowsill, washed the windows. There even is an impressive crucifix: a defeated, exhausted man, who in great humility and surrender bows his head.

There is a pieta too. A Mother of Sorrows with an expressive Hungarian face.

The land is level, like in the Netherlands, brushwood here and there. Large fields lie fallow after the harvest. Better if there is no storm here, all the powdery soil would blow away; there has been a long draught. The grass is yellow, trees hang their leaves; many birches have lost theirs already. My shoes are very dusty. The houses start to show the pyramid formed roofs, which I often saw in Yugoslavia. I am walking the Slovakian-Hungarian border. Most people I meet speak Hungarian as their mother tongue, but they understand my broken Czech very well. All notices have two languages. The Slovaks (or Hungarians?) are quite reticent. They hesitantly return my greeting, but after thawing they like to practise their English. Today I received a bag full of grapes and vegetables; everything from their own garden. Somebody else asked whether I needed help. Yet another person came running after me with the telephone card I had forgotten in the telephone booth. But they are not as sweet as the Czechs, however they are much tidier.

Last night I slept without a tent under the branches of an old, wild olive tree. Through the branches I see the wide starry sky with five shooting stars. I dream that I sleep there. In my dream a large animal approaches. Is it a roe deer? I can't see; it is too dark. It lies down around me, its soft, warm belly pressing against my head and shoulders. It has lost its way and wants to be with a human being. I feel with my right hand for its nose. It has large nostrils, a round nose with hairs protruding. It is licking my fingers. With my left hand I feel its feet; it has small round hoofs. It is a little horse. We lie together for a long time, enjoying each others company. Then I hear a car stop. A woman is calling. She is the owner. The little horse stands up and joins her. I lie in my sleeping bag enjoying the memory of the little horse's warm belly and sweet company. Then I wake up. It was not real; it was a dream!

Tuesday August 29, 25 kilometres west of Komarno, Klizka Nema (= 'she hasn't got a key')
The most important subject of yesterday and today is: MOSQUITOES. Already at noon I have to don my spacesuit: jumper with long sleeves, long trousers, woollen headscarf to leave bare only a small part of my face — and that with a new heat wave of 32ºC. I walk between the Danube marshes. Somebody called this the epicentre of the mosquito explosion. The tent is reasonably mosquito free, but pitching and un-pitching is torment. Insect repellent cream helps about ten minutes. I am glad to have a soothing cream based on ant-acid. That helps really well against the itching bites and I have used half a tube today. How do I wee? As soon as I bare a square inch of skin, the mosquito army goes for my noble parts. I found something! My waterproof poncho! When I squat the seams are touching the ground. I feel triumphant: got them there!

Last night I slept beneath the dike again. Between me and the Danube there is two kilometres of marshland. So I couldn't get to water for my morning wash. There is a cottage 200 metres beyond my camping spot. That's where I will get some water tomorrow morning to drink during the ten kilometres which are between me and the next village.

I enter into the front garden and ring the bell on the gate. "*Dobre Rano*" (good morning).

"Was that you in the little green tent over there?" She changes into perfect German:

"If I had known you were a woman, I certainly would have invited you into my home".

A woman of my own age now opens the wooden gate. "We thought yesterday, the person in that little tent must be a hero."

I am allowed to wash inside and she prepares breakfast for her husband and two small children and me. The children understand my Czech! I am pleased. The husband departs for his work and the children for school. We talk about illness and want... She has leukaemia and seven years ago this illness has opened her eyes for the spiritual side of life. She calls it one of the best gifts of her life. I am here sitting opposite a Slovakian woman of German-Hungarian descent. And we don't notice anything of cultural difference. The communication is immediate. For three hours we talk about all and everything and both of us feel enchanted.

She tells about the lovely pony they have and points at the little stable in the back of the garden. I feel a pang. "Does it stray sometimes?" I ask carefully.

"Yes," she says. "When she walks around free, she tends to stray, but not very far. The neighbour usually brings her back and sometimes we go ourselves to look for her with the car."

I can't believe this! I tell her about the dream I had about the little night mare that came to me and about her lovely soft belly. And that was 40 kilometres back!

She is very moved: "You know what I like best about her? Her soft sweet warm belly! But I am hardly allowed to touch it!"

It must have been 'Dona' whose soul visited me the night before yesterday. So there was already a connection with this place where I'm having breakfast long before I knew that I was going to come here. I am writing a strange story!

Wednesday, August 30, west of Komarno

I found a child's silver bracelet, but it fitted me perfectly. Two silver hearts dangle from it and in between there is a fish. The fish is of course the Danube and the hearts are Love.

This morning, at sunrise, I take my bath in the Danube; silent hazes drift over it. I feel grateful for creation and for the new morning. I am greeting the sun with Masunaga's mantra. I think of the Great Mother River in the novels of Jean Auel and feel myself a little like Jondalar, having his initiation walk along the Danube to the Black Sea. How would he have walked through all the undergrowth along the river? Because beautiful dikes and roads weren't yet there in the Ice Age. And will I meet a 'flathead' this week?

Lying relaxed on my back in the tepid clear water of the Danube, in the early morning at half past six, eyes closed, I suddenly see on the speckled dark screen before my closed eyes a clearly cut out Valentines heart. It is definitely a pink heart with a yellow rim. What's happening? What is this? I really see it. I don't imagine it... It is a gift...for me! A gift...from the Danube? Does she love me?

The colours are the colours of the sun the way I always paint them in my pictures. It isn't the Danube. It has to do with the sun. I had just sung the sun mantra. The sun tells me that it loves me...good Heavens!

Later, when walking the way again I keep thinking about it. The sun, for me, is a Christ-symbol, the Resurrected, more so than the cross. I am not drawing the sun in my pictures for nothing.

And, how stupid. Fish! The Age of Pisces! The fish dangling between the two hearts on my newfound silver bracelet is not the Danube, but Christ! It is Christ who loves me! Good Lord!

Thursday, August 31, Komarno - Slovakian/Hungarian border town

Lots of news today. Magdalena has agreed to join me for a month and hopefully for two more. I am very happy with this, especially since I have to walk through dangerous Romania. When I apply for my Romanian visa in Budapest I will try to get some information about where these notorious highwaymen are operating. And, very strange, I look forward to that. How irrational can you be? Johanna, wake up! It could be really dangerous! It is dangerous already, but I'm never afraid anymore! Perhaps I should be!

In Komarno new adventures are welcoming me. Via the husband of the lady with the little night mare, I am given an address where I can use the internet. The husband is the director of the Slovakian Canoe League and he introduces me to his friend, who has a computer and is trainer and coach of last year's world canoeing champions. I sit at a table in a restaurant together with half a dozen men and shake hands including the world canoeing champion. Next month he, his crew and his coach will go to Sydney to hopefully become an Olympic Champion. The man radiates with happiness telling me he will take part in the Olympic Games. At the same dinner is the medical superintendent of Komarno's hospital, town councillor and sport physician for the canoe team, the Olympic coach and some more people of name. How did I get into this company? I am snobbish enough to enjoy it. The medical superintendent will arrange a TV program for me and an interview in the newspaper.

He tells me something about Komarno. In the past years Hungarians, Slovakians, Bulgarians, Romanians, Gypsies and Germans have tried to live here in good harmony together. In the new national government there is enthusiasm to work together instead of engaging in the previous constant contention. He hopes for access to the European Union.

Tolerance is very important to him, that's why he loves my story. He is very happy with the fact that they - as Hungarian Slovaks - are in the coalition as a recognized minority. This was not possible with the last government. He was moved to hear that when the canoe team said goodbye to the prime minister before leaving for the Olympic Games, he asked how their - Hungarian- names, were pronounced. Finally they received acknowledgement after fifteen years of toil.

I don't know anything about Slovakia, apart from the fact that it is economically less healthy than the Czech Republic. In this way I learn in passing about local sensitivities and politics. I tell them I am a green socialist and religious in the bargain. The coach says that he is 'green' in a small way. He always fishes the plastic bottles from the river, bags and bags full. I ask whether in Slovakia left wing communism is seen as progressive or conservative. A startled silence follows and then laughter. "A good question".

This morning I participated in a program for local TV. The interview with the newspaper was cancelled because they couldn't find a proper translator. So this afternoon I did some mending in my hotel room. Yes, hotel room! I am completely fed up with the mosquito army. Ironically Komarno means: 'City of Mosquitoes'. My hotel is near the docks. It is very large. The ground floor has all the windows broken, but I have a lovely white room on the first floor with a white bed and in front of my window stands a beautiful poplar with whispering leaves in the wind. Showers and toilets are in the corridor. Those for women are always locked, but the reception gave me the key, so strange men cannot charge into the bathroom while I take a shower.

I'll tidy up now. The washing is dry; the rucksack mended. I will spend my last Slovakian crowns on a nice dinner.

HUNGARY / MAGYARORSZAG

Saturday, September 2

Today I'm five months on the road. Yesterday I crossed the border with Hungary and said goodbye for now to the Danube, which is flowing dead east and then suddenly makes an angle to the south, direction Budapest. I try to shortcut the angle and keep a south-easterly direction.

First impressions of Hungary: there are European Union flags everywhere. They want so much to join! The houses are low. The countryside is slightly undulating with short waves, very fit to hide my little tent in the fields and between the shrubs. I walk through the *puszta*. Many villages have '*puszta*' at the end of their names. *Puszta* really means steppe, desert, but this isn't a desert.

Until now I have walked on 1: 50,000 maps, but the most detailed map I could get now was only 1: 125,000. So not all unmetalled country roads are projected. I have a choice between going for safety and walk tarmac, or risk to lose my way, take my compass and just follow cart tracks and paths direction south-east.

To play safe means getting bored with the traffic and trouble with joints and tendons, so it isn't really safe. The days I could walk on earth paths along the Danube have been like ointment for my feet. So I think I won't go for safety.

The Hungarians are at first a little suspicious of me. They must be thinking: 'Who is this strange solitary woman with a backpack?' And then they become friendly and helpful in an incomprehensible language. I haven't been able to buy a Hungarian pocket dictionary yet. I feel unhappy without any language tool. It was going so nicely with my handful of Czech in Slovakia. I started to feel like a fish in the water. Here I have to start all over again. The word for 'thank you' is '*Gösönöm*',

I know now, but I don't know yet the words for bread and cheese, tomato and even 'good morning'.

I will start a list myself: *'Ejadu'* is 'solitary' and *'koci' means* 'feet', *'sokat do koci'* is 'to walk'. *'Rheumatism'* is rheumatism. An old lady on a bench taught me that. We could not talk together. That is an unknown experience which will happen more often now.

I notice a lack of enthusiasm to start a new language all over again. The notices on the signs give me the well-known 'blind' feeling. As if I can't read yet.

Stop Johanna, don't moan, but it is true I'm a little depressed. Everything was fine with my feet I thought, walking on level country, but after climbing one mountain only, it seems to go wrong again.

On top of this mountain I have lost my way and keep east on my compass. I walk on a lovely wide grassy path. Left and right a red stag, roe deer (eight of them) and wild boars (four, with upturned tails) are fleeing my presence. This long grassy path along high trees ends at a hunter's platform in a tree. Three green-clad hunters with rifles sit on it, angrily staring at me. One of them climbs down and comes towards me with a face like a thundercloud: broad chest, dark eyes, fresh face, big black moustache like a circus director, green hat, green long felt cape. He speaks grumpily to me in Hungarian. After it has become clear I don't understand that, he says in German: "Now you have chased away our game. We can stop for today! What are you doing here? There is nothing here!" I tell him I lost my way because of the bad map. He takes the trouble to point me to the 'right' way. 'Right' way? That is the busy traffic road I have been trying to avoid. Hypocritical vegetarian that I am, I apologize for the disturbance of 'his' game and congratulate myself on wearing a vividly red T-shirt. Otherwise they might have mistaken me for a wild boar on the long green avenue.

I disappear into the forest, in the direction of the main road. It is seven o'clock already and I look for a place to pitch. During the night it rains for a long time. I am happy for this region of Hungary. It has been hot so long that everything has perished. The trees are losing their leaves already. Autumn has come a month early. The corn has remained small because there wasn't enough water.

During the night, when I have to follow the call of nature and open the tent zip, that penetrating sound is answered with the sudden loud burling of a red deer, somewhere close to me between the trees. Even although I shove back into my sleeping bag as quietly as possible, the sound of the zips gets him going again. A burling deer in the beginning of September? It is much too early. It doesn't even smell of autumn yet. There is no morning mist, nothing.

Tuesday, September 5, Budakeski, eight kilometres from Budapest

Wild grapes are growing along the motorway. They have overgrown many other small trees and shrubs, and they offer their small full bunches to the passers-by. I tasted one grape. It tasted very good, but I know that fruit which grows along a motorway is poisoned by the exhaust fumes. These plants have made such an effort to grow lovely fruit and there is nobody who can eat it.

Today also I see the first wild badger of my life - dead - at the side of the road. He is still warm. I see many knocked-down soft dead little birds, one more beautiful than the other. I see flights of sparrows. I haven't seen so many sparrows together for years. The sound of their flying brings me back to toddler age. Yes, I suddenly remember how it sounded when a large flight of sparrows passed. I see wide undulating plains with extensive fields. Harvest is over and the plough has been through, but I also see fields with their harvest of corn and sunflowers still unreaped.

I see broad chested, fat men, but without beer bellies, with clear blue or dark eyes, apple cheeks, always with moustache; families in colourful clothes who are digging up potatoes or picking grapes in the vineyards.

When I pass through a village many savage, neglected, chained dogs bark at me in full decibels. There are dogs behind fences, dogs behind garden walls, one house after the other. They fly against the gates, jerking their chains, ranting and raving, barking and baring their fangs. People can know exactly how I walk. The sequence of hysterical dog barking points out where I am. In the last village 40 dogs, if not more, have bellowed at me one after the other. Every time I jump when yet another Alsatian throws itself growling against the garden fence. They are just as nasty as French dogs, but there is one advantage. They are not walking free.

In the yards I see neglected and fearful cats, ducks and geese. Chickens roam the path. On the country roads I often see carts and waggons with beautiful well-groomed work horses in front. There is a lot of rubbish abandoned along the road. Car seats, deep freezers, washing machines, bags of bones, old iron. In between stand nice, neatly painted little cottages, clean, tidy.

In Slovakia I met Hungarians, who were a minority there. Here in Hungary I hear the same story of a German minority, which has been living here ever since Empress Maria Theresa of Austria invited them to come and live here in the 18th century. They are originally from Schwaben and weren't allowed to speak German apart from in their own homes. Now they will have bilingual schools and the official notices have two languages too. Although they have been an isolated German speaking community for almost three centuries I can understand them much better than the Bavarians or the Austrians.

Further impressions of the Hungarians: open, straightforward fresh people, obliging, polite, but not very friendly and keeping a distance. It doesn't help that I only know a few words of Hungarian yet.

The roads are populated with motorbike groups. They visit special motor cafes. They are sitting astride on their saddled motorbikes, their broad bodies dressed in leather, holding the reigns of their handlebars. They ride through the *puszta* just like their distant ancestors, the Huns of Attilla, rode through the *puszta* on their small fast horses. Like them they have bald heads with thick long pigtails flailing their backs. Here comes the warlord with his armoured warriors on their rearing horses.

At last I know the Hungarian word for: 'parson, pastor or priest'. It is *pope*. Yesterday I spoke with my first Hungarian *pope*; a handsome dark young man in a spotless white cassock with azure sash and a row of azure little buttons from neck to feet. He is a Premonstratensian monk and is interested in my mission. Friendly and distantly he gives me ripe tomatoes (the tomatoes in Hungary are surprisingly sweet, juicy, delicious and much nicer than at home and are called 'apples of Paradise'). He gives me ripe tomatoes and grapes from his garden, invites me for vespers and Mass, lays the Latin-Hungarian prayer book open on my desk. That is welcome. I understand church Latin a little because of my Roman Catholic upbringing. In his sermon he mentions my mission. I hear 'Holland' and 'Israel' and everybody in church turns around and looks at me. Then he asks for a long silence and says a long prayer for peace. He couldn't have done better.

The temperature has dropped from 33°C to 20ºC. A sharp wind blows over the *puszta.* I already caught a cold and now I am feverish. I zealously take Echinacea. And that helps.

This morning I meditated on the sound *Aum mani padme hum*. This is one of the names of God in Sanskrit and placed on the heart chakra. It means as much as: Holy Place, Holy City, Pearl in the Heart of the Lotus, Divine Truth, Source of Sources.

From Budakeski I have to walk along a very dangerous traffic road. There is no other possibility, so I allow myself to take the bus for the last two kilometres to Budapest. There is a bus stop near to a building of special architecture: the *Lauder Iskola.* The road beyond disappears in the abyss, towards the Danube in the distance. I can see part of Buda's panorama already.

I ask a lady at the bus stop of about my own age, which bus number I have to take to the centre. She is eager to help and asks the significance of the The Hague-Jerusalem sign on the backpack. I tell my story. She jokes about the traject on the Mediterranean: if I can walk on the water like Jesus?

The bus arrives, we depart for the centre. From a telephone booth she calls several hotels and hostels for me, because I can't speak Hungarian. They have no vacancies. Then she offers me her house for the night. How help is showered on me! She is a teacher of the Lauder School. It is a liberal Jewish school for primary and secondary education. She is the music teacher. When she stands in front of me I notice on her bag the *Aum* sign, on which I meditated this morning! She has bought that bag last week in the old city of Jerusalem. She doesn't know what the sign means.

She is a widow and has two children of 20 and 22 and a gentleman friend. His apartment is in the old part of Buda. It is full of old fashioned bookcases, old prints, new publications, paintings, etchings, engravings on the wall; rooms with high ceilings and arched passages; lazy leather chairs, old worn Persian carpets and the books he inherited from his father, a famous Hungarian linguist and author: Vargha. Tonight I sleep with them in their apartment. He is pleasantly surprised with

126

my visit. The three of us talk about the possibilities and future of Jerusalem.

Vera says that as long as in Palestinian mosques the verses from the Koran are quoted that the killing of Jews is a deed looked upon with joy by God, she doesn't dare to trust the Arabs.

I could quote in her place a psalm from the Bible that advises to smite the skulls of the babies of the enemy of the Jews against the stone walls. Perhaps Palestinian people quote this Bible verse to each other in their own families.

In each religion selective and abusive use of holy texts has been known to happen. And possibly even some 'devil's verses' might have been included without us noticing! As far as I'm concerned, there are some very unholy verses in both books to be looked at with suspicious eyes.

Their cordiality is overwhelming. I can take a bath and am soaking in there for half an hour. While I'm drying myself with a rough towel I rub the brown old skin from my arms and legs. Now where does that come from? I wash myself every day!

When I emerge from the bath Vera has cooked. She invites me to stay for a few days, if I want, in her own apartment in Pest. I feel blessed. I really need it. My feet do need a few days of rest.

Wednesday, September 6, Pest
My brother writes me on email that our mother has been taken to hospital in an emergency. I am worried. Perhaps I should go back. Tonight I can't sleep for guilt.

It is cold in Budapest and it rains. Budapest is a dirty, beautiful, sad city with strong Eastern influence. The Turks were here too. They built mosques and hammams (bathing houses). The Hungarians in the city look different from the country Hungarians. I see long noble faces, dark eyes with a strict eyebrow line above them, and sometimes the men grow a noble little moustache. They are beautiful, sometimes stern people and they are very helpful. I only need to stand still for a moment on a street corner or they will flock to me from all directions to help. At the bus stop an elderly gentleman and I have a conversation. Then when the bus arrives he steps inside while he insists: "the most important word here in Hungary is love, '*szeretet*' Remember that!"

In Budapest, a big city, I stand a chance of obtaining the best available maps for walking through Hungary and Romania. But it appears that no walking maps exist of those regions I need to walk through. I'll have to make do and that's alright. I knew it had to stop once, the wealth of topographic maps. I have a nice talk in the best map shop of the city. Although in Germany I have been warned not to walk through Siebenburgen and Transylvania in Romania, because of criminal gangs and outlawed gypsies, the gentleman in the shop says:

"On the contrary, it is better that you should pass through that region, because that is where lots of Hungarians live. Also there is a German minority and even some of the towns have German names, so it is much safer!"

Do I touch on some prejudices here? I decide not to adhere to any fears or hopes, but to hug as closely as possible my straight line between The Hague and Jerusalem, which means I shall cross Romania via the south-west.

The word for 'The Lord God' is in Hungarian: '*Urunk Istenünk*'. In my mind's eye I see a wild bearded giant, giving his black giant horse the spurs.

I visit the founding place of Budapest: the hill on which stand the old castle and the gothic church. Inside, the church is painted dark brown with small flowers and ornaments. There is a repeated request on notice boards for silence and respect. And exceptionally; people do comply and walk around without making any noise. The effect of it is solemn and heavy. The pointed arches disappear into the semi-darkness of the high vaults. I sit down on a bench to let everything sink in. Upstairs, near the organ a small choir practises Latin chants. I feel a strange energy, which I have never felt before and with which I feel no affinity.

According to many this is the holiest place of Hungary. What I feel is a male rigour and nobility - I search for words - or self-evident authority, for which I want to bow my head very deeply. If it wouldn't look strange for the public I would like to stick my head into the earth and disappear accordingly. Deep awe is what I feel. Here is *Urunk Istenünk*, the God of Magyarorszag.

While feeling this, I can also see the Hungarian plains which I shall be walking the coming weeks. And behind those plains are awe inspiring ranges of alien wild mountains with alien wild people, to which I shall surrender. I fear all this, but I also long for it.

At the word 'Transylvania' most people will think immediately of Count Dracula. It is that sort of energy that I feel. That strange energy is not only awesome and noble, but also cruel and repellent. The colour is black. And a little of that uncanniness is also stuck on Romania. Perhaps because lots of Hungarians live in Transylvania? Who knows? The words: *Carpathian - Dragoman, Dracul, Bratislava, Krakau,* associate their sounds with our Dutch words *draak, wreed, wraak, grauw, grillig, griezelig, gruwel* (Dutch for dragon, cruel, revenge, grey, grill, horror, ghastly). And why I always associate the word Carpathian with the grasping and grabbing of dragon's talons I have no idea.

The people who live in those regions could have quite a task to process the 'dragon energy' which is anchored in the earth and of which they would be part.

We Dutch in our watery land of frogs, living on sand, clay and water, can judgmentally speak about the difficulties and proverbial cruelty during conflicts in Balkan countries, but we

129

have no share in those. Perhaps people who live there are processing something for Europe which is quite beyond us.

Friday, September 8
My mother is better. She had a minor heart failure because of an emotional issue unrelated to me. I write her a long letter.

This morning I visited the Romanian Embassy for the second time for my visa. A multitude of people were waiting in front of the door. I saw a group of fascinating faces. Are they Native Americans or what? They speak a Latin language; wear light blue denim jeans and jackets, gold crosses as earrings or pendants. They have gold teeth. I have never seen such people before. It is as if they come from an entirely different world. They could be gypsies and I notice my heart jumping for joy at the thought of meeting more of those people, that I shall meet them and talk with them. They were treated quite rudely by the people of the embassy, just like the rest of us and I could see that it had an emotional impact on them, making them insecure.

An official of the embassy promised me that my visa would be arranged within five minutes. Instead however I have to return at 02.00 pm to collect it. That was impossible, because I had promised to go the Jewish Seminar of the Lauder School together with Vera on the coach.

"Could I perhaps get it half an hour earlier?"

"No, madam."

"But Sir, you did promise yesterday I would get it this morning!"

"It is impossible."

Now I have to return on Monday. It is a very strange feeling to know, that my passport is in the Romanian Embassy, while I am here attending a Jewish teachers' congress about education and tolerance.

Sunday, September 10

The walking pause does miracles for my Achilles tendon, that's for sure.

Yesterday I have been celebrating *Sjabbes* (Sabbath) in the lap of Hungarian Jewry.

Lauder Javne Iskola is a secular Jewish school, which teaches also about Jewish tradition and celebrates the Jewish feasts in combination with the ordinary primary school and gymnasium curriculum. The only condition is that both as teacher or as pupil you must be prepared to respect the Jewish identity of the school and live accordingly during school times. Therefore many Christian teachers are here too. You are at liberty to tell others whether you are Jewish, Christian or something else.

The school organizes every year at the beginning of term a seminar for teachers and interested people in a Jewish holiday village in the middle of the country. This year the theme is: Holocaust and raising children in tradition and tolerance.

Vera has reserved a seat for me in the school coach and informed several people of what I am doing and as a result I am pampered by the people with much interest and cordiality. In the bus there is a man who lives in Jerusalem. He asks if I have a place to stay in the Holy City and if not, I can stay with his wife and him, if they are at home that is. "Lucky you!" says the woman who sits next to me. Yossi is about 55 years old. He is a jovial Labour party playboy; a social worker in Jerusalem with the liberated air of a true sabra. He was born in Hungary, but ever since he was a baby, he has lived in Israel. He is secretly worshipped here in this company and he knows this very well and enjoys it.

When we arrive, an hour before sunset, all women change into skirts and dresses to welcome in the Shabbat in the synagogue. I see a true transformation. Easy-going young girls in tight fitting jeans and sexy tops suddenly appear in blouses with long sleeves and formless long skirts. Not many give an impression of actually enjoying wearing one but they comply with the regulations without grumbling. What a strange bunch of unattractive women they have become.

I don't have a skirt with me, but I would love to join welcoming in the Shabbat. As a solution I tie two shawls together and wear them as a skirt. Combined with my walking boots I make quite a pretty picture and am second to none.

The synagogue is a small red brick building on the campus. We women follow the service in a corner of the synagogue separated by a white transparent net curtain. There in the middle the men are. Most wear skullcaps but some of them, including the *gazzan* (cantor), wear the black long coats of orthodoxy. They have large wide-rimmed black hats which are standing jolly and too high over the skullcaps on their heads.

Praying and singing starts. First it has been as silent and solemn as in a church. After that, when the mood improves and we all have sung *'Le chol Dodi'* (Let the Shabbat, the bride come in!) there is a lot of fun and dancing of a polonaise. Many of the smaller children are joining in. It is a wedding after all! The *gazzan* sings well. He is a tall, large man of about 30 years old, with a black beard and red cheeks, an American Hassid with the emanation of Santa Claus. He enjoys it and knows how to get his customers going. Later, at the Shabbats' meal, joined by his black brothers, he knows how to get the whole company singing. It should be accompanied by a little band I think, for all the nice Hebrew songs he starts, are picked up by the congregation too low and too slow. Vera is covering her musical ears.

The Shabbats' meal is rich and vegetarians have well been taken care of; not with the usual fried egg or piece of cheese, but with home-made veggie burgers, humus and aubergines with lentils. Before the meal we all wash our hands ritually. At our table we pray a long time and say *berachas*, blessings, over the wine and the bread. I don't see Shabbat's candles. Was it too late to light them? The sun has already set.

The tiny rabbi who runs an orthodox primary school in Budapest, his family and his guests from New York are all sitting together at one table. The rabbi's wife wears a wig, a long skirt and thick stockings. She is pushing a pram to and fro. There are two little girls in wide velvet dresses with lace collars and a serious boy with jug ears and skullcap, neatly in posh suit and tie and two elder nieces. One of them has a delicate face with glasses, dark hair, fragile lethargic gestures and a tent dress. The other is a serious girl with intelligent eyes, fragile too. She wears a long black skirt and moves awkwardly. More awkwardly than necessary I feel. The mother seems a bit below par, but that is not true. When the little girls are playing too wildly under a distant table, she only has to call them once and shake her head slowly and emphatically and the romping is over.

After dinner we all get a banana for dessert. In the communist past Hungary hasn't seen a lot of bananas and it is a jolly sight to see everybody eating their banana with an ecstatic face.

I get a lot of response on my golden pendant of Jerusalem: the crescent moon, the cross and the six-pointed star. Not everybody finds it a good combination.

In the following days I have been able to hear lectures on the theme 'education in tolerance'. One of the teachers translates simultaneously for me. (The trouble all these people go through for me!) The most interesting one was Yossi's lecture on the future of Israel. It was refreshing to see all the facts and numbers about the present peace process right in front of you, but even more hopeful was the conclusion: (It is the same which I carry within me for the past thirteen years, but now it emerges from the mouth of a liberal Israeli Jew.) "Let the holy places in Jerusalem be God's holy places. Don't make them into something Palestinian or Jewish. Let God solve the problem. It is God's Holy Mountain." In other words: Make space for a third solution.

I have always felt that an *international status* for Jerusalem would be a practical solution, but it never gave me a good feeling. But this: 'Let God solve the problem' does. It is a spiritual solution with immediate advantages for politics. This feels so good! How would politics be if there was an empty chair at the negotiation table reserved for silence, for the times when no human solutions can be found? Silence first and then perhaps: spontaneous inspiration!

It is one of my own great lessons in life: when you have to make an important decision, wait until it *feels right in all of your body.* Take your time; don't pressurize yourself or others to decide before a *physical decision* is taken. That is how I took my decision on walking to Jerusalem.

Through the days I talk with two young men, close friends. One is an athletic muscled young man with a bald head, covered with a black skullcap, and a six-pointed star hanging as a pendant from his neck on his blue T-shirt. However he is a Christian Armenian studying in Budapest. He asks me if the Messiah, Jesus, means something to me in my life and whether I have connections with New Age. He is from Transylvania in Romania. His friend is a Sephardic Jew from Serbia, who is in Budapest to study for the Rabbinate. He is very well informed about Dutch, Westerns habits, painters, thought concepts. He says thoughtfully: "A new age is coming." Greater contrast between two friends doesn't exist. As athletic is one, as fragile is the other. As quick in reaction and movement is one, as thoughtful and slow is the other. The latter is of a silent Eastern beauty, tall and thin, dressed impeccably; earnest long-lashed eyes, olive colour skin, small black beard and moustache, wearing a jolly chequered cap on a black skullcap. Slowly he places his remarks and asks his questions: an observation about the etchings of Rembrandt, his feelings about them. How he tries to look at people around him and to observe what happens. He does this with a quiet sensitive involvement in which he seems vulnerable too. Although obviously young, 24, with all the characteristics of that age - he loves to swim and dive and likes sports cars - a steady light seems to burn in him, and I can touch that. I stand in that light too. His slow pace had got him in trouble in New York and he had tried to speed up, but on the other hand: he wouldn't like to become as stressful as the New Yorkers are. He asks whether I dream and with how many members of my extended family I have a regular contact. He unfolds his ideas about family life and the lack of that in Europe. Fifteen family members seem to him a good average. I count no further than eight. I haven't seen most of my cousins for 30 years, although we all live in the same city. I might not even recognize them meeting them in the street. I don't know their children. "A great loss," he finds it. People with whom you share a blood relation may offer you an extra security, a self-evident welcome when you cannot manage on your own anymore. For the individualist Westerner the connection with the Divine is in this way the only solution not to become lonely in times of need.

Although he is strange, exotic by appearance, clothes and ideas, there still is this light in which we both seem to stand. Perhaps I shouldn't call it light. It is as if the eyes of God have opened in him already and it is in this open eye in which we know each other; something that he is, and that I am, and that is constantly knowing and known.

The following days I see him every now and again. We greet each other from a distance. He is there like a steady presence, an invisible burning candle between the others, touched by the spirit of God.

The last evening there is a dance: Israeli dances of which I know several. My feet have so far healed, that I can dance in the circle wearing my big boots for support. Some married girls wear hats or scarves. The others wear the usual denim jeans. The Hasidic girl with the awkward movements sits against the wall and watches. When I pause between two dances to catch my breath, the disc jockey plugs an Arabian dance tune. I make some movements to go with it. As if being stung by a wasp the girl walks over to me:

"Do you know the name of this music, or who sings it? I find it so beautiful!"

I don't know. Now in her turn she makes some dancing movements which cause a complete transformation in her. She shouldn't do Israeli dancing; she should do belly dancing.

"Why aren't you dancing?" I ask.

"I'm not dancing with men."

She tells me about her Hasidic background and asks whether I know the Baal Shem Tov. Of course I do. She is 19 years old and the daughter of a father who was part of the community around the Lubavitscher Rebbe. Many people believed and believe that he was the Messiah. She tells me that when he was asked whether he was the Messiah or not he answered that that question wasn't important. It was much more important whether they - those who posed the question - where the Messiah.

Then she tells how it will be in the hearts of the people when He has come. Her small white hands gesticulate unconsciously from solar plexus to heart chakra.

"We shall know much more. The knowledge of God shall be without a veil, without reserve. You can compare that knowledge with the preparing of the Shabbat's meal and to taste thereof to see if it has turned out well, and the great meal itself."

While she explains her voice deepens, her back straightens, her eyes shine and I feel how the Knowing opens up in her. The same Knowing that I felt with the rabbinical student from Serbia yesterday. It is not dark or light; it is Knowledge or Wisdom and it feels like a space round her and in her. A space connected to awe, or reverence, or no... it is not that at all. I could call it Knowledge of God, or God who knows us. But how does a young girl like her become so wise? That wisdom is much larger than herself.

She blushes when I tell her that her dancing movements are naturally graceful and that she could be a talented Arabian dancer. She is open and interested in my story, has open eyes and ears for the rest of the world. She asks for my spiritual schooling and listens attentively to my explanations of the meaning of Eastern names of God. Where her wisdom touches the politics of the Israeli Government our opinions diverge.

"God has given Israel to the Jews. You don't have to take more (*so no more new settlements*), but where Jews live you are not allowed to give land back. That is sinful."

And this stands painfully opposite the true story, told by Yossi, who hasn't got this knowing space in him, but who does know about human laws and abused human rights. Here is a spiritual being with knowledge of God and the person in front of her, but without knowledge of equal rights for Palestinians.

Her uncle, the *gazzan* from New York comes to have a chat. He asks me if I am Jewish, on which I shouldn't have replied, because it is none of his business and I can see he is not pleased with the answer. I am impressed with his niece. She wants to exchange email addresses. He is looking uneasy. Then she leaves me to get her camera. She wants to take a picture of both of us. There she goes in her long black skirt and pullover and I see her awkward movements which do not fit her at all.

I never received any answer to the emails I sent her.

It strikes me as odd: Vera, my hostess, doesn't believe in God. But all around her, on her bag, on her bed spread, in her diary, she is displaying the holy Hindu *Aum* sign. The sign for God. And now, when I am shown her favourite coat, I see along the seams the extensive calligraphy of the Arab name of God: 'Allah'. When I point all this out to her she is aghast. She will have to look at this for sure! She is an atheist. What does she have to do with God's holy Name?

Monday, September 11
I could at last collect my visa at the Romanian Embassy. Today I didn't see an official abusing his authority but an exhausted, overworked man, who could only remain standing by being harsh to us beggars. I am no longer annoyed by having had to come back three times.

Tuesday, September 12
Today is my 53rd birthday. Am I walking pitifully by myself on the country road? No way; just love it.

Friday, September 15, Nagykörös (East of Kecskemet)
This week I have had no great encounters or colourful visions. Now I can fulfil my desire to write about the Path, not so much about the Path in the spiritual sense, but in the practical sense, but yet with a capital P.

The Hungarian country roads, the '*foldut*' through the puszta are long, straight and dusty. Sandy! Sometimes they are bordered by little trees and bushes. Sometimes they lead straight through the steppe or through ploughed fields, sometimes through meagre and thin woods. Here and there are small white cottages, some neat, some dowdy. A big, firm woman of about thirty years old steps from a courtyard. She wears a ragged T-shirt with holes, leggings with the same; she is barefoot and has soft kind eyes. She has filled my bottle with fresh water and brings it to me between two ragged, bleeding chained dogs. This is a paradox, which fills me with compassion. Between the barking and the biting, between the despair of those two dogs, who really want love but will never know it, she hands the bottle to me with a courteous gesture worthy of a queen. Dogs are just there to sound the alarm; they are not co-creatures who need love. I am getting the love.

The path is long, but never boring, always beautiful. South-east behind the horizon is Jerusalem. The fine dust of the road is reasonably well-fixed by the worn tyres of cars and carts. Sometimes it has two tracks. In the middle grows grass, mugwort and camomile. I often see the traces of horses' hooves. The dust is very fine; the prints of my deeply profiled soles are reproduced in extraordinary exactness. There is no wind, the traces keep. I see little prints of insects and the slime track of a snail, caterpillar tracks, or real caterpillars. I see the prints of an insect, searching for the grass verge in the middle of the road. It has desperately walked circles, corners, angles, all without finding a way out before finally perishing in the fierce sunshine. I see many beetles on their backs, struggling with their little feet in the air trying to turn themselves. Some have, by their wriggling, made a little hole in the sand around them. I have to bow down many times to put them on their feet again. I, an earthworm myself, am usurping the role of God, but why not? Because on the other hand, how many cobwebs do I have to destroy in a day? I feel sad having to destroy cobwebs. I have a special stick for it, to take along wooded paths, where countless spiders spin and span their webs across the road. The cobwebs will stick to the stick and not to my clothes, where all those fat, furious and desperate spiders would be rolling and jumping their way off me.

I feel grateful for this wide, quiet and unassuming landscape, for the sandy field road. In the vicinity of villages and houses more prints become visible. Chicken prints crisscross the path near the entrance to a courtyard; dog and cat prints, horses' hooves, roe deer and cows and then, on a quiet, empty stretch, the print of a boy's shoe appears, with next to it a girl's sandal. Do they belong together or is it a coincidence? After a mile I see them in front of me, a boy with his young mother. This morning I saw the prints of a man's shoe, accompanying me for at least three miles. The same prints came walking towards me as well. At every farm the prints went inside the courtyard and returned again. It is not the mail man. The mailboxes are in groups at the road side. Or is he the mailman fancying a chat every now and again? The prints make me curious about him. His presence is so strong on the path. On another stretch I see dog prints. A dog has walked here early in the morning. I can see where he just walked, where he was trotting and where he was running. Every now and then he has sniffed at a tree, lifted his hind leg, followed a side track and every now and then he has jumped. He was in good spirits this morning, enjoying his early walk. On the next corner his prints disappear into the thicket and I lose him out of sight. I turn around and look backwards. I see the infinite line of my own profiled footsteps until far behind the horizon. We are writing our names here. This path is guarding our footprints, our scent, our presence, for a long time. It is an archive of memories and it accompanies me already for such a long time, the path to Jerusalem. So many faces it has shown to me, but here, in this flat, unassuming and infinite land of copses, steppe and field, it has its strongest expression and becomes a personality. I talk to it and thank it, that it is so straight and so soft for my feet, and runs so smoothly through the landscape without spoiling it. The Path, usually a friend, sometimes a foe, but always company and always there where my feet are.

This afternoon a nervous man asks me for 70 forint to...? I am immediately suspicious because of a pickpocket trick played on me in Prague a long time ago. I can miss 70 forint, but I don't entirely trust this man. He is fingering around too much in my small change, wants a piece of 100 forint. I give it to him and then go into a public toilet to change the place where I keep my money.

I see a flight of white doves in the blue sky drawing their infinite lemniscates. At every turn the sun reflects from their white flapping wings. It is as if they are representing Spirit offering my mother and me consolation and hope. My mother is at home again.

In the evening: a small adventure has arrived after all. I sit on the bed of a woman, who lives with two tiny Pekinese dogs in a little cottage in the forest. I asked her for water and if I could put my tent outside. I couldn't. I had to sleep in her bed. I had to have a bath. That was nice, because I couldn't wash in the morning, for yesterday I had to pitch on a path which was overgrown and impossible to pass. Dusk was already there and I couldn't continue. There wasn't a drop of water either. I don't mind not washing for a change, but only as an exception.

This is a cute little cottage, straw roof, ground floor only, two rooms and a kitchen; an earth yard, a pig and chickens. Toilet is outside too. Bath is a wide enamel bowl in which I have to stand and throw warm water over me. She gives an example in the nude. That is good to know; women can be nude together in Hungary. That is practical.

Saturday, September 16
I sleep in the moonlit cubicle with pictures of a wedded couple on the wall. I can just about recognize the bride as my hostess of tonight. The groom is a handsome 'Baron Esterhazy-like' slim dark man with moustache. He died ten years ago. The moon throws patches of light on the patchwork blanket. I wonder where my hostess is sleeping.

In the morning I am offered a big plate full of fresh scrambled eggs. The Pekinese dogs stand trembling beside me looking up at the plate with watering mouths. On the way to the toilet outside, the pig tries to draw my attention by grunting loudly. He draws attention to his hunger by demonstratively walking from his empty trough to an empty watermelon peel. He wants to eat. I stand there talking to him for a moment. What pleasant good-natured company he is! He has a different sort of head than the Dutch pigs; less pointed. He has a little impressed snout, which - in a few folds - sits close to his eyes next to a pair of round cheeks, nostrils turned up. His ears are smaller too. He looks like one of those laughing pigs on the assorted sliced meat bags of butchers. In two months he will be sizzling in the pan with all his good-hearted trust.

One o'clock. I just sat down for lunch. I have found a watermelon fallen from a cart. I spooned it clean out. I also found a large white cabbage. It was too big to take with me, but I cut a piece out of it. Sweet, juicy, crisp white cabbage.

Sunday morning, September 17, Lakitelek
I find it rather annoying that I have lost two important objects over the last few days. The first one was the Opinel pocket knife which was a birthday present from my son. I always take it with me in the sleeping bag, you never know. It is more taking responsibility for my situation than fear, because I am not afraid any more. I had forgotten it for two nights already, and the day after my birthday it must have dropped out of my pocket. I have bought a small potato peeling knife instead, but it is not very adequate and it pricks in my thigh while walking.

Secondly I left my forest green jumper in Ilona's witches' cottage. That lovely comfortable woollen jumper, which camouflages me so well when I look for a place in the forest to sleep, which has such a lovely collar against the cold and long sleeves to warm my wrists. I miss it very much.

Later I think about it. I could defend myself with the knife and I could hide myself with the jumper. The message seems to be: 'don't defend yourself and don't hide. Be as vulnerable as you are.'

When I've thought this I feel a load falling off my shoulders. The responsibility to defend myself in case of danger had slowly changed into a heavy obligation. I find I'd rather be vulnerable than armed. This way I want to enter Romania.

02.15 pm
I had such a craving to eat a lovely hot meal with lots of cooked vegetables. I can't bear chips with salad anymore. However, it is not available and it doesn't matter.

I ring the bell at the parsonage of a little church to ask for their prayers for peace. Yes, they will certainly do so AND I am invited for lunch! Boiled potatoes, sauerkraut, gravy. Delicious! And I have to eat chicken. I decide not to tell them I'm a vegetarian, otherwise the housekeeper has to make a special effort for me and fry an egg or so. So I eat chicken, sorry chicken! But lovely. I haven't eaten chicken for years and years. Why doesn't the priest eat chicken? He eats a fried egg. He is a vegetarian!

Monday, September 18, Convent of Benedictine Nuns near Csongrad
I have been welcomed here by ten sisters with so much love, that I couldn't take it in and almost got a panic attack. I was overwhelmed; I couldn't believe that love was all for me. I felt I was drawn into an ecstasy of joy. It also had to do with the fact that I was sleeping on my own in the guesthouse. In the room next to mine is a little chapel, where the consecrated host is kept. In the evening I walked back from the main

building to the guesthouse and suddenly I had the strange impression that Jesus was waiting for me there. I would be alone with him in the house. It seemed as if he was longing for me ardently and all I wanted was to be in that little chapel and surrender, sitting in that sweet silence.

But then my 'shadow' emerged and prevented it. I don't know yet whether it was a good thing or a bad thing or both. I thought: 'You are deceived by a chimera. You are 'only' contacting the energy of the blueprint of ideal man, (Model of Man, Carlos Castaneda) not a real entity.'

Gone was the love and gone was the connection. I thought: 'It is false; it is a sort of involuntary deceit. It is not really Jesus.' Or: 'He wants you to walk an outdated path.'

I was in great turmoil and confusion about this. I decided to put those in my 'simmering pot' (a way of dealing with problems by not thinking about them too much, but postponing this for a few days. Then you look at them properly again later). For a moment it seemed that there was a black malignancy around me, which I also put into the simmering pot. And then I calmed down and sat in a wholesome flow of good gentle darkness. And I thought: 'God doesn't exist. Jesus is no more and I am what I am.' Practical, sober and content.

But now I cannot sense the healing energy of the host anymore. And I could! Now what is the truth? Confusion!

However today I received two reassuring insect messages: a ladybird landed on my hand. (ladybird translates to Dutch as 'Our Sweet Lords Little Beast') and somewhat later I saw a large green praying mantis on my poncho. As if I was told: 'Don't worry; everything is going to plan with Johanna: God's Little Beast and Praying Mantis.

At the large dinner table at night all the sisters are smiling at me with their beautiful wide and narrow Hungarian faces. One sister speaks German and translates for me. I sit there in the centre of their attention telling stories and answering questions.

Sister Justine (70) insists on putting everything I have in the washing machine; even my clean hand-washed clothes. Instead of my own clothes she now lends me a T-shirt and a skirt (although I would have loved to try on a black habit with veil). This morning she tells me as pleased as Punch that she put everything to soak overnight and that especially from my 'clean' socks and sleeping bag liner - too large to wash by hand - a lot of dirt had come off. I get everything back, neatly ironed and folded. Sister Benedikta (26) is my interpreter. She is a slender dark woman, sober and sensible. Inadvertently I compare her to Chani, the Hasidic girl of last weekend. Then I noticed the knowledge and the wisdom, with Benedikta I notice the devotion and unconditional love.

Sister Magdalena, the abbess, is a large good woman with black hair, dark skin and a somewhat male face, in which light blue eyes are kindly scrutinizing me. You couldn't pull the wool over her eyes if you wanted to.

Three very young sisters, who have just taken their perpetual vows, still love it to have giggling sessions together. All of them are pretty, but one more so than the others. She has a face of transparent clarity and serenity. The white-starched little cap, which surrounds her face together with the black veil really suits her. She could have stepped from a romantic picture.

There is also a very old sister in the process of dementia; she helps in the kitchen. Then there is sister Gertrud, who makes my bed in spite of my protest, and who asks me many questions about the Dutch Royal Family. She always comes to the guesthouse with a chiming little bell to call me for service or meals.

There are very old or very young sisters, nothing in between. Sister Benedikta explains: the older sisters entered the order before the communist regime. During this regime they were clandestinely living in one of the few (male) monasteries who were allowed to stay. They couldn't wear their habit and were so-called kitchen aides. Since ten years the order has received back its former convent building, which had been left unattended. There are many new sisters now. After 40 years of atheism they want to lay the faith like a rock in a sea of sand, just like the sainted King Stephen, the patron of Hungary, said. They have a primary school in which most of the sisters are teachers, apart from their agricultural duties on the farm. A statue of St. Stephen will be unveiled shortly. The pedestal is made of stones from the whole province of Pest: stones of the many churches which were destroyed by the Turks some centuries ago.

In the daily choral song in church, the sisters don't sing high and rare like their colleagues in more Northern regions. They have powerful voices and the middle and lower registers are not forgotten. Especially the elder sisters are physically present and not sparing with light touches, little caresses in passing, of which I get my share as well. And I notice that I like it. It must be a habit among Hungarian women. I had already noticed last week at the Shabbats' celebration how physical women are among themselves.

Lunch consists of freshly baked doughnuts with homemade jam. It is nice, but on the sweet side. The young sister with the clear nun's face eats one after the other: eight doughnuts thickly spooned with jam, dripping between her fingers. If she can have eight doughnuts, then I can have six I hope, and, while clearing the table after lunch, I quickly pinch a seventh one.

Her name is Kunigunde and in 1988 - she was ten years old - she walked in pilgrimage with all of her family from Hungary to Poland in honour of the Black Madonna of Czestochowa. Their intention was to pray for a new beginning of Christianity in Hungary. In 1989 there was the velvet revolution and in 1998 - in support of that intention - she took the veil and entered into this order.

Tuesday, September 19

This morning there are little paper notes on the breakfast plates. Mine says: *'Széretet, édes, eros, meleg Széretet'*. 'Love, sweet, strong, warm Love'. The whole congregation comes to wave me goodbye; everybody gives me a tight hug. Even the demented sister comes to me with a very soft face to give me a kiss.

The Abbess gives me a look with her light blue eyes and a cross on my forehead. She thanks me for giving so much to the sisters. I think not! More the other way around! Then I am heavily laden with apples, grapes, peppers and tomatoes, which must have fallen straight from Heaven, so good is their taste. Photos are taken. I play a goodbye for them, the song about the good Canaan, that land full of grapes and grain. And they sing for me about Abraham, who follows his God into foreign lands. They all have filled in prayer slips to carry to Jerusalem and they wave at me until I disappear round the corner of the maize field.

Today I walk through orchards the trees heavy with apples and vineyards full of grapes. Harvest is on. I pass containers full of black grapes. It is like Eden, I can eat as many grapes as I want. It is warm amidst the grapevines. It still hasn't rained. I can see many a dried-out bunch, but still for me, it is riches. A group of colourfully dressed grape pickers has stopped for lunch; men with moustaches, boys. A deadly silence falls when I pass. *"Jo napot"* (hello), I shout happily, "Am I going right for Csongrad?" Yes, absolutely; the group starts to move. A little boy walks with me for a while. I am given grapes again. I start longing for something savoury.

Wednesday, September 20

Yesterday I found in Csongrad on the email many congratulations for my birthday. That was healing ointment! Last week they hadn't arrived yet, still drifting in digital space.

I pitched tent in a pumpkin field next to the river and today I walked over little dikes and between traffic roads, searching for the bridge. I walked many kilometres but did not progress. I met a man who showed me the way; a nice man. He had been a printer, but lost his job after the revolution. Now he couldn't practise his profession anymore. He does something else now: 'blue collar work' and he doesn't like it. His hobbies are archaeology and history. We talked about socialism, capitalism, culture, economy, Europe and Hungary today. According to him, a socialist (I bet he didn't dare to say he used to be a communist) everything is going to pieces. The people are poorer. A few people have become rich and the rest perishes. I don't know enough about Hungary to be able to judge that. I see well-dressed, well-nourished children, clean Trabant cars, discos, cinemas, and yes, sometimes tottering houses and real poor peasants.

He, Laszlo, wants to go to the West. He wants to practise his own profession. I explain that a lot of people in my own country cannot do that either. I say that the Netherlands are rich, dirty, overpopulated and have a spoilt landscape, no clean air, not enough nature and space. The cities are large; a new proletariat is developing, which has no ambition and hasn't learned to have any. I tell him, that, if he comes illegally to the West, with all his education and ambition, he might join this new proletariat, because the official ways will not be available to him. The West is not 'Paradise on Earth'. There are far too many people in the Netherlands; more than 16 million. And I envy the large Hungary, with its 9 million people spread out over that great space. I'm afraid I'm speaking to deaf men's ears. Many Hungarians are dissatisfied, but don't know that is part of democracy. In a democracy nobody ever gets his way completely.

Thursday, September 21, Szentes
Via email I have contact with the Palestinian man I met in Bratislava. Also, a certain Saleh-Ali from Libya contacted me with a detailed peace proposal for Jerusalem. I was touched.

Magdalena from Belgium wrote to me. She would love to come with me, but is not sure now if she can come. It could be that I'll have to face Romania on my own. Nobody has responded to my ads. The last possibility is to ask someone I met in Germany.

I hear a lot of evil things about Romania, which I don't want to elaborate on; never something positive. I hope I will be able to tell the good things.

Towards the evening I walk over the moors. I don't see anybody for hours. There is a magnificent sunset, changing from minute to minute. A soft breeze blows over the prairie and I walk on velvet feet over the grass path.

I come to a smallholding and it is as if I step into an old European fairy tale. I see a small, well-kept but old white farmstead with thatched roof. In the yard there is a wooden well with a long pole resting on a forked pole to draw water. I stop at the entrance of the yard. I want to ask for my evening water. To the left is the cottage, back in the middle is a stable, to the right a tottering shed with haystack, a pigsty and two barking, felted chain dogs. I stand there a moment, waiting. Usually somebody will come out if the dogs keep barking. But nobody comes. Instead of people the animals come.

The chickens are first. The cockerel is on the dung heap. A file of white geese emerges; a large white turkey with pink wattles is in front. Some four cats steal up to me to smell at me. Two pigs stand up to look jollily over the fence of their sty.

149

Black crows sit on the ridge of the shed and a group of pigeons coo in the pigeon loft. A large calf emerges from the shed. She has a rope around her neck. She keeps stepping on it, hampering her in her curiosity to come and smell at me with her pink moist nose and dark moist eyes. Now two red-brown horses with a foal have come forward from their stable and stand outside behind their fence, all three heads in my direction, softly whinnying. In the meantime the dogs have got bored and lied down, every now and again growling at me.

It gives such a contented and happy impression, all of that. This is how healthy domestic husbandry should feel.

Two people are approaching in the distance over a field. It is a couple of my own age, many more dogs and puppies playing around them. All throw themselves at me after becoming aware of my presence. The woman calls them back. I tell them my story. That is going quite well now in Hungarian. I am given water. Under their protesting eyes I pitch my tent under a group of trees. They want me to sleep inside, but tonight I long to sleep outside. Shaking their heads they give in. In the meantime the dogs want positive attention and jump up at me from all directions. The whole pack accompanies me to help pitch the tent. The cats are mixing unhindered but warily with the dogs. A large reticent Dalmatian follows behind, together with a large white Newfoundland dog, which hasn't lost all of his suspicion yet. The woman comes to call the dogs back.

I just arranged myself. Inside it looks - after the meditation - very tidy! Sleeping bag straight on the mattress; rucksack next with everything in it that shouldn't be out. My nightshirt folded on my pillow, which is a nylon bag with all spare clothes. I hear the dogs coming again. There is the woman in her red apron, carefully carrying a jug of warm milk; warm from the cow, for me. The invisible cow, that invisible mother has just given it for me; soft, warm, creamy milk. The woman walks back to the house, the dogs crowding round her legs. It is dark now. I go to sleep.

Friday, September 22
In the morning I'm woken up by a sound at the tent door. A curious cat is looking through the mosquito gauze. Behind her is the calf. While I wash the sun rises before my eyes. Washing, drying, dressing under this solemn Eye in the dawn's light suddenly is a sacred act. In the distance I hear the dogs coming. The woman comes to give me a cup of coffee to help me wake up.

At half past eight I am on my way, looking for the non-existent road to - deep breath - Hodmézovasarhély. How happy I am again today.

Behind me on the road I hear a horse and cart approaching. 'If they offer me a lift, I will accept,' I think. Not because I don't want to walk, but because I would like to sit in a horse and cart once again. The lift is offered and accepted and I sit in the back of the cart, on a blanket to soften the worst bumps in the road. The drivers' names are Talman and Alexander. Talman is a handsome Latin playboy and wears a leather jacket. Alexander is a broad blushing Hungarian. When I tell my pilgrim's story, the mood changes. We talk about Jesus and Heaven now. Yet Talman draws his wallet to show me the picture of a beautiful woman. "She has run off," he says. He is on his own.

Suddenly the cart turns into a road to the east, while I must go the south. I am alarmed and point to the south: "Hodmezovasarhely..." I stammer!

"We are going to (...), there is a post office there too, and it is in the direction of Mako; that is where you wanted to go, didn't you?"

"Yes, but in (...) is no internet cafe." When he sees my frightened face he makes a gesture of shaking out all the pockets in his old leather jacket. "Don't fear," he says laughingly. "I'm not a Romanian!" So far so good for the Romanians.

After half an hour they drop me off at the crossing for Hodmezovasarhely. "*Pusit!*" Talman calls after me. That is Slav for 'kiss' and he doesn't know that I know that.

On my way through the town I am addressed by a young man. He wants a street interview for the regional radio. That's nice. It takes quarter of an hour and afterwards I walk on. It is getting dark. I only have three quarters of an hour to leave the town and find a sleeping place.

I ask the man standing in front of a protestant church for water and for prayer for Jerusalem. He is the vicar and about 30 years old. He has a true protestant face - just like those at home. The communication is difficult, for I don't speak Hungarian very well yet. There is somehow a great tension and I must restrain myself not to fill in unusual silences with my own words. It takes a long time and I am eager to get on before darkness. He wants to say something in English but he can't. I help him. No reaction.

It ends with me sleeping in the consistorial room on the sleeping sofa. His wife came out to make the decision for him.

They have three boys, Adam, Abel and Basilius. There is also a special old, distinguished gentleman with them. He is a retired clergyman, who courteously kisses my hand at introduction. His collar and cuffs are spotless; not a mote of dust on his dark blue suit. He has white hair and a fine bony face. His mouth is toothless. He is 75 years old and speaks a careful and articulate German; he is a good interpreter for tonight.

We have a wonderful meal together. We sing Jewish songs and my Christian pilgrim hymns. The old gentleman tells about his experiences in Russian captivity and that he was once an anti-Semite. At school he once gave a swastika to a Jewish classmate. Later he had talks with a Jewish book seller. "He spoke to my heart and then I changed my opinion." The bookseller and his family were murdered in Dachau. For a moment he stares into his plate. "And I have done nothing." Again he is silent and runs a bony hand through his white hair. "I have a troubled conscience."

Saturday, September 23
The next morning the whole family waves goodbye. I get - oh my joints - a large heavy bag of food. Amongst which a big pot of jam, half a litre of *palinka* (grape liquor) and roasted chicken. They are so good to me! When I thank them and try to explain that it is really too heavy and can't take it all with me, they don't understand this. Waving, and almost collapsing under the load I leave town and give the heaviest things away at the first occasion.

It rains, and I haven't seen a sunrise. I searched on the map for the non-metalled road, which didn't run where it should; it took me two hours to find it. Yesterday that happened too. It costs a lot of extra kilometres. That is part of the deal from now on.

Monday, September 25, 02.15 pm, Mako
With dustpan and brush I will sweep some last Hungarian impressions together:

- Did I tell you that you can drink from all the blue pumps standing in public space in Hungary? They give very good water.

- Another thing I see in every village is a kind of totem pole; black wooden poles, carved full of new and old symbols. It gives a shamanistic impression, and has folkloristic subjects like dancing girls and boys. Could there be a grain of truth in the story that the Hungarians are the descendants of Attilla the Hun and his hordes, who came from Mongolia. And 25,000 years ago, the 'Indians' (Now Native Americans) came to

America over the Bering Street from that same Mongolia? There are supposed to be still shamans in Hungary. I asked here and there, but nobody knows anything about it.

- Hungarians love heroic statues, but they are on very low pedestals.

- Hungarians always ask you what you think about them and then look at you in happy expectation.

- I am very nervous now that I will be going into Romania.

Tuesday, September 26, Nagylak/Nadlac

I sit in the sunshine on the terrace in the back garden of the B&B very close to the border. The Customs office is 50 metres from here.

I would like to write about an intuition I had. I saw an enormous spider. She was a weaving spider and was at least ten centimetres wide inclusive of legs, with a large body. She was at a proper distance so I could admire her without being too frightened. I thought immediately of the Great Navaho Spider, Spider Woman, who is creating the world by spinning stories. She has two sisters, who help her creating the underworld and the upper world.

So this work is connection, webbing and creative work. Again they are a manifestation of the threefold goddess penetrating our woman's world. This time it is not in the form of the three matrons of Celtic origin or the three women at the grave of Jesus, but the three spinsters.

And this is the archetype which has connected to us, three women: Joke, Adrie and me.

I am spinning the first support thread, the story thread, stringing together European countries, and God, human beings and nature. In the web of European paths I am searching the centre, the heart, Jerusalem, earth paths. I spin an endless thread of ink on paper; it doesn't stop; all that thread spinning infinitely from my navel. There are new surprises time and

154

time again. That thread is connected to Joke, my best friend, almost as an umbilical cord, as thick as a cable, a tube for mutual nourishment, because she nourishes me and encourages me by reading everything. She is spinning the second support thread. She is a real networker in her daily work, working for the second goddess. The third is Adrie, who sits in the middle of the (internet) web typing out my letters and putting them on the web. She works for the third goddess.

What sort of web are we weaving together? Which part of Europe are we polishing with Light? A thread of light from The Hague to Jerusalem, prayer, meditations, planted on different places in the earth, an extra point of light there where people pray with us. Tatty bits are there, the thread breaks sometimes, but we tie it together again. It remains a thread of light.

At night
Magdalena can't come. She can't fix it with her work; she is very sorry.

I am nervous but not scared. I have a map of 1:500,000, only showing tarmac roads. The largest part of Romania is on it, that area where the large Hungarian minority lives. The map is called *Erdely*, the Hungarian name for Romania. Many Hungarians wish that this middle part of Romania will be Great Hungary again. The Romanians themselves live more at the edges. The southern part of the country is not on the map. No Hungarians live there. The Hungarian printer didn't find that part important.

I shall have to walk on compass, for the map doesn't show small soft roads. My hip joints can bear some five kilometres tarmac per day, not more. If I can't do it I will have to go home or buy a bicycle.

I sit on the edge of my bed in my small clean room. I just finished the watercolour in which I turn away from the large Christ-sun, running after my shadow, when again I feel this

155

great Love. I experience again how much I am being loved, and this time I don't need to run away. I am in a bath of sweetness, strongly associated with Christ.

And I am loving too: I love my life and my lot. It is the last gift from Mid Europe: *Szeretet*. It was true what that old man said at the bus stop in Budapest.

I am entering Romania.

ROMANIA

Thursday, September 28, 4.00 pm
My first impression:

The Hungarian and Romanian custom officers at the border compete with perfection of uniforms. The Hungarians have brown and the Romanians have grey uniforms.

People predicted I would have to pay bribes to the custom officers, but nobody asks me for bribes. With a cursory look the custom officers pass over my visa without making a note that I entered the country on the 28th of September. So, I have time until November 8, the date stamped into my passport by the Romanian Embassy in Budapest and I hope this will be ample.

Little groups of poorly dressed men are calling to me: "Dollars? Mark? Lei? Change money?" but I'd rather go to the official money exchange. There are just notes, no coins. The note with the lowest value is Lei 1,000. That is as much as two pence. I am the proud owner of two million Lei. It is a fat pile of banknotes to get used to. I must cut every amount with four zeros to have an approximate idea of the value.

There are many horse-and-carts here. It is the normal way of transport. There are hardly any cars. Romania at first glance gives a poor and untidy impression. The people are a bit darker. The Romanian language is more comprehensible than Hungarian, because many words can be traced back to Latin. At the market I see young and old gypsy women in brightly coloured skirts.

One of the three churches which Nadlac boasts, has a very strange late baroque tower with a black spire. To get used to the new country I walk to that little tower. It is an orthodox church; when I enter, I see from the scaffolding, that restoration work is in full progress. The 19th century murals are being refreshed. Pots with pigments, bottles of oil and bags of eggs are lying on the table. There is a large baroque iconostasis. An iconostasis can be compared to a rood screen. It is usually painted with icons. In the middle there is a little door, which swings open at important moments during the liturgy, so that the congregation can look at the priest and the altar. The iconostasis in this church looks like a 19th century Dutch street organ and you expect popular tunes to be played from it any minute. However the atmosphere in the church is not popular; it is very serene. A small dark woman of about forty enters with a pot of paint. She speaks English. We tell each other our stories. A year ago another pilgrim to Jerusalem was here on his push-bike from Austria.

Ana lost her husband ten years ago in a car accident. She tells me how difficult it was; extra difficult with the revolutionary upheaval and the political changes, and how God has supported and helped her. She considers herself fortunate with her work: the restorations of murals. While painting, she seems to connect with the saints and angels she is working on. Sometimes Paradise really opens up. And she sings in the church. She asks me to sing. I play the descant recorder. Ana often thinks of Jerusalem and how much she would like to go there. Perhaps that is why the pilgrims come to this church? The *pope*, in overalls, joins her with some more workmen. They are very open to my story. They also understand that I am on my own; I have the feeling I can ask for prayer slips. They write on them with great dedication. Ana's prayer slip speaks of the longing for God, the coming world and the gratitude for existence. I can put them all in my little cotton envelope, that I made especially for the slips. When it is time to say goodbye Ana follows me and gives me a banknote of 50.000 Lei (about three Euros). I protest. Romania is such a poor country, and I don't need it. So this is my first experience with Romanians. Nobody can take this away from me.

I write this on a country road direction south-east, under a poplar tree which drops twigs with dry leaves with the new buds for next year already underneath. The weather has turned warm and the sun is shining. The Europeans have vilified the Romanians so much, that I walk with great compassion through this country.

The barren, dry landscape, smelling of animal and human shit is turned into a reddish desert by the sun, slowly descending towards the horizon. I approach a river. There is no bridge, only a small passenger ferry, which now drifts slowly towards me from the opposite riverbank. A young ferryman handles the oars and rises up to help me on board. He sings and chats and, having come to the other side of the river, he refuses my money and wants a kiss instead. I feel brave; I kiss him on the cheek. He points at his mouth with a wink, but I refuse that, with a wink. Gallantly he helps me on the quay before taking in new passengers.

Friday September 29

Last night I slept indoors on a farm. A large family lived there, and the grandson, who was 20 years old, spoke perfect English. These Romanians told me that there are a lot of good Romanians, but also many evil ones, and I should take care. The grandson showed me his beautiful little horse. People don't have cars here, but horses.

This morning I drank water which was too cold. It gave me a headache and now I feel feverish and weak. I have no energy to write down my impressions, although after two days in Romania I can tell a lot of stories already.

Yesterday I had an unpleasant experience. Via the main road I entered into the little town of Pecica, via a neighbourhood where lots of gypsies live. My heart rejoiced for seeing so much colour and beauty. They adorn their houses and wagons with lots of ornaments and colours. The women shine in their flowered wide skirts and colourful head scarves. I tried carefully to greet them. Some nodded their heads kindly, but a few gave me a straightforward hate stare and one even spoke aggressively to me, without me being able to understand. A group of street urchins started to pick up chestnuts from the ground and I understood that they were meant for me, so I quickened my step. They pursued me, throwing chestnuts and hitting me painfully. I decided that the best thing to do is to ignore them. One or two times they tried to connect to me in a more positive manner, but changed that immediately in negative when I reacted. They acted kindly to draw me out, to be able to harass me the more afterwards. They pulled and tore at my clothes. I was happy that this morning I put away my watch, my money and my compass in a very safe place. They only stopped when a passer-by told them to. I didn't miss anything afterwards, but my tent hung sideways on the back of my pack. They could have torn me apart like a pack of dogs. I was really sad about this. I would have loved to be able to really talk to them and not to be considered a prey. Original openness and curiosity turned into cruelty. How do I come to terms with this? The language of goodwill and interest they don't understand. The language of authority or defence I don't possess. I have no answer to this and I am sad that a door is shut in my face without it being necessary.

Although I didn't feel well today, I still have walked 31 kilometres. I want to get to an orthodox monastery between Nadlac and Arad before nightfall and I knock on the door of a house to ask for directions. The man who answers the door is in deep discussion with someone else. He takes the time to show me the direction to go, but in an impatient and irritated way. He points at the sunset and says I can't get there before dark. Yet I thank him and I continue on my way. He shrugs his shoulders and turns away to his other visitor.

Half an hour later, while the dusk is quickly deepening, I get lost in the darkness on the *puszta*. I hear from far a car driving towards me over the field and it catches me in the beams of the headlights. I'm afraid this could be an assault. The car door swings open and a shadow emerges. I can't see the face because of the lights. I wait until the shadow speaks to me. It is the man of half an hour ago. He couldn't bear to let me just wander into the dark of nothingness, he says. He is still impatient, but he also offers to drive me to the monastery. I get into the car. It is a ten minute drive, the car shooting like a star through the darkness. Only the dirt road in front of the car is visible in the headlights. A dim silhouette of large buildings looms up at the edge of a black forest: the monastery. There are no lights. "They don't have electricity anymore," the man explains. After a knock on the gate a nun opens the door with a candle in her hand. Yes, I can sleep here for the night. She gives me a large room on the cloister. After I have lit my candle I see that it has a cream-coloured vaulted ceiling painted with golden stars, a couch to sleep on and a small table to put the candle on. The woman brings me a mug of hot milk and I go to bed. I feel crushed and ill and I'm not any better the next morning. Also my bowels have started to protest and I have a splitting headache. I take Echinacea, multivitamins, aspirin and rub ointment on my painful hip joints.

If this doesn't stop I can't go on. This is no good. The reason I feel feverish is also because the season is changing. In the morning and in the evening the temperature is dropping sharply. Even at home I had to take care not to catch cold in these circumstances.

Saturday, September 30
In the monastery there are old fashioned latrines and I cannot wash my hands there. I also see that the nuns are very

economical with water. The Abbess has a delicate, kind face. She wears a clean but much worn black habit, which has been repaired with white yarn; she may not have the money to buy black yarn. In the kitchen there is nothing else but bread, onion and fresh curd cheese. This they give to me for breakfast together with hot milk. It tastes very good and this is riches in the midst of poverty. The church's inside walls are painted with stylish brown/yellow murals from the 16th century. The church is scrubbed clean and in it are many clean but broken objects, with the paint peeling off, like the church pews and the iconostasis. There is a basin with sand to stick candles in. The candles are falling and melting together. The sister puts them straight all the time and scrubs the tallow from the floor.

For a long time I sit in front of the icon of the Virgin. I feel miserable. "God, have mercy upon me, have mercy upon Jerusalem, have mercy on this land Romania. This poor land... the Dragons are ruling here. Saint Michael, tame the dragons, Holy Mary, Sophia, pray for us."

I am in pain but I can feel my heart. God will show me what I have to do. Continue, become more ill, get better? I know I will be able to get to Timisoara and I will see what I must do then. I'm going to walk now. The map is showing not a single road or path, but I know place names of the villages I have to pass. The compass is in my hand and the *puszta* is even and easy to walk on.

While walking I think: 'Perhaps the Romanian water is not entirely clean. Perhaps I should buy mineral water.' But today, walking over the *pustza* I am not passing houses or villages. I am thirsty and have already drunk all my water. How unpleasant! But there, in the middle of the path lies a plastic two litre bottle half full of water. Of course I don't know whether it is good water, but I could take a smell! It looks good, very clear, without drifting particles. When I open the bottle

162

the carbonic acid bubbles into my nose. It is mineral water. It is safe! Now which angel has laid this bottle in my way?

The Romanian p*uszta* is very different from the Hungarian. The earth is black and fit for agriculture. The landscape is endless, without copses like in Hungary and very dry. The grass, everything is yellow, scorched. The wind blows unimpeded over the plain. My road is a '*drum de tara*'; an earth road. During all those hours of walking only one car passes. On each side of the road some grass grows in the verge and here and there a low shrub or tree, where I can take shelter from the burning sun and the hot wind. The cart track continues endlessly beyond the horizon. On the fields and the road the wind makes little whirlwinds, which chase up the dust. It is a lonely road. Very far away, in the distance, I see three dark figures sitting under a tree. They immediately remind me of the three witches of Macbeth. I must go past them. Now, who would sit so strangely along the road in the middle of nowhere? After my bad experience yesterday with the gypsy boys I get a little afraid. And many people told me that Romania is full of gangs of robbers. I try to surrender completely to what is going to happen in a few minutes, good or evil. I'm not walking here for nothing and I hold on to my 'fine line'. I feel that my heart is reasonably open although I am a good deal uncertain.

I come closer and closer. The immoveable shapes all look in my direction, but then I feel a smile emerging on my face. They are women; they are the Three Matrons. Surprised and curious they wait until I have arrived. They are gypsies and 'ear-readers' (poor people who walk behind the harvesters and have permission to pick up any ears of wheat which the harvesters have left behind. Ruth of the Bible book was an 'ear-reader'. They sit on bags of corn cobs, which they picked from the field after the harvesting of the great combines. They sit there like judges or a reception committee. When I stand in front of them and see their friendly faces I know I have nothing to fear. A barrage of questions is aimed at me. Little by little we understand each other. The oldest woman has a red headscarf, big dangling golden earrings, flickering eyes and magnificent wrinkles in her deeply tanned face. She jumps up and gets hold of my arm and I know: here is nothing wrong.

After a time they hoist their heavy bags on their shoulders, tied on their backs with straps of cord and I walk on with my comfortable rucksack with padded shoulder straps. In the dust of the road I see the small prints of their feet coming towards me for a long time.

In a previous letter I have mentioned the 'dragon energy' of the Balkan lands and my secret doubt of perhaps nursing 'New Age nonsense'. Yet I have seen several things now, in which I feel I recognize 'dragon energy'.

One was the church tower of Nadlac and the next one a large house. It had an architecture and ornamentation which I had never seen before, but I knew immediately: 'That is what I mean. That is something of this country, something deep deep down. That is the dragon lifting its head.' They were black ornaments which looked repellent and cruel but were also of great beauty. I found something similar in a candlestick today, in the orthodox monastery. It can't be for nothing that the archangel Michael is venerated so much here. He must keep the dragon in its place. Also the Virgin Mary is deeply venerated here. In the Bible's Revelation she stands opposite to the dragon.

It is half past seven in the evening. When I enter the pink streets of the little town of Jelu, the sun is just setting. In my search for the church and the *pope* I am addressed by a sweet looking, German speaking couple, and they have taken me in. I would rather sleep outside, because the temperatures are still OK, but today there was such a strong southern wind, that I could hardly walk against it. I am afraid it will blow my little tent away. Also everybody says it is too dangerous to sleep outside.

Sunday, October 1
I feel much better today. I rested in a bed with clean sheets. The hospitable lady of the household gave me one of those large enamel bowls to stand in and pour warm water over me with a jug. It has done me a world of good. My hosts are very gentle in providing me with everything they feel I need.

Even when in general the villages give an impoverished and dried up impression, this is not the case in Jelu. Many houses - Hungarian style with just a ground floor and sloping roof - have been painted in beautiful pastels and are well cared for. Many trees along the streets have their trunks painted white. That is to make it look tidy. On Saturday the yards and sidewalks are being swept with brooms just as careful as in Harrow on the Hill.

When I pass through the next village I see a brand new red copper onion shaped church spire. The doors of the church are open. I hear the song of sonorous male voices. Could I attend the Sunday morning service here? I take off my rucksack, brush off my clothes and step carefully inside. The inside of the church looks also restored in its former glory. The colours of the icons are fresh and all the woodwork has been painted. The congregation is standing up in the high church pews or sits on the narrow misericords. The women wear white head scarves and the men posh suits. The children sit in the front benches. There is a place for me and the verger waves reassuringly over to me to come inside. The men's choir sings in Slavic. I understand the word 'Gospodin' (Lord). The music is deep and melancholy and takes me into unsuspected depths. The doors in the iconostasis are open. Looking through it I see the altar with the white altar cloth, the golden crucifix on it, the chalice and the bread. Through an invisible window on the right behind the screen of the iconostasis, sunlight is entering and shining on the altar, while the rest of the church is in shade. It is almost a heavenly vision. In front of the altar the priest is conducting the complicated liturgy, of which I recognize only a few fragments. He is a tall man. Maybe he hasn't been here long, because he wears the robes of his predecessor who must have been much shorter. The glittering chasuble of gold brocade reveals his shining black shoes and quite a length of his trouser legs.

He preaches a long sermon. The people are silent; they listen. At the end of the service everybody goes to communion. But it is entirely different to what I'm used to. The people crowd round the priest, who is holding a basket with pieces of bread. When it is not yet their turn to receive the bread, people are chatting amicably. The verger pushes me kindly in the direction of the priest. I get a piece of bread, but before I can put it reverently in my mouth, I am accosted by someone. Where do I come from? How did I get here? I have to get used to that, but so many countries, so many customs. Chewing the Holy Sacrament I chat nicely back. I'm sure Our Lord won't mind.

More people greet me when leaving the church, but I sit and have a long talk with the young man, who has just recited the Creed standing on the altar. It is one of those young people who speak English so perfectly, saying they learned it from movies on television. I ask him what the sermon was about. This turns out to be a disappointment. According to him the priest was asking for more gifts for the continuing restoration of the church. Not in the form of money, but in the form of food for the builders and the restaurateurs. That is OK, but he concluded that - if they didn't want to give that - they were no good Christians; they weren't susceptible to the love and devotion of Christ. And that is blackmail! It almost looks like enrichment of the church at the cost of poor people and was one of the things that communism fought justly against. My spokesman doesn't understand my protest. So I change the subject to the choir song, which I loved so much. He tells me in turn, that he has never heard Gregorian chant. When I say I know a few chants by heart he asks me to sing them. I sing the Latin Gregorian Creed. He listens just as fascinated as I listened to the Slavic songs just now.

There are many white geese in Romania ranging in the street, as do the chickens, the kittens and the pups. There are not as many dogs as in Hungary, and they are not as aggressive. I see a little bitch enjoying the sun in her private hollow in the ground. She is lying on her back, eyes closed, breathing heavily with satisfaction, legs sticking upwards, basking her nipples in the warm light.

This region is supposed to be one of the poorest of Romania.

I just crossed an oilfield of about seven kilometres wide. There are pump jacks and piles of raw oil everywhere. It stinks. The soil is black earth with a struggling thistle here and there. Everywhere I see small installations and broken iron implements; sheds, which are today - Sunday - unmanned, or perhaps even every day. This all extends on an endless plain, which is easy to walk on, so I keep direction south-east, Timisoara. I will arrive somehow somewhere for sure.

Wednesday, October 4

I'm not going to have company on my walk; definitely not. Not even the contact in Germany, who had promised me half and half. I have received no response on my request via internet. Two people had promised to walk; both of them had to withdraw. Today I heard for certain. Well, I have done my best. So I am in it all on my own - and now - with complete consent. Yes, I'm still a little afraid here in Romania, but until now this has been an unjustified fear. My moment of conversion on

Good Friday in Germany was and is authentic. Following that insight I have tried to find people. Arrangements had been made. I looked forward to company. But I have to walk alone. I have permission to walk alone! The dark months are coming, the shorter days, the colder weather, unknown, wild countries, but I am not uncertain anymore whether it is reckless to do this walk alone or not. I feel safe and secure now. I don't have the feeling anymore that I am 'testing God'. I am sure now that my mission is purely to exercise 'trust'. This is no guarantee for actual physical safety. It is a guarantee that I can fully focus on trust in God, without undermining doubts whether I have made the right choices. I have no doubts anymore. This is good! And that's that. I can walk through Romania with a very good feeling.

I know I am going to Jerusalem - if God wishes so - and I feel tested threefold on the purity of my intentions and my good will. My true wish is to follow God's path, my soul's path. And it turned out that the path of my soul is: to walk alone.

Romania. There is too much to write down. I am camping again. After a week of loving hospitality by Romanians and having slept in their houses and receiving their care, my need to be alone outside in nature has grown almost out of proportion. Everybody advises me against it; it is too dangerous, but I really want it.

This night I camp in a little valley, a crevasse in the ongoing plateau. I am out of sight of the road and the next village. Something in the place reminds me of Dartmoor, but it is flatter, hotter and drier. On the spot where my tent is should be a little stream. It has sunk in the ground, but the spot is still damp and grows some strongly scented peppermint plants and purple moor grass.

Every now and again a horse and cart rattles over the road behind the hill. The sunset is awesome. I sit in the silence, in the grace of this wide land.

Thursday, October 5, 11.30 am, Birda

The landscape diversifies. It is less spoilt by monocultures of corn, which do not leave an inch for ordinary nature or by deserted industrial complexes or premises which pollute the horizon with their old iron ramshackle installations. That horizon is around me 360 degrees. A country road goes right across, an earth road from one village to the other. Usually there are about fifteen kilometres between them. I take my bearings from the church spires, which haven't disappeared, even after 45 years of Ceaucescean rule, but are often in decay.

A dead fox lies on the side of the road. The fox has no tail. It has been chopped off. Can a fox live without a tail? I hardly see blood on the small wound. He has no shot wound and he hasn't broken a bone. It is a perfect adult fox, who lies with broken eyes before my feet. Somebody stole his tail, and his life.

No intimate sand roads here, no copses, but dry steppe and barren fields; very rarely a tree at the side of the road. A tree is like a protecting angel, giving shade with its trunk and leaves.

I've walked through the forest for three months without getting bored one single moment. And now I am walking through this steppe, more beautiful and unspoilt than in the first five days, and I have the feeling I could do this through eternity. However this morning I see at the horizon the first foothills of the Carpathians. It is a mountain ridge in this south-westerly part of Romania and I probably will need three or four days to cross it. The day after tomorrow I will enter the mountains, the first mountains since Krems on the Danube in Austria. Almost two months I walked through level country; land of great diversity. The mountains will rise to 1.500 metres, about 4.500 feet. That is high, and cold. I will need a jacket, and gloves.

This morning, every morning, I am outside. Every sunrise is a gift. Every day it is different. Every time I have only the same words for it.

Friday, October 6, Berecuta, Serbian-orthodox monastery St. George

Yesterday at sunset I arrived at the monastery of St. George, which is situated just outside the little village of Berecuta on the long white road, which, basking in the sunshine, smells of earth and rocks and the perfume of sun-dried herbs and foliage. The monastery dates from the 15th century, and was built on the sacred site of a 12th century cell, where a holy man lived in seclusion. The East European style of building and decorating has been replaced by Serbian Baroque in the 18th century, which I do not find a complete success.

When I arrive I see a happy orthodox nun, dressed completely in black, standing in front of the gate. She is flirting - as it were - with two workmen, who are busy doing some building. She stands in front of the round gate in the long white wall, which is built around the monasterial court. I can see rising from behind the wall a spire formed in eastern fashion as an onion bulb and a round church dome.

Sister Iphegenia and I connect immediately. She only speaks Romanian and a little Serbian and we use our hands and feet, while I speak a little Italian and a little Czech, but this is no hindrance to understanding each other at all. She leads me inside and I am given grapes and water while she takes off her glasses to listen to me attentively.

Iphegenia is alone here. She lives on her own in the monastery, prays three times a day the choral chants, cleans and works. The monastery has been uninhabited for 45 years during the reign of Ceauscescu and time and nature have taken their toll on the buildings, which have been rapidly decaying. She is going to rebuild it. There is a happy similarity in temperament between us. I feel very much at home with her and we both feel '*felicida*' to have met each other.

She tells me about her 'vocation'. She has been a nun for only three years, she is my age and happy for the first time in her life here in the monastery, after being a librarian for 25 years. It is difficult to live and travel on your own. Yes, she agrees to that, but she also loves it. Her bishop has put a nun or a monk in all the decaying monasteries in the country, which have been given back to the people by the new government. They must bring them back to life again and re-ignite the practice of worship and to give help to the people. 'They have to light candles everywhere in the country'.

She shows me the chapel. Like in all other churches I've seen in Romania, the interior is old, in decay, but clean. The 16th century murals are beautiful, but I wouldn't mind if she gave the totally over-the-top baroque altar screen to a passing American for his antique carrousel.

Two little oil lights are burning and the flames are moving gently within their glasses in the semi-darkness in front of the icons of the stern Christ the Redeemer and of the tender Mother of God. This is the third time that I feel in front of her icon a strong and deep affect. Maria Sophia, quiet, compassionate, worthy, rooted in Eternity. I don't like the orthodox custom of this little flutter, crossing yourself three times in front of every icon. I find it inauthentic and a little hypocritical, but I don't want to break the spell, so I join Iphegenia in doing this. But then something unexpected happens: I notice the effect! It cleanses your aura around heart, throat and head, and the healing energy of the icon has full access to your heart and mind. She is Maria Sophia of Eastern Europe. According to anthroposophy, the next phase of development of humankind will be led by the energy of Eastern Europe. Sophia is symbol of the development of the feminine wisdom in human beings. Here in Romania I have already met many women, who carry this wisdom naturally in themselves. And often they are very simple, uneducated women.

The darkness gathers. I sit in the choir benches while Iphegenia recites and sings. I think of the mythical Greek Iphegenia, who was sacrificed by her father King Agamemnon to the Gods in order to receive a favourable wind for his armada to Troy. She was left behind in front of the altar of the God of Winds Aeolus on an island, where she served for twenty years.

My Romanian Iphegenia sings her heart out. She stands in front of this browned, dilapidated altar screen in honour of the Holy Spirit, another God of Winds, with her head lifted up and her hands raised. She sings Byzantine hymns with a strong Eastern influence. She has a dark, deep Mediterranean voice. When the prayers end, she leads me back along the lights burning in front of the icons. She bows, crosses herself, murmurs a short prayer. It is completely dark in the church when we return to the door. Then, suddenly, on the threshold, she turns around to me and offers me a gesture that I recognize from mediaeval paintings and carvings: the salutation of the angel Gabriel to Mary, the salutation of Mary to Elizabeth, a woman's salutation: a light bow, hands crossed over the breast, but the face lifted up in eye contact with the one saluted. The body bows, but the head does not and the face is open, so that the crossed hands in front of the breast do not say, 'I close myself for you', but 'I know your heart as I do my own; I protect your heart as I do my own'.

In the shadowy kitchen another oil light is burning in front of the icon of the mother of God, but here we eat bread with honey and drink the fresh warm milk of Iphegenia's cow. She has no other food than that. I take out my recorder and play the age old songs of the Dutch pilgrims travelling to Jerusalem. She wants me to sing them. I sing, and she sings in harmony in her mellow dark voice. It is beautiful. And then we are silent, knowing our cup is flowing over. Hand in hand we walk, wiping the tears from our eyes, out to our bedrooms at the open cloister. Behind the dome the starlit canopy of the night is spreading high and wide.

The next morning Iphegenia bids me goodbye, while I take my first steps of the day on the white earth road passing in front of the monastery. The last thing I see is her tiny figure, dressed in black, alone and minute, standing in front of the big gate in the high white wall, waving until I am out of sight.

Saturday, October 7

Let's write down quickly some impressions and not an extensive essay.

The days are shortening. Sunset at seven, sunrise at eight.

Two young men, speaking perfect English, want to practise it and have never had an English conversation with someone. I praise them to Heaven; they deserve it. Their English, picked up from television is admirable. They have unbridled ambition and few possibilities.

Old women with black headscarves sit on benches under small linden trees. Rows of white geese roam the village roads. Flocks of sheep graze the plains. A young shepherd leans on his staff, Astrakhan hat, wide coat. In his eyes I see nothing but the blue sky. No spirit, he is all soul. Nothing is awake.

Another shepherd. The same peace, the same empty gaze. His flock is grazing the field behind him. He has three dogs, who bark at me. He leans on his staff until I have approached. Then he walks with me and asks where I am going. I notice what he is doing; he protects me against his dogs. He stays between them and me until I have passed his sheep. Then he stops and lifts his staff into the air as a goodbye. He and I in that wide land and his pure gesture. Romania.

A little orthodox church in Semlacu Mic. Oh, how beautiful, how beautiful. I can't stop saying it, seeing all the stately, refined murals from the 15th century painted in earth colours. This iconostasis can stay. The light falls in slanting beams through the lantern in the high dome, shining on the colourful carpets on the floor.

I have come into hill country today. It is greener here. A girl of about 20 years old with a gentle face and missing teeth, like many people of her age, gives me a pound of costly home-made sheep feta. She says the shops are closed and I cannot buy anything anymore. With indignation she refuses my money.

An old *babushka* with a wheelbarrow full of firewood has to rest time and time again. I don't mind pushing that wheelbarrow for a while. She doesn't want me to. I give her a big quince, which has been given to me yesterday, and she takes it rather greedily. She puts her hand in her pocket and offers black grapes. I think: 'Oh, she still has nice grapes!', but they turn out to be bitter sloe berries. She sits down and speaks. I understand 'morire de fama' — to die of hunger. As a goodbye I give her money. She doesn't laugh. Isn't it enough? I feel miserable. I want human contact. She wants to eat. I feel like a walking purse; she is hungry. How much and to whom do I give money in this land?

In rich Germany I had to spend lots of money. Money comes to money. How can I do this in Romania? I spend little, no money comes to no money. I want to give. But I don't trust dramatic despair stories. I feel lonely when I give money.

Timisoara

A grubby little boy. His face expresses nothing. His body is in survival mode. He walks along the small tables on the cafe terrace with three tiny bunches of wild autumn crocuses. Blue purple crocuses bound together with taste and care. Who did that? Not he. Their colour is almost luminescent in his dirty hands against dirty jacket. Does he hold his soul in his hands? The wild crocuses are luminous; he isn't. My companion of that moment buys a bunch for me. I look at the child. I look into his eyes. Am I allowed to do that? To look this child in the eyes? As if I want to say: *God sees you in your misery; I see you.* The boy looks back. He has expressionless eyes. Not empty, like the shepherds, but dull; hard and defenceless at the same time. Now he sees me. Something is moving inside. Do I become a walking purse or do I remain a human being? My own desire for human contact kicks in. My companion gives him twice as much as he asked. "He was not asking enough," she says. While he turns his back on us I see a smile appear on his face. We are not allowed to see it. Happily he walks off with the money.

Now a little girl presents herself at our table and a moment later an older boy. They have seen it. Another little boy arrives. They get nothing. The two of us exchange looks unhappily. There are always coming more when you give to one.

She is 22 years old. She is a religion teacher and teaches children of 7-15 years. She has just started the job and loves it. We speak French together. I asked her for directions in the square. How do we deal with the misery around us? She tells about the Romanian orphanages. There are too many children and not enough carers. They lack a lot of love. Once per week she collects a little girl and takes her for a walk and will not abandon her in the future. That is all she can do.

When I get back to the Netherlands, I must do something for the Romanian orphans. Only then I am allowed to enjoy the cosmic nourishing compassion that I experience in front of the icons of the Great Mother, and that I carry with the small laminated image of her that Iphegenia gave to me.

Wednesday, October 11, Steierdorf,

It is autumn. I am in the mountains and the mixed forest is full of colour. It is cold up here. For the first time I have to close my sleeping bag during the night and put on extra leggings. Every morning a robin wakes me up by 'ffrrrts ffrrrrts, ffrrrrts', making nosedives on the flysheet and tweeting on a thorn bush in front of the entrance. It seems to be the same one every day.

In Oravita, just before entering the mountains I am received royally by people of the Catholic church. I am staying with the sexton, a German lady, who does everything to please me. She even prepares for me a hot bath of preciously saved-up water, heated up in the washing machine. I protested, but I had to. And it was lovely I admit. There is hardly any running water in town. There are the mains, connected to each house, but nobody ever knows when the water will flow. That is why my hostess always keeps the taps turned open, in order to hear the water coming. The two nights I stayed with her, she has to rise in the middle of the night to collect the trickle in buckets and water bottles. This way she has saved a whole bath full of water to do her laundry. In that precious, heated water, I have to take my bath. After that I sit in a not very clean, untidy, unfixed house, feeling clean and fresh close to the kitchen range, which is burning comfortably with logs of wood. What goes for the water goes for the gas and the electricity. You can't count on it anymore. That is why Lotte has taken this old fire range back into use.

The evening before I had a very good talk with the young (and very handsome, but that is not the point) priest. Everywhere I find people with whom I can really talk. With Lotte's family we took an outing and visited on foot an orthodox monastery a few miles up in the mountains. Long ago it was built near a holy spring. Little water rivulets run from the rock into a deep basin from which the monks draw water.

Where the basin overflows it forms a little brook running parallel to the path. The sacred mood in the chapel is very impressive. The family kisses a blackened icon, is blessed by the present monk, and returns to have lunch on the roadside. It is a lovely family, who has made me feel very welcome. After we eat lunch, the wrappings are thrown into the brook. Son-in-law breaks off a young birch tree (ow) to make a walking stick for Lotte, to walk more easily on the stony path. They are so gay and warm that I guilelessly dare to ask if it is normal, that rubbish and garbage are dumped around all villages and towns and along all the roads. They take it good-naturedly and I tell them something about recycling and natural beauty and that the money is lying on the street here. It becomes quite a discussion, where complaints about the mentality of the Romanians, the government, the economy, no work and not enough money are clearly an issue. Lotte's pension is around 30 Euros a month. Could that be true? I already ate for at least two Euros with them. It is very cheap here. I am getting a little fed up too. Everybody complains about the others not doing anything. But they don't do anything themselves either. It is quite shocking to discover that under Ceaucescu the people looked more thriving and better dressed on the family pictures than now. "But," Lotte says "we didn't have enough to eat. Now we do. Only, there is no choice."

Secretly I love this frugality. Everything is there, but not in 80 different brands. Western abundance feeds me up to the back teeth sometimes.

6.30 pm. I sit here on a spot with a panoramic view of the surrounding, closely forested mountains. The autumnal colours are definitely to write home about. Down by the river the pigs are being fed. The whole valley resounds with their screaming. I have still six kilometres to go to Bozovica. I walked the whole day over the tarmac road down in the valley. It was a bit boring. Luckily there was not a lot of traffic and I could walk on the grassy verge.

6.55 pm. It is dark enough to pitch my tent now.

Thursday, October 12, 4.00 pm, Eftimie Murgu
I slept so wonderfully last night. Eight o'clock I am in bed. I wake up at three. I slept for seven hours on end and if I wanted I could rise and walk on. But I am so comfortable. It is dead quiet.

Not a breath of wind stirs and the full moon shines clearly on the plateau where my tent is. The river beneath is shrouded in mist and around me rise the moonlit mountains. Far away I hear a dog barking. A twig cracks; there is a mysterious peace. I am warm and dry and happy. Round half past four I must have fallen asleep again. At first light, half past seven, I wake up, very well rested. The eastern mountain range shimmers orange with the sun behind it.

Now I leave the mountains for the plain before entering on the next range. This afternoon I visit a nice little town. Bozovica. Good mood, nice shops. One sells cheese, the other meat, another soap. I am hungry. My food is finished and I treat myself with fresh bread with cheese, peppers, oranges and local herb biscuits.

I call my brother in the Netherlands to ask about our mother. He has shocking, unexpected news. We all thought it was going much better with her, but suddenly it seems that my mother will not be in the land of the living for very long anymore, and I must come home soon. Next Monday he will have a talk with her GP about the prospects. He advises me not to make a decision until Monday or Tuesday. That would fit very well. Hopefully I will have arrived then at a 'red' road, a motorway, near Orsova on the Danube. From there I can reach Bucuresti and the airport easily. My mother's health is deteriorating quickly. In the night I lie awake with remorse.

On the map no road is indicated, but there must be a *drum forestiera,* through the mountains from Eftimi Murgu to Orsova. It will be much more efficient to take that one. Otherwise I have to take a detour of five days through the valley and the tarmacked road via Lablanita-Baile-Herculane to Orsova. A big part of it is 'red road' - motorway; dangerous because of the fast traffic. But here everybody advises against taking the forest road. This is nothing for a woman alone. "Up there are bears and wolves". How I would love to see those, and how fearful I would be too!

If I take the forest road it will cost me at least three days to climb straight south-west along the river from the valley here, go over the watershed and take direction straight south-east, along another river down the mountain to Orsova. I have to take food for three days. There will be water no doubt.

Before going into the mountains I write in a letter to my friend: 'I am so precise, in order for you to know my whereabouts if I will get stuck, and where people have to search, when I haven't called my brother on Monday or Tuesday. To be honest, I don't think that it will be as bad as that. Bears and wolves on the road? They are so well-fed at this time of year that they wouldn't fancy a leathery old woman like me. To be sure, I shall hang the food in a tree each night, away from the tent. I will post the letter here in Bozovica. When you get it I am either breathing my last breaths at Mountain Svinecea Mare, or I have run on and will soon collect your letter in Drobeta-Turnu-Severin. Love, Johanna.'

Friday, October 13, on the road
No, I haven't seen bears or wolves yet. But I have seen some dogs, three, who are straying in the forests and are a bit afraid

of me. Just now I passed a little shed in the middle of nowhere. Next to that a beautiful yellow dog sat howling lonely to his echo. When he saw me he started barking of course, but in contrast to other dogs, who stay near their home, this one walked with me, barking and all, for at least half an hour, further into the woods. I talked a little with him. He stopped barking and walked with me at a safe distance. I had visions of him coming with me. I was going to buy meat for him and smuggle him through the customs. In my heart I knew it would probably be better for him to stay here. He didn't look bad or hungry. All dogs are loose here. They don't seem to have a bad life. They are not aggressive or mean. They are treated with a rough affection. Sometimes they are caressed; sometimes stones are thrown at them when their boss's mood is not their way. They are a bit scared of me. I carry this huge impressive rucksack and they tend to make a circumferential move to smell secretly at my behind. This yellow dog became quite friendly and perhaps he would have walked with me longer, if I hadn't picked up a stick - not to beat him - but to help me up a steep stony path. Dogs don't like long sticks. I saw him leave with mixed feelings. Better like this, but pity too.

So, I am here, somewhere in the mountains. Yes, the way to Orsova exists. Yesterday morning people told me: 30 kilometres, six hours of walking. That sounded perfect and I entered the impressive cleft in the rocks through which the road to Orsova leads. I was so happy. The higher I came, the more flaming and fiery the autumn forest became. But...? The road follows the south-west direction and not the south-east direction indicated on the map. It goes through all sorts of meandering valleys, so I am not really progressing. In this way it will take longer than two days. Towards the evening, at a fork in the road, I stop a - rare - car and ask which way I have to take. The driver seems to have run away from a Tolstoy novel. He wears a black felt hat without a brim, has blue eyes, a black beard and red cheeks. "It is another 100 kilometres." I freeze on the spot. That is a lot. I will have to make rations. He says with gleaming eyes that I can come in the car with him. In the back of the car I see eight woodcutters. No thanks. I go on higher and higher into the mountain pass. That should be OK. I should go higher and higher. But the direction is not OK. The direction is south-west and I must go south-east! Strong gusts of wind blow downwards from the pass. I look for a sheltered camping place near the river, which has now shrunk to a brook. The setting sun shines on orangey-yellow mountains. Beams and rays of the glowing sun shine through the forest and on my tent. I am excellently camouflaged by my red and orange fleece. Everywhere there is orange light around me. The leaves on the trees, the leaves on the forest floor, everything is orange and red. I am too cold, otherwise I would feel like one of the biblical young men walking in the fiery oven. From a decomposed trunk just in front of me an enormous salamander climbs sluggishly. That is a message. In mythology the salamander is a being of the fire. He stays in the fire without changing, without being hurt. And this is not an ordinary newt, it is a fire salamander. Black with big yellow and orange spots.

During the night I can't sleep. I am in the fire. In the fire of my thoughts about my mother, who has become seriously ill and is unhappy and I could give her consolation if I were at home. I think of the pain in my family. Of the temper, the unjustified anger, the suspicion, the deafness, the blindness. We wound each other with our wounds. I lie in the fire of my thoughts and feel devoured, ill. This is not good. Let go of your mother. This way the mill is grinding the wrong way. I know I am on my way to Jerusalem. I know it is good that I am going. And it isn't good to go back, only in case you must, when your mother will really die. I think of the message of the fire salamander and I know: "*Everybody of your family has their*

181

own soul, their own path. Don't assume that you are their saviour. Your mother has her own soul, her own path. Let it go, let go. Unbind yourself. Fire all around me, family pain, pain about my own part in this. The salamander stays in the fire without being devoured. Slowly, slowly I become more peaceful. The sick and desperate feeling diminishes and I can finally fall asleep.

Saturday, October 14, 02.00 pm

This morning it is misty. I wash at the brook, eat my ration, meditate, pack and walk. I reach the top of the pass and see that there are more sandy paths here. Which one do I take? The eastern one, the south-eastern one? I decide for the last one, it is the correct direction and it looks very used.

A raven crows in the wood near to me. It crows and crows. I feel it as a warning. In fairy tales the raven is often an adviser. I close my eyes, make contact. I see the raven, large, black, on a branch, but I also see that his eyes are watery and red. Now what? Somebody told me once, that I shouldn't believe fantasy creatures with red eyes. I really don't know. I follow my own common sense. I take the south-eastern road. The raven keeps crowing, flies with me. How large they are, ravens, how deep their voice is! "I don't know whether I can trust you," I say. "I have to think for myself in the first place." The road soon turns in south-westerly direction. I keep following it, but it keeps going south-west. It branches off, but the main road keeps going south-west. That is NOT good, what to do?

At the next fork in the road I go south-east again, a narrow forest track. I see a blood track - not a good sign. Drops of blood. A dog overtakes me; he doesn't even see me; he has his nose near the ground. He runs like a tram on an electric line, following the track of blood.

Now I am sitting in a little valley in the sunshine near a brook. My second ration has been eaten. The mineral water is finished. Now I must drink natural water. I don't feel worried. I continue. It is three o'clock in the afternoon.

05.45 pm.
I should have taken the eastern road, there at the first fork on the top of the pass. That raven was right!

Since 03.00 pm I search for roads to the east and the south-east, but they take me west or south. On the map I see that I am led into an uninhabited, mountainous spit of land; the Danube is flowing around it. No way I want to go there! What is happening? I have food for a day and a half. I hope the water I drink from mountains streams is OK. It tastes fine. I am lucky; the weather is dry and not too warm. It has actually been a wonderful day, the only thing is that I'm not going in the right direction. Will I get to the airfield in time to be with my mother? Did my subconscious make me take this way, not to have to go back? Please, let me be in time, let me find the right way!

Sunday, October 15, 10.00 am
Last night I had a beautiful camping spot next to a mountain brook. I didn't hang the food in a tree after all. All that nonsense about bears! This way I have the food close and can eat breakfast as soon as I wake up. These rations leave me quite hungry.

Yet I had a big fright during the night. I was woken up by a sound that seemed like two heavy footsteps through fallen leaves and cracking a dry branch, very close to my tent. Is this a bear after all? I tried to follow the advice of the nuns in Hungary. Keep dead quiet and don't breathe. The first wasn't difficult at all, I was petrified by fear, but the second was impossible. No breathing! My heart was pounding like mad and my breath went three times as fast. Impossible to suppress that. 'Well,' I thought, 'this may be the end of your walk. This was one of the risks, go for it!' But nothing happened.

In the morning I eat my ration. The buckle of my belt finds a hole which has never been used before. After that I find a road taking me south-east. Finally it does. It is dark under the leafy canopy. The brook mumbles beside me.

12.45 pm

I'm very excited now. What happened? I walk along the brook. The path becomes wider and more accessible. The mountain stream is wider and deeper, waterfall, deep basins, ferns, moss and lichen. They take me through a deep high rocky chasm. Perhaps I am lost, but it is a very beautiful way of being lost. I enjoy every step. I don't feel worried for myself. This river will contribute to an even wider river somewhere further along the road. I guess somewhere between Dubova and Jeselnita on the Danube.

What do I see in the mud on the road? I can't believe my eyes. This must be a bear print! And a quarter of an hour later another three! They are not very fresh. (I'm glad and sad). Or could it be a big dog? Near to it are prints of red deer and dogs. They look very different. I see another print of an enormous wide and long naked foot, the upper part of the sole. Is this also a bear print? The back foot perhaps? So it is true, that there are bears in these mountains. I have found bear prints!! They cross the road to go to the river. Perhaps a bear is looking at me right now! I know that they do that, making a detour to hide in the shrubs to look at humans. I am afraid and very happy at the same time.

04.00 pm

I still follow the Delicious Crevice. Giant heads lie in the running water, rocks with faces; ferns, lichens, crooked trees, falling leaves. The sun grows warmer. General direction south-east. I am content.

I meet another dog. First it barks, but when I say only one nice word to him, he becomes my friend. He is limping; he has blood on his left front leg and a deep scratch over his nose. Is it the blood track of yesterday? He is very thin and a wild dog, but still he wants a human boss. A quarter of an hour later we meet another dog. When they see each other they stop dead in their tracks and look at each other, 30 yards between them; they are very tense. After three minutes I get fed up and walk on, telling them they are both nice dogs and everything is OK. The other dog sits down when we come nearer. It doesn't dare to go to my first companion, but comes to me for a caress. Only later they dare to meet each other. I might collect a whole pack around me. They are lovely, but what to do with them?

Four o'clock. A wide perspective opens. I see a high barren ridge of rocks in the distance, a mountain lake at its foot; small sailing boats are drifting on the water; holiday cottages on the banks. I am back in the civilized world. But where? I sit down to rest. The second dog continues. The limping one cuddles up to me. In the tree in front of me two woodpeckers are hammering away. A black tit, a wagtail and a robin are joining the party. When I am rested I take water from the brook and walk on. The Limping Dog, when he hears a pack of dogs barking in the direction I'm going in, turns around and leaves me.

This isn't a mountain lake; it is a side arm of the Danube. I have come out ten kilometres south of Eselnita. From there it is eighteen kilometres to Orsova. I made a big detour. The wrong choice of yesterday morning cost me one day, but I got something good for it in exchange! I walked most beautifully; I found bear prints, and now I greet the Danube while she flows through a magnificent chasm. On two sides the rocks tower thousands of feet high. The high barren rock ridge in the distance turns out to be the far side of the Danube and already Serbia. The river is the border. The evening sun shines on the crests of the high cliffs. The Blue Danube flows sweetly past; it is blue from hundreds of blue plastic mineral water bottles drifting in it.

On the Romanian side of the river a giant's head is hewn out of the rock face. A severe and strict face looking with warlike intention at the Serbian side of the river. It is the mythological Romanian king Decebalus. I don't like this really. It reminds me of those four American presidents, hewn out of a mountainside in a US National park. The presumption! How dare they! Did they ask the mountains for permission? This one hasn't been finished yet. It seems as if a mountain spirit looks out of the rock. It isn't the king yet, it is still the mountain and I find it beautiful. Better leave it at that, don't touch it anymore. I hope the money for the project has run out!

Going downstream, the Danube leaves the chasm and evens out in a much wider space with lower mountains at each side. The sun approaches the horizon. I look for a camping spot, but it is difficult, although there are plenty of forests and fields. Everything is sloping. I can't pitch the tent anywhere, so I crawl in my sleeping bag against the upper side of a small haystack. In this way I can't roll of the hill. I greedily eat a double ration. Rations are not necessary anymore. The night sky is studded with stars. The moon is still full. I look out over the valley of the Danube. After leaving her one and a half month ago in Hungary I meet her again here in the south of Romania.

Monday, October 16, 10.30 am

The dew was heavy, the night wind cold. I am not cold, but the wind on my forehead gives me a headache. I wrap my socks around my forehead. In the morning everything is as wet as if after rain. The dew has penetrated deep into my rucksack and the sleeping bag.

The sun rises behind the Serbian mountains and it gets warm quite soon. All my wet things are drying fast. I'm going to fold them and pack them and then it is time for walking again. My adventure in the mountains has had a happy end.

Countless holiday cottages are being built along the Danube. Apparently this will be Romania's new Gold Coast. Some are very beautiful, small and modest, with interesting Romanian woodcarvings. Some cottages are home made with rough material. The Romanians are not such excellent builders as the Germans, but I see a lot of creative ideas. It is such a relief to see something built in this country instead of buildings slowly decomposing. Between the modern houses cowherds walk the dusty paths. Each cow has her own name: Jeannette, Bianca. Little old houses stand among the new; there are small meadows, fields and woods in between.

Now I will post the 'mountain letter'. I don't know anything yet about my mother.

Tuesday October 17, Orsova

I can't believe it. My mother is recovering fast. Remember I wrote about my 'fire ordeal' in the night of Friday/Saturday! Then I let go of my entanglement with my family, especially my mother. And I hear that since Saturday she is much better! Could there be a connection?

Above Orsova stands a hill overlooking the Danube. On top of this hill stands the Convent of St. Anna. It is a rich convent, being supported by people from Germany with high quality second hand furniture and goods. There are twenty young orthodox nuns here. I haven't prayed here yet, but I have eaten! After six days of white bread with processed cheese I indulge in a meal of vegetables, soup, homemade yoghurt, quark, potato salad, delicious red wine and a small piece of fish. I say true grace. Sister Ambrosia says that everything is ecologically pure and from their own large vegetable garden. Orthodox monks and nuns are always vegetarian. Her twin sister and her mother are here too as nuns. They embroider liturgical robes and paint icons behind glass. They have three milking cows in a very clean stable. More Jerusalem pilgrims pass here: by push-bike, by donkey. Sister Ambrosia keeps me company while I am eating. Because I am so hungry it takes a long time. She sits next to me in peace, hands folded in her lap. I wouldn't be surprised if she was practising the virtue of Patience.

After dinner she shows me the complete convent. Everywhere it is spotlessly clean, even in the cowshed. I am given a small room with a fresh bed. I would like to pay the ordinary guest price, but she doesn't want that. "You are doing something for God and we are doing something for you."

The following morning she brings me a goodbye gift. It is a little bottle with holy oil. It is only three quarters full. It must be her own little bottle, which she is giving to me now. The oil has been blessed by 24 holy priests. She makes a little cross on my forehead with it and says that I must do this whenever, being on the road alone, I am afraid. "You will not be afraid anymore and will be able to decide in all peace what you will have to do in that situation."

Here I stand with this precious gift in my hands, her own treasure spared from her heart. Like in a fairy tale I am helped by those who cross my path. I think of the little Tsarina, who wore down seven pairs of iron shoes while trekking over seven iron mountains to find her beloved and was helped on the way by the sun, the moon and the stars.

The little nun in front of me gives me her peaceful and even-tempered look. Do I feel something of impatience under her calm? She doesn't give that impression at all. When I turn around to wave before disappearing behind the chapel I see she has already gone into her little office.

Wednesday, October 18
This morning I had to walk along the motorway. There is no hard shoulder, only about 50 centimetres to walk beside the tarmac. Large heavy lorries from foreign countries are racing past me on half a meter distance. Every time I'm almost blown over; it is dangerous. I do have a good view of the Danube though. After ten kilometres I no longer want to put up with it and turn into the road to Manastire Vodita. It lies one kilometre inland in a little valley, next to a small brook, called Vodita (Little Water).

From afar I see a typical Romanian wooden chapel. It reminds me a little of the Norwegian steeple churches. Near to it are well kept buildings *in statu nascendi*. The small brook flows past it. However some years ago Little Water must have been wild and wide. A track of devastation is visible on either side; a washed away bridge, many uprooted trees, loose timber, a wide dry river-bed with many stones and gravel.

The church is new. When I enter I see every space on the wall is painted, but because of the still and non-obtrusive style the effect is harmonious. Peaceful devotional lights waver in front of the icons. In the baroque style everything which is inner truth is manifested outwardly and by this the secrets become vulgarized, but here the mystery remains in place, inside, and becomes truly visible because of that. It is beautiful. If ever you want a spiritual holiday, visiting monasteries and convents in Romania is an absolute must and they can use some tourism and foreign currency.

This is a monastery for men. Impressive *staretses* (monks) are walking around; young men dressed in black cassocks and black high headgear. They have long black hair bound in a ponytail, ditto beards and moustaches and velvety soft and sparkling eyes in pale transparent faces.

One of them, the abbot I think, is in the church with visitors. I want to ask him if the monastery takes guests for the night, but he avoids looking at me. I have the feeling he rejects me, and in turn I feel resistance against his displayed importance. I soften towards him when I see how shy he becomes when two women kneel down to ask for his blessing. He gives it and then disappears hastily from view.

A moment later he has sent a junior brother into the church. He wears a less smart habit full of dust of the masonry work he is doing. I like Father Cadeniki much better. He is my son's age (20) and humility himself. No, the monastery doesn't take guests, but I am allowed to camp behind in the valley next to Vodita. That is a safe place. He gives me a coloured brochure of the monastery as a gift. I read that this monastery is very ancient. Titillating detail: the original count Dracula was a sponsor of the abbey when it was originally built.

We can communicate in English, but not enough to go deep. While with religious women I have an immediate emotional connection without much language, the communication with Father Cadeniki is via the head and concepts and not with feelings, and that is more difficult. If I have understood correctly, protestant evangelical preachers from the United States have built many chapels here and made converts with aggressive sales methods. They have alienated the people from Christian Orthodoxy and - worst of all - accused Orthodox monasteries of homosexual practices. Almost with tears in his eyes he says: "We are here for God! Not for that sort of thing!"

When I tell him of my pilgrimage, my two children, my divorce fifteen years ago and being *singula with God,* he interprets as follows: " You have born two children and now you purify your body - being alone, not 'knowing' a man - for God with this walk." He likes that.

I pitch my tent behind in the gulley, a place of silence, safety and rest. I feel so safe, that I light a little fire in the dry bed of the river.

Thursday, October 19

This morning, after a deep meditation in the small church Father Cadeniki takes his leave from me. He just told me that the monastery is very poor. The church has been financed by benefactors, but the monks have to work hard to earn their own living. I want to put some money in the box, but he gets a little angry with me. "Keep your money!" he says, because he wanted to give ME something. And now I get a real gift; something very pretty, a miniature foldable altar the size of a small book. Unfolded it displays two tiny icons, one of the Mother of God, the other of the Christ. So rich, so poor are the people here.

Yesterday I saw that he gave a loaf to a poor family; a young couple with a baby. They were dressed in rags, something like 'our' city junks and I expected to see degenerated faces. But that wasn't true at all. They had ordinary, young, decent and clean faces. The man looked depressed; the woman had a sweet face and a torn scarf around her hair. I almost didn't dare to look at them; I couldn't bear their misery. Then they were gone too fast. I was full of shame during the night for not having given something to them. I was too afraid of their poverty. Today I asked the monk for their address. He didn't know. "Many people are very poor, but we can give them only food."

Drobeta Turnu Severin

No mail, again no mail! Poste Restante doesn't work anymore. Such a disappointment! I can ask again tomorrow, but I haven't got much hope.

I wanted to take a hotel and thought that would be possible in a little town like this. There are two big hotels; both cost 45 Euros per night. An average wage here is 45 Euros per month, and after I have seen such poor miserable people yesterday without a cent, who were grateful for a loaf, it is impossible to pay 45 Euros for a room for one night. I would die of shame if I did.

So in this town there are no letters, no gloves to buy, no hotels and I couldn't reach my brother. There was an internet cafe but the computers were old and slow; it took me two hours to send two short emails. I can't buy any maps here either; not of Bulgaria and not of Romania. I'm walking off my present map; for the south of Romania is not on it. Now I'm really inconvenienced. God must take it over from me and I went into a cafe to treat myself to two nice cakes for consolation and to be able to go to the toilet, but then it didn't have a toilet!

Friday, October 20
I found a roof and a bed for five Euros with a nice woman of the Catholic Church. It wasn't easy this time. The priest wanted a guarantee that I wouldn't make any problems. They had them before while giving people lodgings. I could give him the telephone number of the priest from Oravita.

It was OK. I could go to bed only at 11.00 pm, for my bed was in the living room and I had to watch television with the family, quizzes and the All-you-need-is-Love-show. It was nice to be in a house which was so clean. Everything was old, but the electricity worked and there was running (cold) water.

Now I'm on my way to Bechet, the border transit town from Romania to Bulgaria. I guess it will take me ten days to get there. Without a map I only have a sequence of village names direction south-east, and a mouth to ask directions. The country is flat here. I am walking along the river a little outside of Severin. It is cold. I wear three pullovers and bought a thin woollen cardigan at the second hand shop. There are no shops with new clothes, but there is the Park Hotel for 45 Euros per night.

Saturday, October 21
I can't keep up with everything that is happening!

While I am meditating in front of the tent this morning I hear two men approach. They come to see how the land lies with me and have an uncertain look on their face.

"Just a moment!" I say cheerily while I blow out my candle. "I'm praying!"

There is no harm in it; it creates trust and brings potential lasciviousness down to a manageable level. I notice that I am a master in that. The two men, one older, one younger are quickly reassured. The older one, a thin man in a black suit with black side whiskers is carrying a pumpkin under his arm and has looked at my tent from afar with his binoculars, but as soon as he sees that I am a woman he comes to greet me courteously with a hand kiss. Many men do this here. It is a pleasant, romantic, slightly flirtatious but respectful gesture. They have problems with strangers sometimes in this region, for on the other side of the Danube is Serbia. The old man sometimes ferries foreigners without passport over to the Serbian side of the river, for money. I tell them my story. The old gentleman lays down his pumpkin and spontaneously embraces me. He is glad that I am not a problem. The other man wants to go to work, but the old gentleman decides to help me with packing. He finds my camping gear extremely interesting. "Good bye," he shouts to the other. "I'm going with her to Jerusalem! You go ahead and work!"

It is difficult to describe the intense fun that he radiates. He decides to walk with me for a while. I don't mind. After a few failed efforts to hold my hand longer than I want, he takes his leave with: *'drum bun'* – 'good road' and, with a resigned shrugging of the shoulders: "I love you, baby."

I walk on. It is a cold but beautiful day and I feel infinitely happy and energetic.

Many gypsies are living here and I feel my heart opening more and more with a longing to really get to know them. On the other side of the road horses and carts full of hay pass by. On top of that hay lie red and blue skirted women with dark faces, flashing eyes and naked tanned legs and feet with golden ankle bands. They look curiously at me and wave and shout! I call across the swift traffic of ordinary cars, which flits between us, that I don't understand them because I'm from Holland, but I feel a wide smile on my face, because how magnificent they are! Those strong free women with their colourful clothes. I see their teeth white and gold in their dark faces. Five good natured smiles flash at me from the other side of the road.

'It will happen,' I think while walking on. 'I shall be able to tell all of Europe that it will have to withdraw its d....d shadow from d.....d Romania. And also the Romanians themselves have to do that. I have heard so many stories about murder and manslaughter, theft and drunkenness of the gypsies, that some of it must be true, but my experiences are hopefully different. At a gas station I get water. There is a large car full of people next to the petrol pump. The car door opens and a gypsy woman in her forties with a wide yellow skirt with red flowers and a blue blouse with a green scarf asks me: "What is the time?" It is an obvious pretext, but that is fine.

"Quarter past eleven." I say while we look at each other in enjoyment. Again I have to tell her that I don't understand her next question. Then they drive on and I walk on.

In the next village I look for a shop to buy bread. A man is kindly showing me the way, but, he says: "Today there is no bread." What to do? Tomorrow it is Sunday; every shop, if any, will be closed anyway. There are no restaurants here in the country side and I'm starting to get hungry. The man stops a passing young woman.

"Come with me," she signals. On the other side of the street I pass a gate in a high fence and behind that, oh happy surprise! stands the gypsy woman of two hours ago who asked me what time it was. We immediately recognize each other. I have to come in. I receive a homemade loaf. Fish is fried for me, coffee is made, coca cola poured. The whole village sits on the settle and stares at me. I want to give the children a biscuit, but they are not allowed to accept it. Her name is Georgetta and her husband is called Laurel. He asks me everything about my walk. They have a young daughter and an older daughter." One is wearing blue jeans, the other is traditionally dressed in gypsy skirts and has long thick plaits reaching the hollows of her knees. I feel happy. I have to stay the night, but no, it is too early for that, and I know I will have to watch television and also everybody is smoking.

Suddenly there is panic at the door, a dog is growling, things are falling and breaking, children are calling outside. The man who just helped me find bread falls into the living room. With a face expressing pain he grabs for his thigh where the dog has bitten him and then comes towards me with a pledge. I understand from him, that this is not a good house. It is much too small and I have to come with him. Eat and sleep with his family; that would be much better. He has a large house and I can have my own room.

"Come, come." Just now he has been friendly to me. The family around me freezes, but they stay polite. Of course I won't go with him. He complains to Georgette and Laurel. They react very reticent. He is angry about their dog and turns to me again: "Come, come!" and then disappears through the hole of the door, annoyed about the hole in his trousers. When he is gone Georgetta says that he is mad. No, not mad, but drunk! She shakes her head indignantly. "He is not a good man, asocial!"

This is the world upside down. Not the gypsies who are drunk, but the Romanians!

Georgetta asks if I'm not afraid on my own: *'frica',* and with the knife she uses to cut the bread she makes a flashing gesture of piercing somebody's heart. Suddenly her temper becomes visible. On the TV at this very moment a woman is raped in an American film.

"Yes, I often am a little afraid on my own. But I am not really alone," I say, and point to the sky. This gesture is always good to finalize the discussion about being alone on the road.

It is time to say goodbye. I can walk for another two hours before darkness. I thank and wave.

After two hours I see a little hotel along the roadside. It is the first ordinary hotel I see in Romania. I can stay for seventeen Euros and have a private room, a bucket full of hot water to wash myself and my clothes. The room is not heated. I sleep with my pullover on. The toilet is a squatting toilet in the garden. The electric light works even though it has been dark outside for a long time. I buy privacy, time and light to write this letter.

Sunday, October 22
Last night the temperature dropped to -7ºC. The hoar frost is thick upon the field. When I leave at 09.30 am the sun is shining but it is still cold. I wear all the pullovers I have. I don't have any gloves, but I wear my thick winter socks over my hands which is satisfactory. For breakfast I drink sweet Turkish coffee and I go. So happy I am, so happy to be on the road!

In Vanju Mare it is market day; cattle, horses, sheep, goats and vegetable market. In the bleak winter sun the white breath of human and animal rises up above the market place. In the pale backlight the Astrakhan hats of the men and the backs of the horses and cattle have a shining rim. The women wear long winter coats and woollen scarves over their heads. On the roads there are long files of horses and carts, carts drawn by oxen with pigs and calves in the back; real farmer's carts. I get many invitations for lifts but I don't accept any. "Just in times of need," I say, "I am *pelerina*".

It is half past twelve. I eat from Georgetta's good bread and home-made jam. It is time to finish and post this letter. My mother is really much better. How lovely for her and for me and my family.

Monday, October 23

Last night I pitched camp near a little brook. The sun had already set and I didn't expect anyone to be out in the dusk, but I was mistaken. A flock of sheep passed my tent and a sturdy shepherd with his dog walked behind. As soon as he saw me he let the sheep continue and came over to have a chat. I was kind and polite but hoped he would go away soon before it got too dark. I felt vulnerable for there was no house in sight and nobody else around. He sat down next to me and said it was cold and couldn't we cuddle up warmly together in the tent? I politely declined, but was worried. I smelled a lot of drink on his breath; he became impatient and aggressive and touchy and tried to put his arm around me in quite a forcible way. Then I stood up shaking and asked him urgently and with trembling voice, please would he go away; it had been nice talking to him, but I really wanted to go to sleep now. Then I zipped open the tent, disappeared, zipped it back and laid down trembling on my sleeping bag, dressed and all. I thought: 'You vowed you would not defend yourself by weapon: this may be it! And yes, this was the risk you took with open eyes when you started on your pilgrimage; he may come in any moment now; there is only half a millimetre of fragile fabric between the two of you. He is drunk, he is aggressive. This is what you chose: now deal with it.'

So I lay on my back trying to surrender to the idea of being raped and robbed and left to die here in the middle of nowhere. I thought of God, and that my soul, if not my trembling body, was safe in him, but it didn't help much to reassure me. I heard the shepherd's loud breathing and snorting on the other side of the flysheet. Then after 10 endless minutes I heard him stand up and walk away. It was completely dark by now. I crept into my sleeping bag and slowly relaxed, grateful and surprised. No harm had come to me after all.

The night was very cold. The next morning a hoar frost was on the tent and the grass around it. I shouldn't sleep so close to water anymore. It makes the frost thick. I can't sleep out anyway. I survived tonight, but it is too cold. I'll have to ask for shelter from now on. Also I won't be able to write as much as I do. I cannot take long breaks anymore, for I am cooling off too much while sitting at the roadside. But I will keep writing every week.

Wednesday, October 25

I must write, I have to write. About the iron and the cement which are used to build clumsy wells, sidewalks, road crosses, foundations. And also about the old-fashioned pretty cottages of loam, straw and wood with the Turkish decorations and the Greek columns; about the creative ideas which appear in the private new homes and the brittle quality of the building materials and the slightly slanting perpendicular and horizontal lines in which those ideas are made manifest. I must write about the fields full of frost in the morning, about the hospitality of the people, who take me in and also about me being eaten by people's curiosity. I must explain ten times a day about what I am doing. My Romanian is becoming very good. Last night I slept under a dragon's roof; seven black crows were sitting on the ridge. I feel and see the dragon everywhere here. I see him in the decorations on the roofs, the shape of a farmer's cart, the finishing of a drainpipe. What is the gift of the dragon for this land?

I must write about meeting great-grandmother Aurelia with the white cap over her forehead and black headscarf tied over it. She doesn't understand anything. About her daughter, the grandmother of my own age: Maria, with deep scars of five operations in her belly, goitre and a heavy smoker's cough. About grandson Beat (7), the Blessed One, son of her son, who is in prison for three years, and her runaway Roma daughter-in-law. Seven men, Maria shows with her fingers. Not a good woman! Is son a good man?

The woodstove is being fed and water put on to heat for washing. I get stew with filled cabbage rolls and hot camomile tea. It is lovely warm here in the kitchen. I can wash with warm water. I bathe my poor feet, what a blessing! "Women amongst women," says Maria. Her husband has fallen in love with a younger woman last year and has left. I am tired, empty. I cannot talk so much.

Great-grandmother sleeps with her great-grandson in one bed. Grubby little boy sleeps with dirty clothes under dirty blankets. I sleep, clean nightshirt, clean body, together with Maria under dingy sheets and blanket. I would have preferred to sleep in my own sleeping bag. "We are sisters," Maria says. "We sleep together." She puts the sleeping bag away. I cannot sleep. Until deep in the night the radio is trumpeting while everybody sleeps. I hear *'Milosevic'*. I hear *'Barak, Arab, Palestine, Jerusalem'*. What is the matter in Israel? I don't know anything! And I stay awake. Next to me Maria is snoring. It is wonderfully warm in bed. After half an hour I feel soft itching over my body. Are they lice or fleas or bedbugs? I feel petered out, sucked empty. I can't do this. I need to be alone; I need silence. After two hours I climb out of bed, turn off the radio, shake my clothes and crawl in my sleeping bag. I don't feel itching anymore apart from one or two. Sorry Maria, don't worry; I am still your sister! In her sleep she puts her hand lovingly on my head.

In the morning, in the new grey light, I rise. Babushka lights the heater with tinder, kindling and wood. Lots of wood, for me, luxury! Coffee is coming, fresh Romanian coffee. Beat rises and puts on his dirty socks to go to school. He often makes a shy eye contact with me. He doesn't need to wash but has to pray for breakfast. He prays: sign of the cross, silent prayer, sign of the cross. When he goes to school he lets me kiss him firmly on his two cheeks. After Maria has had her raucous morning cough she lights the first cigarette of the day. She sits in her dressing gown and smokes one after the other. I pack up. I want to give her something for the night. She refuses. We are standing opposite each other in front of the small icon of the Annunciation. Maria prays for me with her eyes closed. I pray for her with my eyes open. Compassion, unconditioned acceptance of her lot, my lot is flowing through me; gift for me from under this dragon's roof. We embrace softly saying goodbye. I pay easily and discreetly without her noticing. As a last gift she fills my water bottle from the well in front of her house. The bucket breaks the thin layer of ice on top. The well is bright green of algae. The cold water streams over Maria's wrists while she fills my little bottle. Perhaps I want to call my book:

Walking in the light
About the goodness and the dignity of the people

This morning I see the dragon on the wall of the Orthodox Church in Caraulia. He eats sinners deep down in hell. Devils pull people from the staircase leading to heaven. They try to hold on to it, but there is no mercy. Many devils have another face right on their solar plexus, the place of the ego. It is very chaotic on the left side of the staircase, where screaming sinners fall into Hell, in the wide open mouth of the dragon. On the right side of the staircase serene figures stride upwards, protected by angels. At the top of the staircase Christ is waiting for them with outstretched hands. The peace and quiet of the right side are in shrill contrast with the left side. This painting is wrong. I long for a Christ who turns away from the sanctimonious ones - they will arrive in Heaven anyway - and turns to those poor wretches, clinging to the celestial ladder. Wasn't that his message? When you can't do it yourself he will help you. He must go and help that poor bloke, the son of Maria, who - having a crush on a wild and free woman - has committed manslaughter and theft, and is in prison for three years.

What is the gift of the Dragon to Romania, to Europe? Who shall help the little dirty Beat?

Maria? Aurelia? Sancta Sophia? *Domine Ajute*. God help!

A few loose impressions of today. I have seen ox carts again. The carts are special carts and the patient oxen have special harnesses and draw the cart in a slowly rocking heavy gait. I am offered a mile on a horse and cart with two nice women, mother and daughter. I sit on the firewood. We have fun and laugh together. I see that the horse, Daniel, is hurt on his left hind leg. A horseshoe is loose. Sometimes he limps or stops, but he must continue. I'm sure they have no money to repair his hoof. They are dressed poorly. The horse is thin. When I am dropped off two kilometres further I give them something for the horse. I point at the loose horseshoe. Vali, the daughter, becomes pale, grabs my hands and kisses them. They are very happy. But gone is pleasure and equality, because now they are grateful and I am their benefactor.

Kelims in red, white, green and blue hang over the fences to dry and to air. I see women sitting outside and spinning. They have a large distaff with two clouds of wool and large drop spindles, no spinning wheels. The land reminds me of Afghanistan. The shepherds even wear the same sort of clothes. The green meadows are infinite; flocks of sheep graze in the distance. People ride on donkeys. In 1972 in Afghanistan the austerity of land and men seemed to be natural to me. It was an agrarian and nomadic society in her natural development. But here I know of the recession in economics after the forced development under Ceausescu. I look at the electricity pylons with the broken power cables sweeping the ground; the deserted factories in decay; the thinly populated kolkhozes and people who complain and don't complain. *Domine Ajute*, God help.

Thursday October 26
I camped again last night. It was feasible. During the day it is hot in the sun, I guess some 20 degrees, but as soon as the sun sets it drops below zero. I have not been able to wash myself for two days, having run out of water. Am I giving lice a chance to survive? I have not washed my hair for two weeks. Yesterday at five o'clock I had my last meal and I am hungry, but I hope for a snack in the next village.

I walk across the wide arable lands south of Afumati. I've walked off the map by now. I only have the names of the villages I have to pass before reaching the border with Bulgaria. I know just about where I am; my compass is indispensable, but I wish I could look on a good map.

I walk in the midst of an endless plain of monoculture three hundred and sixty degrees around me. After a while I see a little cloud of dust on the horizon. The cloud comes closer and closer. It is a jeep. It stops and five people climb out of it to inspect the irrigation canals which cut through the land from north to south and from west to east. I'm walking south east, so I have to cross them at an angle, which is an effort, for constantly I have to descend and ascend the sloping deep and high talus, but there is no water in the canals. "Irrigation canals *totalement kaputt.*" They are a French-Romanian team of engineers and are bringing me the good map which I longed for a quarter of an hour ago. Everything I need seems to fall from the sky.

I ask them in French if they know anything about the situation in Israel/Palestine. "*C'est la guerre là maintenant!* It is war there now!" They tell me that a month ago, Sharon, who wants to be elected prime minister in the next government, has made a provocative visit to Temple Mount, pretending that he wanted to pray there, and bringing with him many policemen and soldiers. Immediately afterwards the second intifada has broken out. Peace talks are non-existent at the moment.

The team goes back to their work and I walk on over the endless fields. I see one little tree, about a mile further on. The rest is silence, blue sky, wind feather clouds, a dry irrigation ditch running from here until far behind the horizon. I walk on the earth road beside it. It is hot in the sun. What am I doing here? It is war in Jerusalem. I am on my way to a war. I have been praying for peace for seven months already. One drop of peace please, a little more peace please. Result zero! But my walk is not about results in the first place. I feel more and more strongly, that the only important thing now is, that I have to be there; that I have to go there - however small and insignificant my contribution - to offer our prayers for peace against all expectations of death and doom.

October 27
I found out that today is Friday and today I hope to reach Bechet, border town with Bulgaria. My visa is officially running

out today, but I think that it won't be too late to pass the border tomorrow.

Also it is the great celebration of Sfant Dimitru, Saint Demetrius. On the way the women are slipping me all sorts of goodies and the men are a little tipsy drinking their fruity Romanian wine.

I am walking along the Danube again. I can't see her. Between the river and me there are wide grassy wetlands cut through by little creeks. Wild horses and groups of geese are grazing there.

Many synchronicities are happening to me today:

I lost my bottle of water. When I pause I am very thirsty and there is no water near. A horse and cart are passing. The driver descends from his box seat to bring me a watermelon and a hand kiss. What a lovely hand kiss! He enjoys it and I do too and yet he stays exactly within the safe bounds of the etiquette. And I do enjoy the watermelon as well. When it is finished I am no longer thirsty.

I pass a village. The drivers of two horse and carts are having a terrible row in the middle of the road; they rant and rave. The woman roars; she is furious, a dark menacing fury. I have to pass. I glaze over my look, invoke dumb invisibility and steer ahead; this is all part of the deal. When I pass she calls to me menacingly: "*Domina, unde va!*" Three times: "Woman, where are you going!" I know that when I answer and tell her I don't understand everything she says, she will be even more infuriated and might attack me. At this very moment a large Alsatian dog jumps barking and whining between the horses. They start to rear and the woman has to direct her attention to her horses and I can pretend that I am so much gripped by the spectacle of rearing horses, that I haven't heard her. That was true Deliverance.

In the peeling door opening of the only hotel in Bechet two drunken men are hanging against the posts. All the rest of the hotel is hanging too. As I look at the first floor I see dirty and torn net curtains. Some windowpanes are broken. I'm not going there! But what else? After asking in a shop I am offered shelter with a family again. I am sitting on the settee right now. But something is strange. I feel something not quite right but I have to sleep here first; only if I am murdered tomorrow morning I can afford to get worried.

It is a beautiful clean room; we agree that I sleep in my own sleeping bag. They want some money for the night. Of course, fair enough. Seventeen Euros. I find that quite a lot for a night on the sofa, but OK, they help me. I want a bucket of warm water to wash my hair, but I have to pay another three Euros for it. OK, go for it.

Grandmother sits next to me on the bed and asks me for more and more money. She makes a pitiful spectacle, theatrically grabbing her chest when she coughs, clearly play acting. She tells me about her drunken husband, but I believe she is drunk herself. She wants more of me, but I am glad I don't understand her. The daughter has written prayers on bits of paper and asks me to bring them to the Biserica di Santa Croce in Jerusalem. Most of the prayers are about money. I feel the daughter is OK, but grandmother isn't. Of course I will bring the prayers to the Church of the Holy Cross.

Saturday morning, October 28, 11.15 am
I have arrived at the Danube again and am waiting for the ferry which shall carry me to the Bulgarian side of the river. The only thing that still can go wrong is that it will sink in the middle. I believe that my walk through Romania has had a happy end. Better than that: it has given me much goodness and hardly anything bad. It is a beautiful, but poor and primitive holiday country with lovely and interesting people. All my initial fears have proved to be unfounded. This can be put in the Public Relations. They need some international currency here! I spent

205

an exciting and moving time here and I am happy to be able to say: Bless you Romania, thank you for your great hospitality!

When I compare Germany (rich) with Romania (poor) I find several things the same: Both peoples don't trust their countrymen and speak about being careful, travelling alone is dangerous. Money is the second subject of conversation for both.

And what is the difference between those two? In Germany they always thought I was carrying so little. In Romania they feel my pack is much too large.

BULGARIA

Saturday afternoon, October 28, 03.00 pm

The border ferry crossed the river from Bechet in Romania to Oriahovo in Bulgaria. I feel melancholy; this was my last meeting with the Danube. She will follow her way further eastwards to the Black Sea, while I will continue south.

On the ferry a Turkish lorry driver on a Dutch lorry presents me with a map of Bulgaria 1:500,000. I didn't have a map yet; I couldn't buy one anywhere, so I am very happy with anything that gives a few indications of where to go. Everything on it is written in Cyrillic. That is what I will have to learn now. Romanian was easy, a piece of cake after the difficult Hungarian. Now I have to learn once more another foreign language. It is exhausting.

First impressions: Bulgaria reminds me of temperate Greece, or the Mediterranean. Still, it is cold today. According to local people it will only take another two weeks before it starts to snow.

To get used to the new country I am in a hotel and take it easy. From its vantage point on the hill ridge my window presents a wide view of the Danube with Romania and the plain through which I have been walking over the last week. They have promised the shower will be warm tonight (for it isn't now).

I have an immediate problem here. The modern, slick cash dispenser in the centre of Oriahovo doesn't work. I still have some money to pay the hotel, but after that not much left to the next cash dispenser or bank, which will be in the city of Pleven. I think I need five days to get there. So, this will be rationing. I can feel temporarily how it is to be 'poor'. The sending of this letter also has to wait until I have money to buy stamps again.

06.00 pm
It is cold in my room. I went down into the restaurant to sit near the burning coal heater putting my cold feet up in front of it while learning the Cyrillic alphabet. The staff consists of a mother with a son, a mother with a daughter and a dangerous looking dark young bloke with greasy black hair and a shady look. The last one kindly invites me to sit with them and pulls out a chair from under the table. On the seat lies a revolver. He had forgotten about that. He gets shy while the family laughs at him.

At night the shower isn't warm, it is just not ice cold! When I lie down to sleep, in the room next to mine two young people are making love. The cries of their ecstasy make me feel all the more miserable.

Sunday, October 29
I sit at the side of the road and write. I am tired, I have no energy. Can I cry against your shoulder for a moment? I am halfway to Jerusalem as the crow flies; walking distance a bit over half. I've so far to go yet. There is a war in Jerusalem. I am on my way to a war.

A new country demands so much energy: new alphabet, new language, new money. I don't want to do it anymore. I just don't want to learn everything again. But in the end it is the cold that does me in. I long for a private place, which isn't cold and depressing. I yearn for a hot bath in which I can soak for an hour and rub off all my old skin. I yearn for a warm, light room with a nice little bed lamp and a very thick book to read luxuriously in bed. *The brothers Karamazov*, *Tess of the d'Urbervilles* or *Jane Eyre*. I crave a few days of rest, but I can only do that when I arrive at the Aegean Sea, because I must keep ahead of the snow. I long for not having to explain in difficult foreign languages what I am doing. For the first time this walk I long for a travelling companion. Just for a moment, to lay my head on his/her shoulder to rest.

Monday, October 30
A donkey cart passes. The driver urges me to accept a lift and I am tempted, for I sometimes consider these days whether it would be advisable to hitch a lift to the south to keep ahead of present frost and cold and start walking again in warmer regions closer to the Mediterranean so I can sleep in my tent again.

This is a lift, so I climb in the back, but I notice pretty soon that I want to walk, not ride. On top of that the driver becomes a bit lovey-dovey. I should never have agreed. The cart has good speed, I cannot jump off, so at the first occasion I will escape, the sooner the better. I am still having this thought as the harness of the donkey gets tangled up. The cart has to stop and I am gone! Thank you up there!

In the evening it gets very cold. Another night frost is on the way. In Galovo there is no church, no monastery, no little hotel. I explain to a group of women who stand gossiping along the road. An old gypsy woman takes me into her cave. It is a cellar with a high little window; the room is swept clean and tidy. It is all that is left of a ruined house on top of it. What a wonderful crone is she! We don't understand a word of what we say to each other. At times she gets irritated by that; in spite of that I really like to be with her. After half an hour a young woman knocks on the door. She has come to see how we are doing. I hear the old woman complain: "She doesn't speak anything: not Bulgarian, not Russian, not Romanian, not Gypsy, not Serbian, not Greek." And I realize that I have never learnt any of those Eastern European languages in school, although there is a wide world of people who live and care, who speak these languages. I have only learnt the languages of West European countries. My pride of knowing how to speak several

209

tongues disappears as I hear how many my hostess has been trying out on me! This poor old woman living in a ramshackle hovel speaks about six!

We sit at the little cast iron woodstove in the middle of the room. It is very old and I can see the fire raging through several slits and chinks. It is red hot and it is very warm in the room. I don't see an icon, but there is a photo of her deceased husband. On the window-sill there is a row of well-kept potted herbs. A string of dried chillies hangs on the wall. Under the window there is a little table with a clean cloth on top. Although she invites me into her bed, I am allowed to sleep on the floor on my own mattress in my own sleeping bag. As soon as dusk has fallen she lights a candle. I am not offered anything to eat or to drink. (While she thought I didn't see it, she has quickly hidden her own little saucepan with her dinner.) I share my own bread and cheese with her, which she accepts greedily. I also give her the little guest soap of the hotel and a little icon of Jesus. Looking at it she raises her eyebrows and shrugs her shoulders.

She would love to have my golden Jerusalem pendant. I can see her eyes light up when she sees it, while she nods and signs to me to give it to her. No, I laugh, putting my hand on top of it. Instead of that I give her some money for the night. She gets tears in her eyes and starts a complaint about the loss of her husband. She lifts her skirt and points at her knickers. "*Sama, sama*" she laments. "Lonely, lonely!" She has a beautiful long, finely boned face, sharp black eyes, a beautiful mouth and a skin full of wrinkles. She has that matter-of-fact power, which I find so attractive and so scary in gypsies; a no-nonsense attitude and very fast-changing moods. I cannot find out whether she has children and whether they visit her sometimes. She is not a hostess who devours you. When it has become clear that we can't understand each other she turns her attention somewhere else. I play a few songs for her on my recorder. She likes that and I feel like being very loving to her and I am, and for a moment she becomes soft and sweet.

We go to bed. The candle is extinguished. My hostess puts a last branch into the black burner. She soon sleeps, but I don't. It is too hot in the room. I cannot close my sleeping bag for fear of smothering. Soon I feel itchy little beasties on my skin. I feel small beetles walking over my pillow and sleeping bag.

Then, up in the ruins of the house, I hear sudden clattering. My hostess wakes up and sits stock still in her bed, listening. She lights a match. The clattering dies away. My hostess goes to sleep again. Now there is something in the chimney which makes a noise and in the corner of the room I hear quick little feet and gnawing. Under the bed something scurries in my direction. I hear a patter. That is not a mouse. That is perhaps a rat! The gnawing goes on for a long time. Outside a dog starts to bark in the night and stops after a while. I fall asleep. I dream of my hostess sitting in the room at a small loom, weaving. I wake up again. It is four o'clock at night. My hostess has lighted a candle and is spinning with her drop spindle. The candlelight and the light of the fire shines reddish on her old face and hands. I have landed with the Great Spiderwoman!

It takes another four hours towards dawn. My hostess spins and knits. I wait. After two hours I rise, I wash, hopefully, all the vermin from my skin. Breakfast, pack up, meditate. My hostess looks on in wonder. I pray aloud and ask if she wants to join. "*Sto?*" she asks. "What then?" Just like with the singing she gets soft and sweet. I pray the Our Father and the Hail Mary. She shrugs her shoulders contemptuously. I just love her.

It is good to stick to this routine. It keeps me going, but I am not exactly rested. I won't be able to travel like this very long. I am waiting for first light. It comes at quarter to eight. Outside there is a thick hoar frost on the grass. I am on my way. The sun hasn't yet risen. My hostess is surprised at my early departure: "*Rano!*" A short greeting, good bye great grandmother, thank you very much for your shelter; I might have frozen to death without you!

Now I am here at quarter to eleven sitting on the endless ploughed field. No shrub, no tree, no bird. I am continuing south-east. I will post my letter here in the village of...? Illegible and unpronounceable Cyrillic. Addressed to my friend from: Johanna Frozen Fridjof van Fessem. I write at the stamp depicting a weightlifter: "Yes, it is heavy; it is a feat of strength."

Tuesday, October 31, Gorna Mitropolia
Summer has returned. I could camp last night. I slept twelve wonderful hours on end from 08.00 pm to 08.00 am. I even lit a fire this morning. It revived me; immediately I see everything from the sunny side. The sun is low and is white instead of gold.

I find Bulgaria a male country in contrast to Romania. There I enjoyed women and the feminine. The light is different here on the south side of the Danube. I only expected this in Greece: clear Mediterranean light. The slanting perpendicular and horizontal building lines, which I found paltry in Romania, I find picturesque here. Bulgaria seems slightly more prosperous and cleaner than Romania. I miss the horse-and-carts, that hunky-dory clacking on the road. There are more cars and more donkey carts. The farmers' carts are painted properly, but those in Romania had rubber tyres, in Bulgaria the wheels are still of wood, rattling over the cobble stones.

I have fallen in love with king Midas, at least, with his ears. How large donkeys' ears are, and how soft. They are black outside and white and fluffy inside. They can turn in any direction and they are so sweet! I can't get enough of them. And I love the little hoofs and legs of donkeys. They have such cute hoofs! I sat on the box of a cart next to a woman and I had a very good look at the donkey. They are sweet and rough at the same time. How can they call it an ass?!

Most people speak only Bulgarian and Russian here. That is nice and peaceful, for I can keep saying that I don't understand anything: 'Nerozumim', which is Czech for: 'I don't understand' and similar to Bulgarian. The conversation dies out naturally under my kind look, for I need some rest after the intense experiences in Romania.

But I hear people say: "She's from Hungary", or: "She is Polish or Russian". I keep smiling courteously. People try to tell me about their poverty and being without a job. They speak about the abandoned ruined factories near the villages. Somebody tells me that after the revolutions in 1989 people wanted higher wages. They went on strike and let the factories perish when they didn't get higher wages. There's a responsibility too for the workers. But perhaps the managers have fat Swiss banks accounts. Who's to say?

The Bulgarians nod their head YES, when they mean NO, and shake their head NO, when they mean YES. I enter into a grocery and ask if they sell bread: The lady shakes her head, so I leave again, but she did have bread. That special sign for YES is done by women in a very gracious way. I try to copy it, because it is beautiful. Many men cannot make that complicated roundish movement, which brings on a lot of misunderstanding.

Wednesday, November 1, Pleven
I managed to get here in five days and there are plenty of money dispensers here. Also I managed to buy another pocket knife. It is a hunting knife and it looks very dangerous, but I can lock it and put it in my pocket. The little fruit knife, which was always sticking into my thigh, I left on the side of a fountain.

Why am I so tired? What are the symptoms of the Weil's disease? Because, I find fleas on my body, do they come from my night address in Caraulia or from that in Galovo?

Saturday, November 4, just out of Pleven, 09.10 am
There was a sharp frost during the night. I was in the tent from 07.00 pm until 06.00 am. There was heavy dew, so also a heavy hoar frost. I revive by my morning fire. I have a cold and haven't slept. It is too cold to camp; I don't know how to go on. I can sleep with people incidentally, but not always. It is too exhausting. I lost my trust a little. In Pleven I slept for two nights in one of those dilapidated concrete mass hotels. 35 Euros per night. So expensive, yes I fell for it. The bed was clean and the room had a small bathtub with lots of warm water. But how shall I go on? There are none or few hotels on the way. Churches and monasteries are not to be found or, if they are, in a state of decomposition. It so seems that I will have to travel south more quickly. Is my walk petering out? Where can I find my trust again? What does it mean? It doesn't mean anything. Just: it is winter in Bulgaria, autumn really, for during the day I walk on in sun tops and shorts, bent under a load of winter coat and jumpers on my back. Sorry my friend; this isn't a happy letter.

09.45 am
The tent has thawed and dried. I will pack and go. I've got eight hours before the next dark night will have overtaken me. I have six hours of walking, two hours of rest. I can do some 22 kilometres when all is right, but I fear the hardships of the night.

Sunday, November 5, 11.30 am
But I was graced. Last night it was mellow; that was lucky beside all the unhappiness, for the cough which I caught at the

old gypsy woman's house doesn't heal. Something nice: there is much more choice in food here than in Romania and I indulged in pastry cheese pasties, cakes, walnuts, coffee and a sour sort of yoghurt. The last did me in. Everything all whisked together in my stomach didn't give me a good night's rest.

And I NEED a rest. A fixed place for some days, for I don't like it anymore. I've had enough! This is my first great dip as far as walking is concerned. I have been on my way for seven months now, and my mood has suddenly switched. I am in deep need of a companion.

This is also due to the reactions of the Bulgarians to my 'story.' When I tell the Bulgarians why I am walking they don't respond to the spiritual side of it. When I tell them I am a pilgrim walking from the Netherlands to Jerusalem, they translate that to 'tourist excursion' and point the way to the nearest bus stop. There is no way to illustrate that I am travelling on foot, and whenever I do make it clear the reaction is: 'Bravo, good sportswoman, achievement!' Men look at me with indulgence and amusement and say: "God doesn't exist."

In Bulgaria the villages have no church. Is that because the communist regime has destroyed all organically built-up old villages to establish a large, new infrastructure and to build new villages everywhere? Without church of course.

Portraits of Lenin and Stalin are still everywhere. Nobody took the trouble to take them down. Maybe Bulgaria was more communist than it thought.

Tuesday, November 7, Agatovo
Believe it or not, tonight I have heard, about two hundred metres from my tent, a pack of wolves howling against the moon. A second pack, I guess about one and a half kilometre towards the south-west, was answering. And even further away the dogs started barking. It was magnificent; I felt so

privileged. I wasn't afraid at all. Wolves howling is very different from dogs howling. It is less tragic and emotional. It is very light, somewhat etheric. Such a pity I couldn't see them. I could have of course, if I had stuck my head out of the tent, but I didn't want to risk them going away.

Every night I have new flea bites. They must be multiplying on me. How is this possible? In Pleven I sank myself completely, head over heels in the bathtub and I washed all my clothes. Every morning I wash properly and shake my clothes and sleeping bag, but every night I am scratching.

I am arriving in a mountainous region which is very beautiful. During the day it is hot like in summer, but the trees are already bare and look wintry.

Wednesday, November 8, Horska Kosovo

Last night was a tragedy. I had to sleep inside because I had arrived at Horska Kosovo in the darkness and couldn't find a camping place anymore. People kindly put me up in a workman's house. It looked neat and clean, but was also depressing. Anyway, during the night I itched out of my bed. I slept in my own sleeping bag. I don't know whose fleas they were, my own next generation fleas or the fleas of the workman's house who threw themselves on the first warm human being who entered. When I went to the toilet, four fell off me on the floor and one jumped onto the white door. I had new bites everywhere. I couldn't sleep from misery and disgust. In the morning the shower is warm, oh, luxury. On the bathroom floor I find six fat fleas. It means that I am getting more and more fleas instead of less. In the past, poor people used to have fleas all the time. It was quite an ordinary thing. Maybe St. Paul had fleas too. Why else did he tell the Corinthians: "I have been given an itch in the flesh. Three times I have asked the Lord to take it away from me." Maybe even Jesus had fleas sometimes, so why not I?

Full of hope I dress in clean underwear and T-shirt and wash what I have worn since Pleven, and now I sit at the side of the road for lunch. I itch. Are they old bites or new fleas? I check. The bites are new! I didn't have them this morning. It undermines me. It is revolting. I must stop writing about it otherwise it will become an obsession.

With the exception of a day in Pleven I haven't eaten any vegetables or fruit. After my request for vegetables this morning in the former *kolkhoz* shop, the lady behind the counter gave me three wormy, wrinkly apples. 'Vegetables are not produced!' I was already grateful for those three apples. When the lady behind the counter saw that, she gave me a lovely big beautiful tasty apple from her hidden stock. That was nice of her.

Half an hour later I walk into the next shop; a small light is burning in front of the icon of Our Lady. People overload me with vegetables (paid for) and fruit (gifts), grapes and a strange sort of yellow apple called 'Julia' (a large quince) which tastes a bit wry and bitter, but must be a great gift as it is offered with great care and joy.

Now stop worrying! You shall not want!

Thursday, November 9
It is a soft clear night. Dogs are howling in the distance at the moon and one is close here, in the forest. I am on a meadow near a tiny spring, in the shadow of a small oak tree. It is a kind place. After pitching the tent I sit for two hours in the mellow evening enjoying the rising moon. A bat flutters by, a small animal scuttles around the tent, it scratches itself (sic!). The next morning I discover my little oak tree has abundantly rained lice on my tent, and yesterday evening, in my hair. The Universe has a sense of humour! I am being eaten by fleas and this little tree by lice. I feel a togetherness in fate with my protector of tonight.

Seen on the road: small horse chestnut tree in full leaf; its blossom candles burning! But it is autumn and not spring! Garden vines are growing over the cottages in colours of golden yellow and glowing red. The leaves fall on the ground and give off a golden shimmer of light from the earth. In the middle of it an old babushka in blue working dress and headscarf draws water from a well.

Friday, November 10

I have arrived on the northern side of the two large mountain ranges, which cut through Bulgaria from west to east. My next stage is to walk in about six days through the mountains to Stara Zagora (Old Garden). A secondary road runs along the mountain railway. If I am suddenly caught by beginning winter, I can mount the train. The winter strikes suddenly, people predict. Around November 15.

I have the strange idea, that, after crossing the mountain ranges I will have arrived in the land of eternal summer. For the moment I am grateful for the mild weather.

Something which strikes me here in Bulgaria is that in contrast with other post-communist countries which I have passed, the showy heroic monuments in honour of the noble working class and peasantry have not been taken down. And something of the true meaning which is behind it starts to imprint itself on me. I can feel the passion, with which idealistic communists have tried to infuse the despised working classes with their true worth and the invaluable contribution they made to the greater good with their hard work. Islam and the Orthodox Church had not been able to do that. They always emphasized more the smallness of human beings in relation to the Divine Mystery.

What a pity that the communist experiment failed. It was really worth trying, in spite of all the terrible mistakes which were made.

The people here shrug their shoulders about 'democracy' and point to all the closed new restaurants and half-finished projects, which were set up hot-headedly after the Velvet Revolution. The house wines are still good and have been for centuries, with or without revolutions.

Saturday, November 11
The monastery of Drianovo is situated in a deep rocky gorge next to a little brook. High cliffs tower over the domes of the monastery. Around 1870 it was the scene of an important battle between the Turks and the Bulgarians, in which the scimitars were brandished all around and the holy place went up in flames.

Next to the monastery are two hotels, built for guests, complete with souvenir shops and cafes. It was a grave disappointment. I had looked forward to being fed with some spiritual nourishment, but it is a really commercial place. The *staretses* are walking around in their black cassocks, being very handsome. Their hair gathered in ponytails at the back, their black beards and their smouldering eyes, but can they be approached by ordinary human beings? Especially women?

I am here for two nights in the hotel, because my washing hasn't dried in one day. I want to go on tomorrow. The temperature has dropped again. O, please dear Lord, keep the snow away for another week please? Until I get through the mountains?

Sunday, November 12
I was too hasty with my judgement on the *staretses*. I ventured with another guest who spoke a little English and is a born Bulgarian, to accost one of the monks to introduce myself and to ask for a prayer for peace in Jerusalem. The same patriarchal Rasputin, whom I saw this morning leading the mystic liturgy in the old church, proves to be a gentle, uncertain young man,

who is very interested in my mission, speaks three words of computer English and feels frustrated because he really wants to talk with me and he cannot. He insists on exchanging email addresses. This morning he has seen how I make the sign of the cross and he teaches me the orthodox one and what it means:

Thumb, index and middle finger of right hand together means The Trinity.

Ring finger and little finger folded in palm is connection of God with people.

Touch forehead: purifying thoughts, opening for the Divine.

Touch stomach: purifying emotions

From right shoulder to left shoulder: connect soul with heart.

Together this brings Power. He says: 'Dynamis'.

Then he holds his right hand in front of me. I look at him in puzzlement until my companion - with an embarrassed nod of his head - makes it clear that I have to reverently kiss his ring.

In retrospect this commercial place wasn't so bad. I met a few interesting people here.

Monday, November 13, Triawna

In spite of my good intentions I can't wash this morning. The washing water is frozen. The sun has just risen and shines blindingly on the mountainside, the frosted meadow and the frosted tent. Ice crystals are glistening everywhere. Direction south-east I see the steep ridge which I have to tackle today. Muglish is my direction. I have to wade through two rivers today. The mountain range is only 1.300 metres high, so it is not too bad, for more to the west I can see summits of 2.400 metres. Old rural villages have their typical architecture; heavy square black slates as thick as pavement stones are on the roofs. The walls are made of tailor cut stones, which, without cement are fitting together perfectly.

This letter will be posted before I start my second large 'mountain project'. According to the map there won't be any villages for 40 kilometres. So, take food for three days.

From: Johanna, the Flea Queen.

Tuesday, November 14

I am in the middle of the mountains and spend, high and dry, a very mellow night. The frost is in the valleys! It was a peaceful place directly under a ridge in a beech forest. The trees are all bare of their leaves. The light is clear; the leaves are crunching ten centimetres deep under my feet. It is still. It reminds me of the wintry beech forest near Aachen in Germany, the wood on the verge of Winter to Spring. I am here in the same sort of forest, on the verge of Autumn to Winter. Yesterday evening it was cold; a bleak wind blew through marrow and bone and I brushed large quantities of dry leaves against the tent for insulation. I went to sleep at 06.15 pm. Tired, thirsty but content. The wind subsided during the night and there was a great silence. The moon threw black shadows of thick branches on the tent roof and I had a great desire to see a bear.

In the morning there is mist in the valleys. Here on high, in the dry woods, there is no dew. I don't see any bear prints and I don't see any springs or brooks. Everything is dry. I am thirsty. Since yesterday noon I haven't had anything to drink, but I have been climbing constantly. I have plenty of food, but no water. Even my dreams were about drinking. Down in the valley, twelve kilometres away, there is the village of Seltse. I HAVE to descend for water; pity.

I am sitting here in Seltse and people are making a fuss, because apparently I have been sleeping among the bears. Very dangerous; a young man imitates a bear attacking me and speaks angrily: "What would you have done if a bear had come down on you?" But no bear came down on me. There you see, I must have felt their presence last night!

Wednesday, November 15, Muglish, 04.00 pm

Here I sit, in the middle of a scorched plain between two mountain ranges after just emerging from a path through a wild steep gorge. Earth layers have turned 90 degrees and peak up as razor sharp pinnacles. They look like guardians. Like daggers they impale the sky on their blades. I can see faces in the stones everywhere. At higher altitudes nature always seems so much more alive and animated.

Sometimes I feel like Bilbo Baggins the Hobbit on his way to find the dragon's treasure. Recently I had to walk an uncanny train tunnel, in darkness, stumbling on a narrow path along the rails, while I hoped there would be no train coming. (It wasn't likely and this way I made a shortcut of 30 kilometres.) So I walked in the darkness, the other end of the tunnel a pinpoint of light ahead of me. Sometimes my right hand groped into emptiness instead of touching the stone wall. I could feel the Orcs coming, but I wasn't carrying a Ring of Power.* Sometimes I think I am wearing AURYN. And then I can be gentle with everything which comes to me from the hand of the Little Empress, dark or light.**

Thursday, November 16

In Jagoda (Strawberry), just before the next mountain range, I am warned not to go on foot over the pass. In that region bandits are infesting the roads. I only need to hop into the van going to Stara Zagora, but I feel down to my toes, that I don't want that. Those bandits? I am quite curious to meet them. I imagine a band of robbers with curved, silver shod daggers sticking in their red sashes, wearing red fezzes, riding on stamping horses. I might lose 45 Euros - or more.

I must walk a four lane motorway. I search in vain for more narrow roads. Those four lanes do make it safer for me though.

---

* Tolkien: The Hobbit

** Michael Ende, The Neverending Story

The oncoming cars can take their detour around me with a lot of space. It is rather boring, but never mind, it is only twenty kilometres, so less than a day's walk. Because I leave here late in the afternoon I have to look for a camp higher up the mountain; hopefully out of the way of the mist and the frost, which are in the valleys. On the narrow path leading upwards and away from the main road, I am met by a herd of white goats, accompanied by a white dog. The large buck with curled horns as thick as my arms watches me warily until his herd has passed. Behind the last animal the goatherd follows: a woman with long blonde hair in light blue denim jacket and jeans. It is almost as if an angel is passing with her white animals.

Friday, November 17
I am walking on the main road again, just before entering Stara Zagora (Old Garden) south of the big mountain range of Stara Planina, when a car stops and a woman jumps out of it and beckons to me. I recognize her as the blond goatherd of last night. For some reason she stayed on my mind a long time after she had passed, she felt familiar, well known, although I knew I had never seen her before in my life. It is this laughing woman who now, gesturing with hands and feet, invites me to join her. I don't hesitate for a second and get into the car. Galina, the goatherd and Hristo, the driver tell me in broken German, that they live in a spiritual community based on the teachings of spiritual teacher Peter Danov and they invite me to stay with them as long as I want, and to exchange ideas and experiences.

Hristo (which means Christ) is a carpenter and makes beautiful furniture, but his passion is building violins. Galina gives the furniture the finishing touch and polishes it. Valentina, a beautiful dark woman, cooks and takes care of the household. Boyko, an elderly man takes care of the herd of goats. Nadia, Ioana and Hristo are the three teenage children

223

of Hristo and go to school. Valentina has taught herself English and can practise this now with me for the first time in her life.

I stay with them for a week, sleep in a beautiful little room that Nadia has vacated for me. It is a little room with wooden floors walls and ceiling, with colourful patchwork blanket and patchwork rug; a little altar. Outside there is a clean shower, giving warm water all the time. I drink plenty of goats' milk and eat the good food of their little garden. In the evening we talk.

The commune wants to live a natural life in natural surroundings. According to the view of Danov/Hristo you can reach a certain stage of spiritual development in a city, but you need more pure surroundings to be able to develop further. I doubt whether that is true, but Hristo thinks I am ready to take another step. Which coincides with my thoughts of last week. I wondered what will be my way once I am back in the Netherlands. Like in a black hole I see my house standing among abandoned rubbish, traffic noise and every two minutes an airplane passing over my head. My flat is excellent; I love it, but I would like to live closer to the sea or the woods.

Hristo also doubts my quest, my mission. "You don't have to go anywhere. Christ is everywhere."

But I have a lot of powerful answers to that and I feel no doubt. Of course Christ is everywhere, but while talking with Valentina and Hristo I suddenly realize, that I am fulfilling a very old promise; a promise older than myself. Something has been lost, has been taken from the City of the Heart (Jerusalem). It was cursed once and it still suffers because of that. It is as if I have to carry something back which belongs there. Something, that after a lot of wandering about has to return. I think: 'What could that be? The Jewish people?' But I am not Jewish. I think of myself, wandering through Europe, and all of a sudden I know: I am bringing the Grail back to Jerusalem. That is where it belongs. After all the wanderings of the Chalice through the Europe of mediaeval myths and legends it must be brought back to the place where it originally came from. Why haven't I seen that before! I carry my mother's Grail badge on my jacket! I carry something of the Grail back to Jerusalem to heal something that was broken in the past.

Because of Hristo's doubt I have suddenly become absolutely sure of that. But what is it that has to be healed? Could it be Trust? Could it be the knowledge, that when you lay your life into the hands of the Divine, it can be good and safe; in spite of everything that can happen? That it is surrender and trust in the Unknown, which is the most important, and from there stems love and from there solutions to many seemingly insoluble problems?

Oh honourable Spider woman; spin and weave our story. Spin and weave until the colours become bright and the pattern clear. She is sitting in her attic and spins. I am sitting in my attic and write, a long long thread of ink.

Saturday, November 25

Last Monday I left Stara Zagora in misty weather. The people said: "Now the winter has begun!"

The first few days I walked through a strange industrial landscape. Endless long conveyor belts are carrying earth and ore. Ghoulish black buildings constructed of iron bolts are merging from the mist. Site huts, dilapidated and rusty, are spread over what once was a sweetly undulating hilly land. There is not a human being in view. Everything is desolate like the surface of the moon. Loudspeakers hang on poles all around; a disembodied woman's voice gives instructions. I hear it echo four or five times from every loudspeaker one after another. It is alienating.

Because it is a large area, I also have to camp there one night. O friendly oak wood. It is as if you are still giving summer

225

warmth. Your fallen leaves are dry and the mist which hangs over the fields doesn't enter here.

I continue through a mountainous landscape that could have been beautiful if it wasn't for the wildfire that burned here. All of the forest is scorched. I walk through acres and acres of burnt tree trunks. It is desolate; in my imagination I see the fire run crackling under the trees over the ground on both sides of the road. If I had walked there at the time of the fire I probably wouldn't have survived.

I want to do a ceremony for this land of scorched earth. Under a charred trunk I spread my white napkin on the black earth. On it I place crystal, rosary, icon of the Mother of God, my favourite sacred texts. And I repeat again and again:

'Hamakom asher atah omed alaiv, adamat kodesh hu.' The place on which you stand is holy ground. As if the ground has to be reconsecrated, valued, acknowledged. I say it until I feel better; comforted and reconciled with the destruction around me.

I am walking through a mystical landscape with remarkable stone formations, which are in open spaces between the trees. After another long, cold, humid night, in which I lay awake a long time, I am disconsolate and lonely and feel myself falling back in a long forgotten longing for a partner, a lover. Everything is leaking. The tent is leaking dew, my water bottle leaks, the plastic cover for thunderstorms leaks and I am leaking. Energy is leaking from me. I have no reserves. The new strength that I built up in the spiritual community last week has already evaporated.

Towards the evening I arrive at three huge boulders, leaning against each other. They stand slightly apart on an elevation in the landscape. Low trees are growing around them in a half circle. The whole day there has been a fog and the sky was covered, but now, looking at the stones, above them the sun disk is appearing through the mist; first vaguely in white and then with more and more colour. I lean against the largest rock and cry a little out of self-pity. The sun is now golden-yellow with a pink brim and it seems as if it says: "Í want you! You know that! I want you entirely, always, give me your love; I long for it passionately."

I think of my experiences in Slovakia and in the convent in Hungary and of the First Commandment: 'Thou shalt love Me with all your heart, all your soul and with all your might'.

"I am always Yours, You know that," I say. "It couldn't be otherwise." But I know I keep something back.

"You have no body that can hold me. You are incorporate. You are second choice. I don't want you."

I think of Gomer from the Bible, the adulterous bride of the prophet Hosea. He is an old man, who picks up a foundling from the field and marries her when she is old enough. He gives her everything, everything. And he feels that because of that she should love him back. But Gomer loves the boys of her own age.

"That you give me everything, doesn't give you the right to own my love," I say. "Something isn't right. My earthly love life is unfinished."

"On earth nothing is ever finished. But I see you and I know you. Come to me...!"

When I want to bow my head for the First Commandment everything in me is churning:

"Love doesn't flourish under command! The commandment *kills* the Love!"

I stay behind, full of good intentions and goodwill to obey, but obeisance and love don't belong together either.

I don't want it. I don't want to put God first. I want a lover, a friend, a soul mate. *That* one I want to love and God may have what is left. And I also know that such is not the Cosmic

Law. I complain: 'You don't have a human body, no human means for expression!'

Full of inward struggle I put up my tent next to the large stones. There is confusion in me, but I also know that this confusion, this stubbornness and goodwill is at this moment my sacred ground, the place on which I stand.

"If You want me," I say sulkingly to God, "then You must woo me. I want to be convinced."

I wake up at 12.30 am. It is pitch-dark, cold and damp. I am chilled to the bone, I am restless and I feel lonely. A new generation of grandchildren-fleas is exploding on my body. This is it! Life! That's the way it is sometimes! And: You're not getting a lover. God wants you for Himself. You're not getting it!!

"You don't have a human body," I say. "My two lowest chakras are not responding." But however true and wise this is, it has become an unfruitful argument. It doesn't add anything. Off with it, I think. I don't get it. God is stronger. He wants it this way.

I become still and in this stillness His love comes pulsating ring wise from a dark source and something in me is reconciling itself to the discomfort of this night, to the loneliness here on earth. It is as if I am turning towards and standing straight in front of that dark source, that black hole that fathoms me and knows me, that loves me and always has and always shall and which has been waiting for this moment full of yearning. I surrender, flow into this source of yearning and become fulfilled of sweetness and tenderness, peace and protection. I am received and I know: I married You tonight. And: This is for always.

Over the past days I regularly feel this fulfilment, that knowledge, that I am deeply secure in a loving Consciousness and that my love makes Him deeply happy.

Sunday, November 26, Svilengrad, on the border of Bulgaria, Turkey and Greece
I've arrived at Svilengrad yesterday. I will go into Turkey from here. Next Monday the Ramadan begins. I am lucky. Most Muslims are happy and full of goodwill to make it a beautiful meaningful time for God and for the people. So I will be walking through a land of goodwill. Shall people accept me as a woman travelling on her own?

Wednesday November 29
Thomas Hardy's *Mayor of Casterbridge*, has just come to his life's bitter end in a tottering hut on the side of a swamp, and with a sigh of satisfaction I shut the British classic. It is exactly the sort of book for which I yearned so much a month ago. Then I fill the bath tub with warm water for one of my many flea elimination actions.

This is a very reasonable room in Hotel Svilengrad. The winter price is ten Euros per night. Since the Central heating isn't working everybody gets an electric heater to use at discretion. I am here for the fifth night now. First I had to stay because of financial complications at home where my ex-husband of fourteen years ago is trying to sell our former mutual home. And now I am waiting for a New Tent to arrive. My friend Joop in The Hague was so touched by my stories of a leaking tent and repairs with brown tape that in a lightning operation he begged some money together from my other friends to buy me a new lightweight one person tent, which he has now sent as a Saint Nicholas surprise. I am asking every day at the post office whether it has arrived yet.

I have had fleas for a month now. Five days already I battle with the fleas by exercising strict hygiene to my body and my clothes. The bath tub gives good occasion. But every new day it is raining fat fleas from my trouser legs. They lie on the bathroom floor, I drown them in the bath tub, and I catch them from the bathroom wall and from between the clean sheets. I am getting very good at catching fleas, but it is as if there are more every time instead of less.

Today - being at my wits' end - I finally went to the doctor. I hope he understood my question. He spoke only Bulgarian and Russian. I want to get rid of the fleas. Those flea bites in which my body is covered like stars covering the night sky, will go away soon enough, I don't need medicine for that, but I don't want new fleas and new bites! I have been prescribed medicines with Bulgarian instructions. I don't understand them. I will go to the internet cafe shortly hoping to find somebody who can translate them.

By bathing so much and washing my hair again and again and by checking this cool room, bed, floor and walls on fleas evermore, I have caught another cold and feel weak. Every time I go to another country this happens. This is not a complaint, but an observation.

I look forward to Turkey as if I will meet a bit of 'home'. There might be many people who speak German or Dutch. I might meet Turkish women. I met many of the latter in my work in a language project in The Hague. It is as if I will walk in familiar territory.

I read about present Jerusalem on the Internet. I can read my Dutch newspaper here every day! More and more I begin to fear that the conflict in Israel/Palestine is insoluble if it is kept on this level. Israel and Palestine keep each other hostage. I started my pilgrimage in view of the peace talks that where taking place at the time and the hope that a 'light' solution could be found. But the way it looks now the two parties seem to have chosen for a 'heavy' solution, for this conflict will be solved one way or the other. To pray for peace? This moment it has changed into: wanting to be there; wanting to be with it, with everything which is happening and will happen.

Dream: I carry a key. The key belongs to the synagogue. It is not the key OF the synagogue. I am allowed to carry it for a while. A friendly Jewish patriarch dressed in white and gold with a prayer shawl round his shoulders is my contact person. The walls of the synagogue are full of paintings. One of them depicts the angel Gabriel bowing down deeply for the root and rose of Jesse (Mary) and asks her if she will not give the birthing of Jesus a second thought in connection with what will happen in the future.

I am sitting in the back of the synagogue. Behind the Veil there is the Holiest of Holiest. Four or five high Jewish initiates are holding a ceremony there. One of them however says, standing on the right side, with gloom and certainty: "But Jerusalem is doomed anyway".

I am angry that such a strong curse is spoken in such an important place, for I know the power of words. I know better and call loudly and rudely through the synagogue: "But that is a lie!" End of dream.

Thursday, November 30
I will brush a few last notes together about Bulgaria.

South of the Bulgarian mountains cars are hooting at you when they pass and they pretend to want to run you over by steering straight at you and then sidle away the very last moment; very funny indeed.

You can buy lovely pasties filled with feta and spinach. They only cost nine cents. A cup of tea costs fourteen cent, but knickers are expensive: 1.40 Euros.

It has rained a lot these days. Because there are no gutters to lead the water underground even a short shower will flood the streets.

Friday, December 1

The tent arrived today. It is beautiful and of good quality, though 500 grams heavier and I cannot sit straight in it. I expect it will be much warmer and waterproof! Very important! Because of the shimmering coating it isn't a mustard colour like it says on the instructions for use, but pure golden and ten centimetres longer than my old one, which is very nice. Yet, I was quite fond of my old tent, it served me well; it is almost like having to say goodbye to a friend.

I still have fleas, after all the trouble I have been going through. Big fat fleas jump from my laundered and camphor-treated washing. It undermines me and I am at my wits' end. I don't want to moan, but why do I still have them? Do I have to buy new clothes? But what about my sleeping bag? I can't wash that one. I just can't take it anymore.

In the internet cafe I sit, as the only woman, between dozens of boys, who are playing aggressive video games. On each screen it is war. The players roam through endless corridors, rooms and spaces, Kalashnikovs at the ready, searching for enemies to eliminate. It is of a great alienation and loneliness. From the speakers I hear quick measured footsteps, the rattling of machineguns and the human dead cries penetrating marrow and bone. The boys themselves are screaming with excitement.

And I am sitting here, with my message of peace!

TURKEY

Saturday, December 2

Turkey here! What a lovely country! Coming from Bulgaria, Edirne lies like a fata morgana in the eastern valley. Minarets and domes of the mosques are emerging from the morning mists, the sun rising behind them. Why do I feel that like coming home? This is a country which still lives with God!

Descending into the city everything is lively and happy. The people are extraverted. There is a lot of business going on in little and large shops. The streets are narrow and bending. I give myself a hotel night in a newly renovated real caravanserai. Vaulted rooms with red ochre walls built with large stones half a metre thick. The rooms are grouped round an inner court where the camels, the horses and donkeys used to be stalled. I have a view to the mosques. How those people could build! What power and might! I will salute God in one of them. Kneeling down on the carpet, shoes off, headscarf on, I bow deeply in the direction of Jerusalem/Mecca. Under the large painted dome, which envelops me like a mantle, I am suddenly crying about what in God's name, in Jahweh's name, in Allah's Name, the Merciful, the Eternal, is happening in Jerusalem. O Allah, Merciful and Gentle God, please take away the anger and the hate from your children, just like you took it away from me, when I felt so irritated and annoyed for a long time. Be gracious to them like you have been to me.

This architecture has power and fullness and warmth. The earth here isn't hard, but soft. You cannot hurt yourself when you kneel. The floor has been covered with rich and colourful carpets. The dome above me almost crushes me with her energy, and at the same time she absorbs me. It is very different from the energy of the orthodox domes in the Balkan monasteries. Those are elevating you.

233

Edirne is a real Turkish town with happy people crowding the alleys. There is an abundance of small shops, stalls and products. I am being hailed and accosted. I can read the alphabet again and immediately have found a good little dictionary. The map I had to buy is 1:750,000. All of Turkey is on it with only its main roads. It will become more and more difficult to find small paths.

I love to be in Turkey and I am not at all afraid to get lost in that maze of little streets. Everybody speaks some English or German.

I find a little restaurant where there are three pots on the fire with vegetarian bean soup. I forget the Ramadan and eat two full bowls. Outside it is getting dark. From the TV and the minarets 'Break Fast' is announced in long resonating sentences. The people start to eat, light a cigarette; everybody relaxes. How beautiful to do this all together.

Monday, December 4, between Edirne and Uzunköprü.
My first two days of Turkey have been full of new adventures. I slept in my new tent for the first time. It is much warmer and I am more and more pleased with it.

The map is a horror, almost nothing is on it. So I must use my compass constantly.

The people, especially the men, are curious. It is nice but also exhausting. In one village I have to explain everything to every other man. They find it strange and don't approve.

The contact starts with an authoritarian gesture of the head and the sticking up of two hands in an inquiring manner: "Hey, what you doing there?" After I have explained they understand; the mood improves.

"Where do you sleep? There are no hotels here."

"In the tent." Yes, dangerous. Perhaps it is. I hardly see women in the street.

It is strange. The landscape has a light feminine energy, but I only see men. They are good-naturedly authoritarian and feel responsible for me. A light panic comes over them when they realize I'm doing it all on my own. As if it would be their fault if something bad happened to me: "In Turkey it is impossible, what you are doing."

The children are curious too. I am followed by 40 primary school children in blue, red and green uniforms. One started with: "Hello, what is your name?" And a second later they all were calling this, surrounding me with their tumult so that I had to leave the village immediately.

I am writing this at the side of the road. A shepherd has just sat down next to me. I'm leaving!

Tuesday, December 5

This morning, when I reached deep into the tent bag to get my gloves, I noticed that I was singing a St. Nicholas song: 'The bag of Sinterklaas'. Tonight it is St. Nicholas Eve and all the families in the Netherlands will celebrate 'parcel evening' and unpack their St. Nicholas gifts. I am in the land of Sinterklaas, bishop of Myra further down on the Mediterranean coast. My own family is in New Zealand and Australia. I miss them.

The disadvantage of Ramadan is that I cannot get any warm food or drink anywhere. In the cafes the men sit talking at empty tables. In every little village there is a little mosque, just like a country church.

I am resting a moment on a stone at the side of the road, but it is too cold to stay long. Still I am too tired to continue. I have plodded through the clay for three hours. The land is fertile here, a river plain close to the Greek border. There are military settlements galore. I am not allowed to pass everywhere. The soldiers always ask for my passport. Not because they have to but because they are curious. They like to try their English and German. The officers are first a little grumpy, then they change and want to offer much more help than I need.

The men's misplaced sense of responsibility, the abundant help being offered and the expectation that I will obey them or follow their advice, is getting too much for me already. It is so well-meant and good-natured however! When I walk on the main road every three minutes a car is stopping. I have to explain ten times a day. They don't understand at all why I am on foot: *'ya-ya'* in Turkish. I wait until I am in Asia. If it still goes on like that I will take the nearest boat to Haifa.

Wednesday, December 6, Uzunköprü, 09.10 am
It is bleak, misty weather. I am in a teahouse and many men are sitting at the other tables. Some of them do drink tea (U. is a big town) and so do I. Warm sweet tea, the first warm drink since yesterday morning. A coal heater is burning abundantly. I also slept warmly, thanks to the new tent, on a lovely spot where grass and willows grew, away from the wind which blows over the ploughed fields. The heavy clay sticks inches thick to my soles. I walk wobbly on high shoes; sometimes a layer of clay falls off and immediately adds itself again. I rise in the darkness at quarter to six. The summons to pray sound from all the minarets in the villages around me. The people start to eat until the sun rises and I dress and pack. Before that the big drum is rhythmically beaten while being walked round the village at 03.00 am. The mothers rise and start cooking to prepare the food for the family. In the evening I pick a spot for the tent when I hear the summons for the evening prayer and the 'Break Fast' signal. I am there; I take part, yet I am outside of it. I am too much a wonder of the world to be completely trusted by the people; especially in the villages. I understand it, but it makes me sad.

That I go to Jerusalem as a *Hadj* - a pilgrim, doesn't register. Many think I will continue to Mecca. I leave it like that. That I travel solitary on the roads with God as a friend is much more interesting, strange and incomprehensible. Somebody calls after me: 'ters....' In the dictionary the word 'ters' means: 'wrong, faulty'.

I eat my sandwich near a lovely little spring. I sleep in a sweet sheltered little valley. Birds, there are so many birds. I see herons, egrets, buzzards, a multitude of finches and warblers; other large birds of prey; many trees and brushwood; unexploited small pieces of ground between the fields. This I have missed on the infinite collective fields of Romania and Bulgaria. Of course I know, this is only the beginning of Turkey, the European part close to Greece. In the teahouse where I enjoy my hot tea I hear Arab music. I love it. Outside there is a little boy with a shoeshine stand waiting for me. His face shines when I let him polish my mud-covered mountain boots. It costs one Euro. Turkey is not at all cheap in comparison with the Balkan countries.

Where are the women; the strong, soft, warm women of Turkey? Inside? I'm not seeing many children either. They are at school. Turkey is reasonably modern, much more so than Romania and Bulgaria. There are many cars on the road and not much natural transport. But there are dogs. Nice dogs. They bark, they are afraid of me and my backpack, and right through it I see their sweet soul, their built-in unconditional love. I've been barked at by a lot of dogs, but I'm hardly afraid anymore.

A kind chemist, whom I asked for advice about my flea problem, has offered to wash all my clothes in her own washing machine (hot and clean!) to eliminate all fleas and their larvae and nits or whatever. I went into a B&B and then walk through town. If you ask for something in a shop and they don't have it, they go out to find it for you. I notice I have to haggle; I had forgotten about that. Here in town there is much less suspicion of me, which makes me happy. In a little restaurant I was allowed to look into the saucepans to pick out what I wanted to eat. I fished some boiled potatoes and carrots from between the chicken; beans in aubergine/tomato sauce, salad, homemade yoghurt; such abundance!

I have seen an embroidered toilet seat, with flowers!

Friday, December 8, near Shahin
I sit in a narrow place on the lee side of a reed border between bare poplars. The wind is bleak; so I'll write quickly.

I collected my clean clothes yesterday. Generous Ebru had a full bag of gifts for me to take, to maintain my hygiene! Very heavy gifts: Eau de Cologne, hand cream, soap, deodorant, toothpaste, wet wipes, shampoo etc. More than two kilograms and lots of liras. I didn't dare to refuse, because she meant so well! The family has asked me to pray for them in Jerusalem and especially for her small son Duna (Turkish for Danube) and whenever I will be in trouble I am allowed to telephone them.

Yesterday and today I searched for small soft paths going south and came through lovely landscape: heather, pine trees, junipers, brooks with reed borders, marsh. My right foot sank suddenly in a marshy muddy bit, but I got it out quickly enough. This morning I drank hot tea in the clean house of a Turkish family, warm, close to the heater. I seem to walk in advance of the winter line, because now people tell me that in eight days the snow will come. I don't notice a lot of the 'Summerland'. That is postponed until after Troy.

While leaving Uzunköprü I pass a number of girl schools, where the girls hang giggling out of the windows and call after me: "Hello, what is your name?" Even on the sidewalks I pass teenage girls in school uniform: a tartan skirt just above the knee, blue blazer, dark blue tights. They look nice, English. The girls snort with laughter, giggle, talk excitedly with each other. I notice, and wait, and walk on. Yes, there it is: "Hello, what is your name?" They really want to make contact. "My name is

Johanna and I am from Holland. What is your name?" More giggles, withdrawals, one pushes the other forward and then: "My name is Zeyneb; my name is Zerah." And conversation can start. They are beautiful Turkish maidens with black ponytails, velvet eyes and ivory skin. Snow Whites all of them.

I must stop writing, for my toes are freezing off.

Saturday, December 9, 03.00 pm

A quick scribble in a white sun and a bleak wind. View to a hilly landscape with terraced fields, which are ploughed and seeded. The seed is starting to germinate and so the fields seem to have a green haze which reminds me of Spring. Between the fields there are golden reed borders, bare poplars and many small oak trees still wearing their orange-red wigs. There are many villages here, on the earth tracks. You see them here and there lying against the hillsides. Their white minarets are piercing the sky. The small mosques are usually turquoise or light green, a typical Muslim colour. I see quite a few gems among them. I am thinking about what these slender minarets are doing energetically next to those round compact domes, which remind me of nuclear reactors, and suddenly I know: the minarets are drawing 'honey', sweetness from heaven and storing it in their domes. The people who pray there are being inundated with it and return it by their pious prayer. Such a little mosque works as a spiritual battery between the small houses. It is good to live with God.

Sunday, December 10, south of Kesjan, Thrace

It's the Second Advent Sunday and I have spent such a cold night! I hardly slept. It's taken an hour to scrape frost and ice from the tent — inside and out. Worse, despite having had my clothes washed by machine and not river, there were two new and very live fleas. It was very discouraging, but last night, I was cleansed by nature, the blood-red sunset, then the pink moonrise. She seemed to pale into a yellow-pink aura, shining through the switches of a delicate tree standing alone, behind the tent. The evening mist, which came with it, brought again the moon's gift.

I find myself suddenly in a hilly landscape like I've never seen before. Was this once the mythical Arcadia? It's a landscape of short, yellowed grass, grazed by sheep, and small shrubs, sharp, dwarf holly and gorse. In between are grey stones and boulders scattered to the horizon. I have to make an effort to distinguish them from the many herds of sheep which graze with their shepherds. The landscape is of an unknown loveliness.

The white December sun puts everything into a meagre light. A shepherd shows me the way among the myriad sheep trails. "First find a mountain, then after a kind of precipice, you see three mountains. Take the path around the leftmost mountain through a pine forest. There's a way."

He accompanies me for a while, and I start to feel uncomfortable. But at a crossroads, he points to me the way to follow and takes only a farewell handshake. I am flooded by happiness. Where did that come from? But when I look at his face, he has a shy expression of love and respect. His heart was open to me; that is what I felt. Goodbye shepherd from Thrace, from innocent Arcadia, God bless you, your herd and your dogs.

Tomorrow, maybe even today, I will cross the far range of hills and after nine months, I will see the sea again, the Aegean Sea.

10.30 pm. Today, after my sleepless frosty night it is delicious to creep again into a small hotel. These are better than in Bulgaria and Romania - clean, warm and affordable. I can dry my clothes, because even after two days hanging from my backpack they are still damp.

I arrived in Camlica, about twenty kilometres north of the sea, but found no hotel. I hitched a ride back to Kesjan in the back of a bakery car sitting amongst the fresh loaves. In town my chauffeurs point to the two hotels there. I walk in that direction but at the first hotel, a man comes running down the stairs, to intercept me. I suspect he was waiting, and since I do not care which hotel, I'm sitting here now in the first one! My drivers must have called this friend with news of my arrival. This is one of the things I like about the lively Turks. They are such entrepreneurs. Downstairs there is an internet cafe and at the hotel I can repair my leaking air mattress. I need boiling water to do this and I don't carry a stove.

Here is synchronicity again. When I was still in Bulgaria several things started to leak. My old tent leaked. Then my foldable plastic bottle gave way at an old leak. I threw it out! I bought an ordinary plastic bottle with mineral water which is highly successful. And now my mattress is leaking. That means: *'I'm leaking'*, I'm leaking energy, leaking it into useless activities and thoughts. It is these fleas... I can't get rid of them! They absorb too much of despairing attention. When I was 'talking with God' this morning He said to me that having fleas was a test to see to whom I was going to give my attention. To the fleas or to Him. 'I am a jealous God. I want you all to Myself! Choose between a flea or Me....!'

That helped! I won't spend another second thinking about them. I'll just have to bear with it. My energy leak is fixed now, and so are all the leaks in my practical life; I have a new tent, a new bottle and a fixed mattress.

Monday, December 11 The sea.
Towards sundown I came over the last range of hills which had been taking away the sight of the sea. I could pitch tent in a pinewood copse bordering on a few cultivated acres and the

edge of a wood. Behind it there was the water. Even after sunset the temperature remained mild. I could leave the tent door open and enjoy the sea view' from my sleeping bag. For two hours, I looked at the deepening night. The moon rose. Far away, on the other side of the straits, villages began to light up. A deep peace surrounded me while I fell asleep until I was woken up by ticking on the tent roof. It is raining; it is a sweet rain. I close the tent flap. The sweet rain becomes a thunderstorm with lightning and crackling thunderbolts. The rain is beating the tent roof. How safe and warm I feel in this perfectly waterproof tent.

Tuesday, December 12, Adilhan
After a good night's sleep I wake up at 05.30 am. It has stopped raining. I wash and dress under the last moonbeams and when the moon sets in the west, the eastern horizon starts to glow. I pack up my wet tent; better than waiting for ever for it to dry. At eight I am on my way; on this soft road of shining golden sand, which runs along the coast to the east.

And here I sit, with my feet in the Aegean Sea, on a rocky boulder, which seems to have been modeled exactly to accommodate my bottom parts. The sun shines in my face. Here on the lee side of a little pine copse, the temperature is very mild; I guess a 15º C, even when the sun disappears for a moment behind a cloud. Before me are two small green islands floating in the blue and behind them I see the long tongue of land over which I have to reach the Dardanelles, Çanakkale and Asia. The sea has deep blue and turquoise colours. I have reached it over a soft yellow sandy road, running along this coast to the east. It is quiet. The road is not depicted on any map and it is more than two hours now since the last car, the last human being passed. The pine trees give off their subtropical scent; they have very long needles. The trees are in their contorted way very picturesque and of a clear green. I am so happy to be here.

After nine months of walking over main land I see the sea again. I am so happy. I can hardly believe that I really walked to this place all the way. Here, to this South coast, which makes me think of the English South coast by the very angle the sun shines on it. Via the legend of the Grail, the English South Coast is connected to Jerusalem and it is there where in 1988, I first got the idea to walk to Jerusalem. Now I am here, so much closer already. And I dare start to believe that I'm going to make it for real to the Holy City.

England and Israel, in which Glastonbury and Jerusalem. They are two powerful places on earth. It is Glastonbury, of which the poet William Blake said it is the New Jerusalem. And many old stories recount that Joseph of Arimathea planted his staff there and brought his nephew Jesus to be initiated in the Celtic mysteries. Later Joseph brought the Grail, the cup of the last Supper to Glastonbury to be buried beneath Chalice Hill.

A second realisation comes over me: I bring the Grail from GLASTONBURY back to Jerusalem, over the sea, the land and over the sea.

Çanakkale, December 13

The first palm trees! Today I sailed from Europe to Asia. (I hitched the last tarmacked kilometres on the tongue of land, they were too hard on my hip-joints) The waters of the Dardanelles are crystal clear. You can look far into their blue depths. The ferry is sailing through shoals of blue jelly fish. I can see very well how they swim. Parachute open, parachute closed. They have four black circles in the middle of their body. Pretty, pretty.

Say goodbye to Europe? The progressive powers in Turkey want to join The European market. Our right wing Dutch politician says: "It is not possible; they are Muslims". But if

Romania and Bulgaria belong to Europe, and they do, geographically and mentally, then I would say: 'Turkey for sure too!' Commercially, organizational and infrastructural they are closer to Western Europe than the Balkan countries. They have an entrepreneurial spirit and are much more modern than Romania and Bulgaria. Attitude towards women? Progressive forces are trying hard. At universities the headscarves are forbidden. In the little towns I see many 'free' women walking around. Attitude towards me? Until now it is authoritarian protective, caring, surprised and certainly respectful. I am amazed at how safe I feel here. I don't know whether that is justified. I have the inclination to relax completely here and to surrender to the land and to the people. I force myself to stay aware, because of course, I have to. But I am walking here through the dark backstreets of town, fully convinced that nothing bad will happen to me.

"It is dangerous," people say! Dangerous? I am not a fool. Ido know about the less positive business of the lands and people I have been wandering through. Do I walk with my head in the clouds? Do I have to crash back onto earth? I am still walking the earth, not flying over it, and I am willing to take the risk as long as my intuition says I'm fine.

Today I hear that there are no boats going from the Turkish coast to Israel/Palestine. However there is a ferry from Marmaris, on the south coast to the Greek island of Rhodos. From there you can catch a boat to Haifa. I don't need to decide what to do yet.

Seen: In a busy alley walks a boy with a tea tray; on the tray balance three tulip formed glasses with hot tea, which he - sidling around the passers-by - will bring to some invisible customers.

The gentleman who is in charge of the Tourist Office has taken a lot of trouble to fish from an old archive a hand drawn map of 1:200,000 of this region and made photocopies of it for me. What a wonderful service! Apparently no publicly available maps exist on a smaller scale than 1:750,000. Otherwise he would have known! He also has found a little map for me with all 'religious' places in Turkey; the places from the New Testament, the Acts, the Letters and the Revelations. I had just been thinking of how to get hold of something like that. We have a long talk about the differences and essentials of Islam and Christianity. For him and his family it had been a great step towards the freedom of heart to eat pork during holidays. Still he prays five times a day. Not because he has to but because he loves it. He tells about the difficulties between his wife and his mother, and that he chose for his wife, but visits his mother every day. So she doesn't live with him. This was a great battle of conscience for him. I have great respect for the seriousness with which he takes his decisions.

Isn't it remarkable that one of my deeds of personal liberation was to stop eating pork?

Thursday, December 15, Intepe
I am lodged here in a pension which is run by an Australophile Turkish family. Many Australians and New Zealanders come here. Their grandfathers fell in battle at Gallipoli in the First World War, when imperialist England tried to extend its sphere of influence (ice-free access to the Black Sea). The Turks, under leadership of Kemal Ataturk contravened this attack in sea and land battle. Now all the fallen rest together on the other side of the straits. The memorials of both sides have been erected on the battlefields between the mass graves. I can see them from here across the water.

I am on my way to Troy (*Truva* in Turkish). The battle of Troy is much longer ago, and seems romantic and mythic, but of course it was all about the same stuff: power, sex, money and the conviction that their own culture was best.

So here I walk, between the olive orchards and the sea. I have an olive twig in my hand and another one sprigs from my rucksack. Salaam, Peace, Baresh.

In the pension I met an Australian couple. The grandfather of this man fought here. He is fascinated by all films, books, articles about this battle. He loves it just as the young boys love their aggressive computer games.

And here I walk, with my olive branch! And dare to think that all people who love virtual fighting and dying perhaps should try it for real. Maybe they will have second thoughts about it then.

Seen here on the coast: billboards of hotels with dolphins! Are there dolphins here? I immediately want to swim with them like every other staunch New Ager. I'll keep my eyes open!

Friday, December 16, Troy, Amphitheatre
I am sitting in Troy in this strong south wind which blows the letter I'm writing from my hands. Next to me sits a dog; she has been walking with me since yesterday afternoon. It is not a pretty dog; she is actually quite ugly and unattractive, but she is sweet and charmingly insolent. How am I to get rid of her? I can't bear to chase her away with nasty words. I am not feeding her, for she will hang on me forever afterwards, but I am nice to her. I had disappeared through the gates of a camping near Troy, thinking that I had seen the last of her, but this morning she sat waiting for me there and was extremely happy to see me again. She is visiting Troy with me, for I cannot shake her off. This morning a beautiful male dog has joined her and they play together. I feel like Artemis, the spinster forest walker and huntress accompanied by two dogs. The old myths are coming closer. Cassandra, Apollo. Aeolus, the God of Winds has the upper hand today. Agamemnon would be content with so much wind in his sails. His daughter Iphigenia

worships in North Romania before the Altar of the Great Breath of God. King Priam is in his palace and drinks his wine without a care, while Cassandra is walking the streets of Troy grinding her teeth and wringing her hands. She sees how the Trojans hack a breach in their own perfect walls to draw in an enormous wooden horse, a farewell present from the Greeks. In the distance I see the beach where Achilles killed Hector. I see Troy's magnificent walls from the Iliad right in front of me: seamlessly joined hand cut stones, impeccably laid and polished into perfection. Between those walls is also visible carelessly piled rubbish sealed with sand. Troy counts nine building periods by different peoples, starting around 3,000 BC. The time described in the Iliad is around 1,300 BC.

I am here in the off-season, and with the exception of my two dogs, I am here all on my own. In the old temple of Athena I have started to tune in. They seem far away, the old Gods. What I start to feel is Great Power in the form of stone parapets (the walls of Troy) and then 'stone breast'. And then I see Artemis of Ephesus with her bunches of breasts, a mother milk fountain, which protects her vulnerability. Diana-Artemis-Kybele are overlapping female figures. I know that the love I feel for people, animals and nature while on this trip, also protects my vulnerability in solitary travelling.

The wind blows in the temple of Athena. She is related to Sophia and the Shekinah. She was born from the head of Zeus symbolizing wisdom and ratio. Paris scorned her offering for the sake of Aphrodite/Helena. He lost his head and had to bear the consequences.

The wind blows too much to have a ceremony. I lay down three 'As' of pebbles; one for Athena, one for Artemis and one for Aeolus. At Athena's A I lay an olive branch held down by a pebble. Aeolus must keep his fingers from it! I feel akin to the two women without a man. The third goddess has disappeared. I do miss Aphrodite!

After Troy I walk on. I have run out of money and I must take the bus to the next town with a cash machine to be able to buy dinner. Of my last liras I hope to buy a nice meaty bone for the dog and then jump into the bus without her.

I feel very ambiguous. I would be OK with her staying, but it isn't practical. How will it be when I want to go into a hotel? Does she come with me on the ferry to Israel? And I will have to educate her, which I am not keen on at all. I can't educate anyway. I still don't understand how my two children turned out so nice. If I say yes, to the dog, she must come home with me later, because abandoning her after taking her on would not be fair on her. How do I keep a large dog in a little upstairs flat in The Hague?

The dog loves to get a kind word. Full of trust she walks with me the six kilometres towards the bus stop. On the way there is no shop and no butcher. The bus is coming. I get on and say: "Goodbye darling". The door closes into her face. I couldn't even buy a bone for her. I still see her astonished face in front of me. I'm off. I don't look back. I feel miserable about it all the rest of the day and the following night. She thought she had found a friend. Her story didn't have a happy end.

December 17
Third Advent Sunday. Of course there are no preparations for Christmas in this Muslim land. The 26th of December is the end of Ramadan, the Sugar Feast and not Boxing Day. Still I have bought four candles to remind me of Advent. Today the sun is shining. I am even wearing my sun hat. I walk through pastoral landscapes. In the distance looms a special rock formation on a round mountain between the rocky hills. Three standing stones looking out over the land; impenetrable thicket around them. Two of the rocks seem to wear a veil. Three ladies seem to stand on the summit. There is something sweet and soft emanating from them. I decide to climb

towards them and meditate there. The narrow path winds sun wise to the summit, but it is overgrown with dwarf holly, pine trees and a wild olive before it really gets there. Alright, I'll do it here. I weave an advent wreath of pine twigs, holly and olive. I don't even need to stand up to cut them off. Three candles for three Advent Sundays, and there I have my traditional advent wreath and coming Christmas is manifest through and through. The emphasis is on the Roman Sol Invictus (pine branch and holly branch) but it is a well-known mood, which is always with me before Christmas. I look at the three 'matrons' on top of the hill: You have given me Christmas. The birth of the Sun. The birth of Christ. *Veni Veni Emmanuel*. It fits. It fits and belongs in the landscape. When I descend the hill after the meditation I think of the dog. Perhaps God has a way with her too. For there isn't a sparrow falling from the roof without Her knowledge.

Wednesday, December 20

Christmas is approaching in reality and in me. The landscape is full of shepherds with their flocks, caves where sheep seek shelter, fields which have sheepfolds and are walled with fieldstones. There are oxen, asses, shepherds and shepherdesses. The plane trees are enormous, crooked and hollow; I fancy furnishing them with colourful hangings so I could live in one. The hills are covered in rocks and boulders. Around them the grasses are grazed down to a millimetre and everything has a cared-for and groomed appearance. It reminds me of England's moors; only in this country the sheep aren't afraid of people. The sunrise and sunset have a red colour here, less pink. In the evening the naturally pink hillsides bask in a fiery red, the sky red above them. The trees, the houses, my skin and my tent, everything glows red.

The authoritarian hailing has disappeared. People greet you happily or shyly or make an enquiring gesture. That is much nicer. Still they are curious as always. Sometimes they pull the dictionary from my hands from pure studiousness and eagerness to communicate.

Last night something might have gone wrong. I was already in bed. It was 07.30 pm and dark, when there were footsteps and the beams of torches around my tent. I open the front flap and put on my friendliest face. Four figures are standing in the darkness in front of me: two elder and two young men. The faces change from worried to relief when they see me. I am very close to a little village down in the gully, which I hadn't noticed. People have seen me and so they came to see what was going on. I get an invitation to come and sleep inside, but I am bedded already. After the initial shock I feel quite relieved.

This morning I rise and want to dress as usual, but then I see that one of the elderly gentlemen wants to pay me a visit. When he sees I want to make my toilet he disappears discreetly and returns when I am ready. He peers curiously into the space of my tent, where my luggage and sleeping bag lie. Then after careful information whether I am married or in a relationship he proposes marriage to me. I am touched and thank him and say that my great friend was Allah (*'Buyuk Arkad'*) and that I don't want to marry right now; he accepts that.

In the afternoon I ask in a village where I can buy bread. A sort of wild looking robber's wife with strong features invites me to her yard. She wears three headscarves turban wise on top of each other. The last one is red and knotted in the back of her neck. She is wearing a dirty embroidered waistcoat and harem trousers. She serves me a hot meal in the yard, including a large piece of pickled cucumber which she has spared from her own mouth, because I can see her teeth printed in it. When I offer to pay she gets really angry, so I eat obediently. A dingy bowl contains a piece of goat cheese. Even in Romania I haven't eaten such delicious goat cheese. She also offers me fresh, tasty, crusty bread which has been picked off the ground by the look of it. Everything tastes very good. In the meantime the robber's woman continues to sort out the new olive harvest, burping and rasping like a dragoon and looking frowningly at me if I do not eat enough. Whatever I can't finish I am given to take away.

On the way I am often invited to stay, but always in the morning, when I still want to walk a long time. I think they don't really want me to say yes. I don't mind. I am still pursued by the flea trauma.

This afternoon, before Assos, a very old couple like Philemon and Baucis, are inviting me into their new little house. They are very proud of it. I can see that it has just been built. It is a house of one room, one door, one window and a flat roof. It is freshly painted all pink with some flowers over the door post. A fig tree and thorns stand on the side. Outside I see some goats and an empty sheep stable. Their herd is grazing a bit further on. I am allowed to warm myself at their brand-new wood burner that is standing in the middle of the room. Against the walls big bags of wheat and beans are piled up: their winter store. Fresh bread is baked every morning, but I am not given anything, because of the Ramadan. But I do get warmth, cordiality and smiles.

And just like St. Paul I walked on foot from Troas to Assos, where I arrived this afternoon. Here, on a high promontory jutting into the sea, are perched the remains of a Greek temple. I don't know to whom it is dedicated and I am just considering, whether I shall climb to it or not - I already walked 25 kilometres - when I am accosted by a lady in a car, who asks me whether she can help me with something. "Perhaps she knows to whom the temple is dedicated? "To Pallas Athena," she answers and would I like a cup of tea? She is American and lives here. In Assos she has found a group of people all concerned with 'spirituality'. She herself is writing articles about 'The Great Mother' and translates medical reports for Turkish orthopaedists. She also paints stones. She takes me to a little cafe called 'Lembas' after the elf bread in the Tolkien trilogy. It is warm and cosy in the cafe and Övgü is giving me dinner. Ovgu is a Turkish woman fascinated by the books of Tolkien and Ursula Le Guin. We are kindred souls and Arlene, the American lady, jumps from one subject to the other. She cannot believe that there shall be peace in Jerusalem. Tears come to her eyes. She is Jewish. She will give me a prayer slip to put in the Western Wall. I tell her about my own prayer slips, but then she turns to another subject. She tells me about her life and ways and tells me about the isle of Lesbos, the women island just in front of the shore here. It protects that corner of Turkey against surplus rain and wind. They never last for long. Arlene herself looks like the Great Mother with her full body and magnificent face. The owner of the pension where I am staying is quite the opposite. Small and delicate her name is Oja, which means' lace work', which suits her well.

Later I am sitting in a colourful little room of her B&B next to a little whizzing woodstove. The wind is wailing around the house. We are expecting snow. A basket full of logs stands next to the heater to be put on the fire whenever needed. It is so comfortable here that tonight I have been able to take off my jacket, thick woollen cardigan and walking boots and I feel snug and protected.

Thursday, December 21
This morning I climb to the terrace of the Athena temple. On the way up I pass the ruins of a Christian church, which was built here in honour of the fact that St. Paul and St. Mary are supposed to have spent the night in Assos on their trip from the Black Sea to Ephesus. Another story tells, that Paul met St. Luke here to speak about the composition of 'the Acts'. I like

to think that Luke met Mary here too and spoke with her about what she 'contemplated in her heart'.

The church has been changed into a mosque, but the plaque which describes it doesn't mention anything about the Greek and Christian origin of the place.

Up on high, on the acropolis, the ground plan of the temple is clearly visible. Many columns are still standing. The sky is clear, the wind bleak, the sun white. The sea extends peacefully and wide into the distance. The columns stand out clearly against the sea and the isle of Lesbos on the horizon. The panorama is of a quiet clarity. The goddess Athena is opening my mind. Nothing is there and everything. I see her for a moment. A transparent giant-like woman stands in the middle of the temple, helmet on head, olive branch in hand. There is silence, clarity and the white sunlight reflecting from the sea.

Friday, December 22

The winter solstice has begun; the longest, darkest nights of the year. Tonight, twenty years ago my son was born under a full moon. I could see its luminous silhouette through the closed curtains while I was in labour. But tonight I sleep in my tent, protected from the icy northern wind in a sheltered corner of an olive orchard. I leave the tent flap open lying in my sleeping bag to enjoy the remnants of a waning moon, but I have to close it because of the frost. My son has his birthday today. It is almost Christmas; it is almost the Sugar Feast (end) of Ramadan and last night it was the first night of *Hannukah*, the Jewish light feast. Arlene from Assos has given me as a farewell present a very special *Hannukah* lantern. Eight pebbles painted by her with the sign against the evil eye and a bigger one, the *Sjammes* (the servant) who will light the little lights one by one; each night of *Hannukah* one more. Her evil eyes aren't evil. They look like islands surrounded by a blue sea. These pebbles I carry with me until New Year, when the feasts will all be over.

Saturday, December 23

The cold wind is blowing through marrow and bone. I bought locally hand-knitted woollen long tights. They are itching but also comfortably warm.

I sleep under very old olive trees. Sometimes their girth is the size of three men. I heard that such wide trees are often more than 2,000 years old. Imagine, older than the Romans. In that same orchard 80 generations have knocked the olive branches with sticks to let the olives fall on tarpaulins and the women have sorted them out and gathered them. It has become a well-known sound. The ground is littered with little olive twigs which fell down with the olives. Two hundred kilograms of olives for one tree is quite normal. This morning, waking up in an old olive garden, I had the feeling as if there were people around me, but when I looked I only saw those big old trees. I walked around one of them, slowly tuning in. He had a peaceful, still energy, humble, not demanding; serving, enduring, like a lamb or a donkey.

The tarmacked traffic road to Kuecuekkuyu is a horror. The international traffic is thundering over the dual carriage way. I am blown off the road by the wind many times. I am looking for small paths, but there aren't any. There is only one road along the coast. The hills, fir trees and olive orchards are disappearing and the coastal strip is being built up by villas, apartments and hotels. I see little restaurants, buffets and bar/discos everywhere. They are closed because it is winter. Inside the chairs are sitting upside down on the tables. Outside there are blown-over fences, the Venetian blinds are flapping in rags over the windows and the shutters are banging. The people wear woolly hats. They say it hasn't been so cold for years. My land of eternal summer is an illusion. Still the seawater is lukewarm. The palms, the agaves, the fig trees are all there. After a frosty night I want to sleep in a hotel. I want a warm room with shower. The room is beautiful, but stone cold. There is no heating. I don't take it and will camp again. Everything is tuned in to summer here. So I will continue to feel cold. I am surprised about my equanimity. Could that be because the oxygen level on the coast is so high that you get into a good mood in spite of everything else? One hotel's name even is: 'Otel Oxygen'.

But the good air is spoilt by the exhaust fumes of the traffic road and the destroyed coast. You find villas and rubbish tips next to each other. It is a common habit to throw rubbish in the street. Sometimes it is difficult to find a clean place to camp.

Monday, December 25, Burhanye

Christmas Day. I had hoped to find a quiet spot in a pine tree copse near the sea to celebrate Christmas night, but it was not to be. Between two apartment buildings under construction I found a small place under a high tree. I couldn't see the sea, but I could see the stars. I knew: it is Christmas Eve. Everywhere in Europe now the families have come together. Even here in Turkey the preparations for the end of Ramadan are in full swing and the families have come together to celebrate that. I am alone under the stars. That is what I chose. I don't feel Christmas; I am cold. I pitch my tent between a cowpat and a horse dropping. Or perhaps the ass and the oxen have been here. And then I sing a Christmas carol from home: 'Between oxen and ass, there sleeps the gentle baby, and the sweet angels in swarming procession...'

I look deep into the starry abyss: 'O Christ night, greater than the Day...'

I had intended, if I had woken up at midnight, to open the tent flap, light a candle, look at the stars and to keep vigil and to listen - to see if I could 'understand the animals' and undergo the very special atmosphere of Christmas night. But it is too cold round midnight. I am shivering in my sleeping bag. I don three extra jumpers and sleep on, disappointed with myself.

I am wide awake at 05.00 am. It is pitch dark. Now I light the candle and think: 'It is Christmas' and sing softly all the carols that I know. And especially those songs which sing about cold and poverty, about distress and hardship really speak to me at this moment. I am 'a child lying in the cold with trembling limbs' but I am also Mary who sings and the angel bringing glad tidings. I sing myself towards Christmas, with comforting tears here and there, with missing my family, but also with a knowledge of that soft inner light which shines in me at every Christmas: the sweet Child in the manger.

At seven the candle is burnt up and dawn has come. When I look out I see a covered sky and on the other side of the bay, on the mountains, I see Snow. Lots of Snow. I have a white Christmas.

After rising I treat myself to a good campfire. It takes a lot of time, but it is also beneficent. The dead branches which have fallen out of my 'Christmas' tree smell aromatically when they burn.

Noon. I walk on the beach beside the sea, southward. It smells of seaweed. The sun is shining and the temperature is mild. The water is tepid, clear. Little waves gently lap the beach. It is the only sound I hear. I see nobody. I walk along the narrow beach past all the deserted luxury hotels with the empty swimming pools in their paradise gardens. Nobody is there. I have the place to myself. I feel wonderful. Christmas has disappeared.

At twelve o'clock the muezzin in the next village is calling for prayer from the minaret. The dome of the mosque sticks up from the houses like a glowing turquoise. I look for a shop that is open, because I haven't had anything to eat this morning.

Somebody helps me to find bread. He doesn't have to; I'm perfectly capable of doing that myself, but that is the way it goes. He invites me for a glass of tea, and yes, I would really like that, preferably eighteen glasses. But of course that won't be possible.

This 40-year-old man doesn't have a very pleasant face. He looks run down, but the cut of the coat he wears is proof of certain style; the look in his eyes is educated but also sly. We sit down and we chat a little. He speaks very good German. Gradually his face is changing. It is no longer sly; the whole miserable story of his life is coming out. From initial success in business he descends into a failed first marriage. Alcohol, a second marriage. He has children of which he is very fond. Alcohol again and adultery. His wife says no and leaves. He loses his job and now? "My own fault, sure. This sorrow, I have wept so much I have no droplet left." He speaks about the loneliness. He has been separated for a year now. He sleeps in the teahouse here. His desire to 'belong', his need of company, intimacy, sexuality. The chatting up mode has completely disappeared. I only have to listen. His face is almost beautiful now. His growing sincerity has moved me deeply. His situation hasn't changed, but he says now: "I want to stand on my own two feet, just like you!" But when he disappears for a moment and comes back I smell fresh alcohol on his breath.

Because it is Christmas I treat myself to a hotel room. I find a nice room with an electric heater and—unexpectedly, a little kitchen, and then I know: I will go shopping and make myself Christmas dinner, and make a big pot of herbal tea of which I can drink as much as I want. I lay the table with a white cloth, my advent wreath and the four advent candles. I happen to have a red ribbon with me. There are tangerines in abundance, most of them bought, some of them picked from trees. In the cupboard are white china plates with golden rims and a silver-plated tea tray. I put them on the table with silver-plated cutlery and a wine glass. I have been able to buy a bunch of Turkish mountain sage and I smudge the room with its fragrant smoke and lay out my white napkin with the white and pink quartz crystals. I boil new potatoes, onions, aubergines, tomatoes, eggs. I have baklava as a sweet. When the candles are burning and the electric light extinguished, it is Christmas in my room. The candle flames reflect in the silver tea tray. For a moment I feel a lump in my throat seeing just that one plate, but so much goodness is on it. And then I think of all the sweet Christmas wishes on email and all people who think of me today and then I am no longer alone. And now, in the light of the last candles, sitting at the Christmas table, I will write this letter to an end.

Wednesday, December 27
The wind has turned from north to south-west. The snow has thawed on the mountains and last night is was mild.

Today it is the great end feast of Ramadan. *Bayram* they say here. Sugar Feast they say in Holland. All day long prayers resound from the minarets. The large Turkish drum is not only beaten at 03.00 am, but the whole day long. The people look beautiful in their new clothes. This morning I woke up at six o'clock because of a very musical and passionate call for prayer. Some imams really can't do it; they are tone deaf, but this man puts his complete heart in it and I decide to go to him to ask for his prayer for peace in Jerusalem. In Thrakija I started to gather courage to ask for the imam at mosques, but only in Anatolia have I started to really do it. The proprietor of the camping at Troy has written a Turkish text for me. I have copied that text and every time when I tell an imam about my walk I offer him this paper text and a twig of olive. In general the men react surprised but also gentle and sometimes even enthusiastic. They often touch their heart, which means agreement and respect.

Coming into the village everything is muddy from the rain. I ask for the imam. It is a big and important feast and he must be busy, but my message doesn't ask more than fifteen minutes. The man who sings so beautifully and sincere is tall and has the same soft eyes as Omar Sharif. He has a clarity in his face, which I sometimes have seen with Muslim people just coming out of prayer. In Arabic this clarity is called '*Nur Allah*', the Light of God. He listens attentively to my story, sends his boy away with a message and invites me into his poor home. His son is coming back with a blossoming pink rose. It is for me! He calls his wife and daughters. The eldest daughter in harem trousers and headscarf speaks English. Then he sees the wart on my left hand. He takes my hand and asks if I want to get rid of it. Yes, of course! In his house, after having consumed a plate of baklava and several tulip glasses of tea, his wife sits down next to me. In her face too *Nur Allah* is shining. She takes my hand with the wart; takes a sniff of what seems to be pollen, makes a circling movement around the wart, whispers something and says that the wart will have disappeared in a few weeks, sprinkling the power on my hand.

Friday, December 29
I walked 30 kilometres along the main road direction Ayvalik. Come on, don't moan, just do it. My feet are hurting from stumbling over the coarse stones beside the road; I am nauseated by exhaust fumes, my Achilles tendon is playing up after three months of silence. Raging traffic. I can't do it. My foot pilgrimage stops here when this isn't going to change, because right now I don't feel like looking for small paths all

day long and criss-crossing the land either. Last week I only had walked ten kilometres as the crow flies, while I had been walking for six hours.

The landscape is still spoiled by apartment buildings under construction and hotels; they are all empty and deserted. In Ayvalik I sit on a bench at a square near the sea. I am writing my letter. It is still *Bayram*. Several women, old and young, are sitting on the other benches. When I look up from my letter and smile at them they rise *en masse* to approach me (twelve women) and invite me to come with them to eat, drink and sleep. I like it and go with them. I am crowded by women; on each side they walk arm in arm with me. The girls take turns. We arrive at a back street. I am placed in the middle of a big shed. There are mattresses along the walls. I am given tea. Many more women come to see me. Finally there are about 30 women in a close circle around staring at me. They are a group of workers from another village who are here to help with the olive harvest. Their husbands sleep in a similar room. There is chatting and giggling. They look beautiful in their wide flowered harem trousers and colourful headscarves. One question after the other is fired at me. One woman speaks a little English; another one a little German. A third lady is cooking a meal on the cooker in the middle of the space. I am fed with soup, bread and beans. Why don't they eat as well? No, no, heads are shaking; hands are being rubbed over bellies. "We are not hungry."

There is a little mother with her son of five years old. I understand that the boy is deaf and dumb. The women shake their heads in compassion behind their hands, so that I can see it, but the boy can't. The child looks deeply unhappy; grey, angry and sorrowful at the same time. I am invited to join the olive harvest tomorrow. I can earn eight Euros a day. It is tempting, a special experience, but I think I will walk on. Time is running out. I am not staying to sleep. The group's matriarch

- my age - walks with me for a while, together with the girl who speaks German, the little mother and a few little giggling girls. On the way we meet their men. Between this colourful group of women opposite the group of their dark men, something is going on of flirtation and playfulness, but everything is invisible.

The son of the matriarch is the father of the deaf and dumb child. The mother asks me if there are good doctors in Holland. Her husband translates. I say that deafness and dumbness is congenital and cannot be helped. But then the husband says, that there is nothing the matter with the ears of the child. '110%' of hearing. So the child isn't deaf! The picture shifts completely. "He doesn't speak," says the father. He is already five years.

A refusal to speak! A child with such a sorrowful grey being. I already heard with my own ears that there was nothing wrong with his vocal cords. I look in the dictionary for the word for 'sorrowful', 'heart' and 'psychologist'. But these people probably cannot pay for such an expensive treatment. With hands and feet I try to make clear that their child is sad, and perhaps that is why he doesn't speak and while I do that, his despair and rage are entering my heart. I can feel the child. I can feel that there is something rotting inside. The mother has understood. She has tears in her eyes. I look in the dictionary for the words 'healer', 'magnetizer', 'laying on hands'. But I can't find them. Then at long last I look for the word 'holy' and 'man' and 'woman'. Perhaps they can pay to go to a holy man or woman, a healer, to heal the child. To take his despair away. The man is pleased. They might do this. I promise to pray seven days for the child. It is in my heart now; I carry it with me, but I am a little alarmed by the way people ascribe authority to me.

I have an hour of daylight left to find a camping place in nature, but the little town keeps stretching itself along the coast in rows of villas and polluted beaches. When it is already very dark, I take a sudden turn from the road to the right, out of the light of the street lanterns on to a little peninsula. It is a high cliff planted with pine trees and picnic tables. Once out of the light I hardly see anything. The wind blows from the south-west. The pine trees sigh and wail. Something white is vaguely visible in the darkness, a little house. It is deserted. On the lee side of it I put my sleeping bag on a ridge of concrete. It is too dark to pitch the tent and I cannot find a level place. I am quite comfortable on my ridge. The pine trees rustle over my head. I can hear the sea below and the traffic on the boulevard. There is peace. I am curious to see tomorrow where I ended up.

At first light my little house turns out to be a public toilet. I can wash at a tap. There is a clean loo. How well I am taken care of!

Saturday December 30

I refuse to walk along the motorway today. Along the coast there is a plain, being built up with new houses and apartment buildings and I take the roads which run from one building plot to the other. It is boring; it is a detour, but ten times better than the motorway. I touch the motorway at one point and do some shopping at a fuel station/supermarket. It is twice as expensive as anywhere else and I am annoyed I have to pay more for a loaf than in the Netherlands. I know I'm cheated and I tell the proprietor. He shrugs his shoulders and I need bread. Three little girls with nice faces come for a chat. They look fashionable and clean and they say: "Money, money, money!" I'm getting more and more annoyed, but they are children. I tell them not to ask for money; they are too good for that. A man from the garage comes for a chat. I tell him something about the pilgrimage. He says that he knows a good B&B for 35 Euros per night. I tell him I don't need one and point at my tent. He keeps going on and on about the B&B. The price is already dropping. I say it is too early to stop, only midday and I don't need one. "Good pension, video, porno, porno, sex, sex." I don't answer; I'm furious. He leaves. I eat yoghurt and bread. The strong wind blows the tub of yoghurt from my hand. When I save it quickly, the loaf blows from my hand into a muddy pool. I am getting more and more furious. The man returns: "Sex, sex, porno, porno..." I explode: "I am Hadj! No alcohol, No smoking, No meat, No sex!"

That is enough. He will throw away my empty yoghurt pot for me and I leave. I walk on top of a dike, guiding a traffic road between the sea and a lake. The seawater sprays over it with every new gust of wind. Like an autumn leaf I am blown between the traffic. It is dangerous and I am still furious. I decide to walk at the bottom of the dike. My anger subsides. Fields, newly built little villa villages. Building plots in a barren plain. To take shelter from the wind I rest in the half-finished porch of a large half-finished house and just want to resume my half-finished letter, when again from nowhere, somebody approaches me. It is a young man with two puppies. "Tea, warm tea," and he points to the house opposite; the house looks nicely finished and lived-in, there are curtains in front of the windows; I am going with him. I would love some warm tea and I think to find his family there. But he is alone there, doing odd jobs. His family is in Ankara. He leads me into a small room with a small purring wood burner. He is sitting on the bed; I am sitting on a chair. He offers me an orange, chocolate. It takes an extraordinary long time for the kettle to boil. We talk about his family, cowherds from mid-Turkey. He works in a hotel in Ankara. He is about 30 years old. He has three small children. I tell my story. I feel good with him. I know it is risky. A woman accepts an invitation of a man and sits with him in his bedroom! In a Muslim country! I tell my story about the peace of Jerusalem. He loves the story and I see how his eyes rest in growing tenderness on me. I mellow, become receptive to receive more of that tenderness. We look into each other's eyes, keep silent, then speak on about the difference in perspective, about men, about women, about the soul; all in Turkish with the dictionary between us on the little table. He only speaks Turkish. How is this possible? He is respectful, tender, in control of himself; and inwardly beckoning to me. I feel that I open up. I want nothing more than being with him in this tenderness, together with him on that bed, and I feel sadness too, because he is married and I don't want that. I don't want to be happy for a few moments at the cost of another woman, even although nobody would ever find out in this deserted, sandy plain without any other inhabitant.

I tell him I have no man anymore and I have no responsibility towards my father or brother. Just towards God. He explains that in Islam the man is responsible to God and the woman to the man. The woman has to take care of her honour. In Muslim eyes I would have lost my honour already, sitting with him in his room, but he really doesn't give the impression at all that he despises me.

I must go, with pain in my heart. I could have got something I really longed for, but I have remained faithful and he hasn't abused the vulnerable situation in which I was. There has been tenderness, respect and real contact.

When we say goodbye at the front door, an elderly man emerges from the blowing sand, a basket with bread on his arm. He gives my host two loaves. He doesn't look at me, but I can see from his face how shocked, confused and sad he is because he sees a woman, coming from the door of the young man. I wish I could tell him, that nothing untoward between us happened, not a single thing.

Tonight I camp ten metres from the sea. It is soft still weather when I pitch the tent, but it is the stillness before the storm. After sunset bolts of lightning start to flash over the sea; thunder, flails of rain and sleet; two enormous bouts of wind descend on the tent. It doesn't give! Wild and high waves come very close.

Midnight. The outside of the tent is full of sea foam and seaweed, but inside I am dry. Through the chasing clouds the clear crescent of the moon and the stars of Turkey emerge and submerge.

All night long I dream about sexuality and tenderness, and that I first have to clear the shit before I can be in bed with someone, but I don't know what the shit is.

I dream that I'm invited for a confirmation/*bat mitzvah* of young girls. They are about thirteen years old. I follow them. The party is in the Upper Room of the Last Supper. They are dressed in debutante white and are waiting for me. I climb high steps, but I cannot find the way to the Upper Room.

About New Year's Eve, December 31, 2000

I had to do something terrible on New Year's Eve. I am well on the way and towards evening I want to find a place in an olive orchard as usual. I leave the road for a clay path leading under the olive trees. Because of the rains the ground is soggy, slippery and muddy. I hear a car approaching on the clay path. The car stops. The owner opens the car door. It is clear that he has seen and followed me. Again I have to give account of what I am doing, but perhaps I must; this orchard might be his. He is a sturdy elderly man of about 55 years old. He has a beautiful car and is well groomed. With short words he insists that I can come with him. I can pitch my tent in his garden. I cannot get a proper idea of him. His eyes are hidden behind heavy eyelids. There is a great insistence in his words and it is true that I'd rather not pitch my tent in this mud. Certainly not under his eyes, while he knows I will spend the night alone here. I hesitate, which he notices. With great urge he says: "Come!", holding my rucksack in an asking manner, and I go with him.

Perhaps this is something of Providence again. I have no time to really weigh it. I sit in his car a little bewildered, my muddy shoes on a newspaper. He brings me way out of my direction to the town of Zeytindag. Every now and again he says a short brusque word. I have no feeling of connection. His house is large, clean and a bit untidy. Beautiful furniture, but again: no family, no wife, no children. He hasn't got a garden to pitch my tent in. I feel uneasy. He has lured me with him with a lie. What does he want? I ask for his wife and kids. "No wife, no kids." So he is a lonely old man who has found company for New Year's Eve and a guest to mollycoddle. Still I don't feel at ease. I tell him about my mission. No reaction. He listens politely. Then I look up in the dictionary: "I am not a prostitute," and "I am afraid; I am a woman on my own."

He grabs my arms and hands, very tight. He is as strong as a bear and says: "I am your brother," (= honourable), kisses my hand and brings it to his bowed forehead; a beautiful gesture. I still don't know; I cannot get an idea of him for he is so brisk, brusque and forcible. Shall I trust him? Shall I give him a companionable evening? I can shower here, wash several things, sleep. But, the proximity which is entailed in this, can he handle that?

He offers me cigarettes, opens a bottle of coke, puts a glass next to it, switches on the television and the electric heater and says: "I'm going to buy food". I know he will splash out to make me comfortable. I am still doubtful. "Don't be afraid," he says gruffly. I don't know; I would like to trust him. On the other hand, I have had a warning today: dogs never attack me, but today I was bitten softly in my legs. Warning bites, with hellish barking before and after. Even then I thought: 'I am getting a warning'.

He is going out to buy food, and then, to my alarm: he locks the door behind him! He has locked me up! He has captured me! He has caught a little bird! Now I know: get out of here! I hastily put on my muddy shoes again and hurry through the rooms to find a window which I can open. Right, in the kitchen! I throw my rucksack out of the window on the ground and jump after it from the low first floor into the street. In front of his neighbours, who stand chatting outside I rush out of town without looking back. There is enough daylight left to find, two kilometres on, a sleeping place in another orchard. This one is much drier on the ground. Lying comfortably in my sleeping bag I think of the wound I have inflicted on him; possibly an undeserved wound.

Monday, January 1, 2001, New Year's Day

I had to make a leap of 70 kilometres by bus. I didn't like it at all, but I might have offended my host yesterday by running away from his hospitality and I would like to get away from Zeytindag. Also, it rains, no... it pours. My new Bulgarian rain trousers are plastic and rubbish; after two kilometres they hang in rags about my legs. My trousers are soaked and my poncho can't cope with such buckets full of rain. I have to walk on tarmac today; clay paths are no option. Nobody recognizes the large green monster walking along the main road as a human being. Puddles on the road are crossed through enthusiastically by the cars and make beautiful fountains on me. I become miserable. There is no hotel in Aliaga, says the owner of the cafe where I take a rest. He steps out into the pouring rain and tries to stop cars and *dolmus* for me. They all rush on apart from the large bus heading for Izmir, three day walks away. But I don't want to continue in the rain like this. So Izmir it is. I sit in the bus. The main road passes industrial estates, oil refineries. It isn't a nice road, I don't miss anything. This IS a case of emergency! A traffic road; AND it's pouring cats and dogs; AND who knows a case of honour revenge.

Tuesday, January 2, Izmir/Smyrna

In Izmir the sun is shining and a large rainbow bends over the city. The hills around the wide bay are covered by a sea of white houses. Here and there a mosque pops its dome out above them and many minarets are piercing the sky. Along the avenues are rows and rows of palm trees. The bus stops at the large bus terminal outside the city. For a moment after alighting and submerging into the crowd I panic because of the masses of people and buses milling randomly around and then the sense of safety hits me again. And that is for a reason. Like a parcel in the post I am conveyed from one person to the other and arrive with the correct local bus (I don't need to pay) in front of the general post office according to my initial plan. This is on Smyrna's quay and at Poste Restante a letter from my best friend is waiting for me.

Afterwards I am comfortably settled down in hotel 'Bebek' (baby) near to the railway station. It has pink and light blue rooms. It is clean and warm, but the sheets have been used. This is a nasty Turkish habit. In cheap hotels you get the sheets of your predecessor when they are not dirty yet. You are just lucky when they happened to be washed. The sheets are thick cotton 'waffle' fabric. They are more difficult to wash than our thin cotton duvet covers.

I am hunting down some proper waterproof trousers in the old bazaar. I enjoy all the colourful twisting alleyways with their enterprising liveliness. Palm trees, tamarisks, cactus and mosques align the streets. I have to wear a skirt if I want to enter the Great Mosque. I don't have one! So I can't be here for a moment? I pray on the threshold. Over my head I hear the call for the midday prayer. This muezzin is very musical and sings straight from the heart. I am touched.

In the tourist streets the merchandise is very different from that in the 'real' streets. Everywhere I see signs against the 'evil eye'; not just for sale but also on front doors, fences etc. It is unpleasant. These talismans look very much like evil eyes themselves! And everywhere those eyes look at me maliciously. Or perhaps I've got the 'evil eye' myself and that's why I don't like them!

In the bazaar the same sort of shops are placed together: one street full of sewing machines, clothes, sweets. I must get away from a street of butchers, the cobblestones under my feet slippery with blood. There is a whole quarter full of jewellers; they have very small shop windows full of gold; gold displayed on white, on yellow satin. It doesn't miss its effect, the gold. Shop window after shop window I wallow in the radiance of so much precious metal. Precious stones are here too; ruby, amethyst, emerald. It gives me so much energy! Especially the yellow gold, not the white-yellow gold - an amalgam used in the Netherlands to make the gold harder. I don't like the red gold either, but I do like the real glowing, nourishing yellow gold. There is a lot of yellow glowing gold here. But, what is even more delightful, I come home completely charged with gold energy and I don't even have to buy some! All the gold in the shop windows is mine! All rings, bangles, heavy golden chains, tiaras, earrings, pendants, all mine! Tomorrow I can go back and look at them again.

Elated and a little drunk of all the gold - I never saw so much together - I come back into my hotel room. I have been wandering, but have not erred in the maze of twisting alleys.

Tuesday, January 4

So much has happened again today! I dreamt last night of the Hebrew song about water: 'Mayim'. In my dream I see blue waves of water flowing through my field of vision while I dance the Mayim step.

In the afternoon I stand in front of a posh carpet shop. I love oriental rugs; my eyes are feasting on them. There is a wicked pleasure in me. Just like with the gold of yesterday I enjoy myself intensely and it doesn't cost me anything! Rich I am, rich and blessed with healthy eyes.

The proprietor steps outside and invites me in; that is how it goes here. He speaks English very well and I say I just love oriental rugs, but that I don't want to buy anything. He says, that it doesn't matter, because: "we want to show the rugs anyway". And now I get to see the grandest Afghan, Persian and Turkish carpets, one after the other more beautiful and rich. There are also magnificent woven *kelims*. Together we interpret the symbols knotted and woven into them. He knows a great deal about it and he shows the difference between these and the - also handicraft - rugs which have been made from a commercial viewpoint. The women make the first ones for their own pleasure. They weave their dreams into them, their thoughts and their stories. The commercial rugs show the same good weaving and knotting work, but the soul is lacking. I fall in love with a small deep red *kelim*. It is just big enough for a prayer mat. The Tree of Life is depicted on it. I can see it through a gate leading to Paradise. While you pray you might become aware of it. For a moment greed is rearing its head. He is a very good salesman indeed; he doesn't push or pull at all. The rugs speak for themselves, but pilgrim's money is not there to buy expensive presents for myself.

Even although I buy nothing I am served an elegant glass of tea and I ask whether he knows a synagogue here in Izmir. I want to visit a mosque and a synagogue today.

I walk through the Grand Bazaar. Contrary to what I thought I am allowed in the old mosque. The criterion was not: 'skirt', but 'no bare legs' and I don't have those. I cover my head with a scarf, take off my shoes and sit on the soft carpet inside the mosque. I am on my own. In a corner a man with a turban sits in front of a low desk and studies in silence the Holy Qur'an. It is peaceful here. And then I feel it again: Allah, the Merciful, the Graceful, as if a protective cloak full of consolation, warmth and grace is wrapped around me. There is fullness, sensuality, abundance. Similar as in Hebrew, the Arabic words of: 'Al Rachman - Al Rahim', mean 'womb'. To be carried in God's womb; that is where I am now; in God's womb full of grace and mercy, safety and love. I cannot pray an Our Father here. The energy is so feminine. I pray the Hail Mary: the prayer to the Great Mother. 'Pray for us in the hour of our Death, when you will take us back into your womb. Amen.'

At the same time I miss something. I look at the elegant calligraphies on the wall. I feel a little blind. A little door is closed. Is it the absence of images of living beings? Faces, eyes, hands? Possibly. I ask permission to lay my Turkish note with the olive branch at the place where the imam always prays. To summon up the imam of this most important mosque of Izmir is like summoning the bishop of Canterbury in his Cathedral and maybe that would be a bit preposterous.

I leave the mosque. The small alleys of the Grand Bazaar suddenly seem trivial and coarse. The 'Nur Allah', the 'Light of God' is still enveloping me.

I walk to the north corner of Izmir, along the quay along the sea. Today it is misty and there is no horizon. In the distance I can vaguely see some ships. The contours of the opposite side of the bay are just visible. The synagogue must be near the German Consulate, but nobody knows where it is. "Synagogue? Do you mean Cinema?"

I step into a small bookshop to ask for directions. The books of course are all in Turkish, but a title attracts my attention: 'Erkek...Mars, Bayan...Venus'. And from another shelf the Dalai Lama is smiling at me. Tolkien in Turkish. Wow, I have walked into a New Age bookshop! When I ask the young woman for the synagogue, the shop door opens and a young man steps in. "Just ask him!" she says. "He is Jewish."

And then we all shout simultaneously: "There is no coincidence!"

Eli is a man with fragile, finely chiselled features; he speaks fluent English and I can tell him in more detail what my mission is. He is a member of the Jewish community here of about 2,000 souls. "A small community," he says. If only he knew how difficult it is in the Netherlands to get a proper '*minjan*' together!

He is also a member of the 'I AM' organisation, a spiritual esoteric movement inspired by the teachings of St. Germain. I say that I would like to speak to the rabbi. Everywhere in the world Jewish communities are vulnerable and this one is no exception. I feel I can make my wish known, but without insisting. He brings me to an old synagogue in a backstreet, which I would never have been able to find myself. It is the *Mayim* synagogue; the Water synagogue.... my dream this morning!

There is a policeman here who searches our bags for explosives. The '*shammes*' (sexton), an old man with a large red birthmark in his face, opens the door to us. Eli tells him my story in Turkish. I sit down in the auditorium. I see crystal chandeliers, dark wooden walls, the *bima* (lectern) and the Holy Ark with the Torah rolls. Dimmed daylight is coming in through stained glass windows with the yellow six-pointed star on a blue background. I sit here, breathe deeply and shake from my consciousness that two people are waiting for me at the door. Over the Holy Ark something is written with fiery letters. I spell the Hebrew letters of one of God's Holy Names one by one. 'S H A D D A I'. A shiver runs down my spine and suddenly there is behind, or in the Eastern wall of the synagogue a Terrible Devouring Presence, in which I recognize immediately the Great Lover. It has the same pulsating energy, the same pulling power. "You are Mine" he says. "I'll eat you raw!"

In this synagogue he carries the uncanny energy of the Covenant between the Pieces (Genesis 15, vs. 7-18) and of the demonic story about Zippora, who circumcises her son with a stone knife, because the Lord of Lords tries to kill Moses in a dark nightly hour (Exodus 4, vs. 24-26)

"You are Mine," he growls with a wide open lion's mouth, in which all and everything could disappear. It is God and He is in Jerusalem and with great power he draws me hence.

But, this God is without hope.

The *shammes* turns off the light. We go out. Eli asks what I felt. I tell him everything.

In this synagogue I experienced something of the Fearsomeness of God, triggered by one of His Holy names, but it was the first time I sensed something like that in a synagogue. The one in Worms, Germany was one and all compassion and light. In Amsterdam I sensed a no-nonsense attitude at first, but when I waited and tuned in, I started to sense not so much the Presence of God but more the power of the prayer which is lifted to God; the power AND the complaint; the yearning for God, the imploring for justice, for grace. In that passionate entreaty also lies the offering of human existence as it happens to be, inclusive of all its sorrow. And in the offering and imploring itself lies the consolation and the acceptance of this - often bitter - existence. This special Jewish tender delicacy has a large eye in my heart. Also there I feel I am coming home and finding ground.

Friday, January 5

I visit the address which Eli has given to me of the spiritual organisation; he has made a phone call first. I am let into a room where a young, distinguished gentleman must be writing important letters and making telephone calls from his immaculate desk. On the walls of the room I see calligraphies of the name of Allah. He has reserved half an hour to speak with me and I tell him my story about the Peace of Jerusalem, the necessity of prayer and meditation and if the Organisation would include the intention of this Peace in its own prayers and meditations.

While we speak together it becomes obvious that the young man has enlightened views on religion and tolerance. Although he is a Muslim, he has eye and heart for all other sincere paths. He is gentle and very well mannered, a being of great refinement and education.

Then why, and how strange this is: quite in contrast with his attitude and conviction and appearance, I start to feel something quite opposed to yesterday's Grand Mosque. Yesterday I felt an abundance of grace and forgiveness. Today I feel an awesome strictness, a dark opaque column of unbendable severity going deep into the earth and looming over me. Faces emerge which look like those of unbending Muslim clergy, distorted into ire and condemnation and there is no mercy and grace, just an overwhelming sense of repression, punishment and penance; do I feel the shadow side of Islam?

There are two more letters for me at Poste Restante. Why moan about loneliness? I am not lonely! I am utterly happy here in Turkey!

For the first time since October 8, last year I could go to communion. I visited the church of St. Polycarp, a martyr from the 2nd century. The church was built in the 19th century on the foundations of the church of Smyrna, one of the seven churches mentioned in 'Revelations of St. John'. This is a fascinating country; this old land with so many different layers of civilisation: Phoenician, Greek, Hittite, Persian, Roman, Jewish, Christian, Muslim. I have to think of an image from the *Kabbalah*. God is sitting on the throne dressed in many layers of different robes, each one even more beautiful than the other. The robes are not God, but His light is shining through all.

So, I was in a church, even a Roman Catholic church and it feels like I've come home in a very well-known place. The *Nur Allah*, the Light of God, is also shining here. It is not like a soft, warm mantle falling around my shoulders, but more like a sweet ray of sunlight piercing my heart and making a space for itself there. The feeling of being 'blind', a 'closed door' has gone. And that is not because there are images of saints on the walls; I don't like them, they are too 19th-century-sentimental. But now another door is closed. I don't feel sensual completeness and holy abundance anymore; no warmth flowing through my body and limbs; only a soft and tender light filling head and heart, however it has forgotten the rest of the body.

When I compare the three great Abrahamic religions then the field of Christianity enlightens my heart and my head; the field of Islam enlightens my heart and my body; the field of Judaism enlightens my heart and my existence. Could those three not help each other in Jerusalem? And why do I feel in Izmir that *Shaddai* is a God without hope?

Saturday, January 6, Twelfth Night
Three wise men were following the Star. After the winter solstice the Sun starts to roll again. I have to go, I must move.

I am here sitting in the sunshine on the quay of Smyrna. This morning I carefully cleaned my boots and greased them with the special shoe product I brought with me from Holland. The shoeshine they use here is not so fit after all to take care of my precious boots. I take them off and look pensively at the soles. They have started wearing off quite a bit. A lot of the deep profile has disappeared.

Large ships are passing. On the opposite side of the bay I can see clearly the hills covered with white houses. Behind me rows of palm trees rise up like stately goddesses.

I put my shoes back on. I am done here. I don't want to wait for letters anymore. The ones of N. and M. took three weeks to arrive. I am going tomorrow. One week of rest is more than enough.

A shoeshine boy approaches me with his beautiful brass shoeshine box. 'No my shoes don't need to be polished, thank you darling!"

"Please Ma'am?"

"No I don't want it."

Splash, a thick dollop of black shoeshine descends on my carefully prepared boots.

"Bugger off!" I shout furiously. "Take it off!"

The child looks perplexed and frightened, but I don't give a damn.

But later I am sorry. I give him some money. Too much! He doesn't even thank me!

Bye, I never will give something to anyone anymore!

Monday, January 8, Gazimir

Heard: toddlers who in their innocence are imitating the lilting call for Prayer: "*Allaaaaaaaaaah Akbar*," God is Great!

I have prayed my Our Father every day for the little mute boy. I just kept doing it even after the promised seven days every time I thought of him. But only today I remember the word: '*Effatha*' ('Open up') from the Gospel. Towards the afternoon I come to a fork in the road. From far off I spotted a large old tree, pieces of fabric - 'clouties' - hanging from its branches. Under the tree is a grave; an erected stone crowned with a turban. It looks special; as if somebody sticks his head - without a face - from the ground; it makes the person who is buried there very present. The man who was buried there must have been a holy man. I keep my afternoon meditation there and tear two strips of fabric from my handkerchief. I have the feeling I must formulate my prayer very simply. A woman comes towards the tree. She places herself at the head-end of the grave. She humbly bows her head and holds both hands ten centimetres in front of her heart, palms open towards it. When she has finished her prayer and has gone I go and stand there too. Hands in front of my heart, palms towards me, head bowed in submission. Immediately there is peace and focus. I ask God, and the Holy Man that he may ask God too, that the boy may open up and that I am allowed to bring a drop of peace, if possible more than a drop - to Jerusalem.

That afternoon it seems as if the olive trees in the landscape are more alive, the grass is extra green. Creation wants to speak to me again. Having been in built-up areas and cities so long I had forgotten that was possible.

Tuesday, January 9

I lost my map, the nice map of 1:400,000 with all the villages depicted on it. Now I only have my compass and the names of the large settlements on the coast which I know by heart. Until Efesus I have to walk four to five days until I can buy another map. But better lose my map than my compass.

I walk along a quiet tarmac road through the mountains. Towards the evening I find a place for the tent in a pine forest. The ground is soft with a thick layer of long brown needles. The trees are tall and wide. Their parasol crowns are swaying softly against the night sky; the stars behind them. The full moon is rising. Her light shines in slanting bundles into the forest and pours moonlight puddles on the forest floor. The tent flap remains open. The night wind sighs through the treetops, but here, beneath them there is no wind and a deep peace. It is dark and yet light. I need that peace badly, because despair has hit me. N.'s letter has touched me more than I wanted to admit. Here is another man, whose tenderness I am not allowed to accept. I have to flee boorish bachelors by jumping from the kitchen window and potential lovers are not free.

But you had married God in Bulgaria! What happened to Him?

That is almost two months ago. That lover is also leaving me, just like the others, and there is the despair, tangibly close.

"Don't give in to despair. It is only despair!" Courageously I try to hold the fort. The pine trees sigh. That is good. That helps.

Then I get angry: "If You also leave me, then forget it! I am not your dancing fool!"

That helps too. I feel relief, but the sadness beneath remains.

"Of course I will come to Jerusalem, because I promised You! Don't worry!"

Wednesday, January 10
I only wake up at 08.00 am. First light has come and gone and the sun shines in the forest. There is such a mild temperature I can meditate outside. God turns from Lover back into a Father. They seem to be two different persons. I prepare my daily tobacco offering for the plants and animals I will encounter on the way and which I might have to damage unintentionally. I want to lay the offering under that tall pine tree yonder, but when I come closer I see that the back of it was at some time hit by lightning. Only half of her trunk remains, and it is hollow and burnt black.

"And God numbed Adam and while he fell into a stupor He took one of his sides, covered it with flesh and formed the side to a woman and brought her to the man, and he said: "Finally bone of my bone and flesh of my flesh." (Gen. 2 21-23)

There stands this majestic tree, on its own, with a gaping hollow side; she has no bone of her bone, no flesh of her flesh, but when I look up I see her crown full of green needles and abundantly covered with pinecones. She lives and bears fruit! She wants to!

Today I had a wonderful walk. I find narrow paths through the mountains and arrive at the coast again. It is nice not having to hold a map in your hands. It is liberating to walk only on compass. I'm on the south coast of the peninsula south of Izmir. It is warm! Really warm and I am wearing my T-shirt. I cover the wide neckline with a shawl not to give offence. I suspect that I've come out much further west than I intended. I want to go to Claros, the Greek name for Ahmetbeyli, a Turkish town. There is an Apollo temple with parts of his statue still there. Nobody I ask knows where Claros is. Have I passed it already? Doesn't Apollo want me to come to his temple? Is he offended again?

Apollo is the Greek (sun)god of the Arts and Wisdom. I doubt the wisdom part. I am not so keen on Apollo; he is too full of himself.

1. King Midas hears the flute play of the shepherd's God Pan. He loves it. Apollo says: "I can do that better!" Midas says: "OK, we hold a competition!" Apollo wins of course, but he gives Midas ass-ears for revenge, because Midas had the nerve to doubt him.

2. Apollo wants to make love to Cassandra, the daughter of King Priam of Troy. Cassandra doesn't want to make love to Apollo. She is a prophet. He is highly offended and makes that nobody will ever believe Cassandra's prophecies.

3. Apollo wants to make love to Laura, a wood nymph. Laura doesn't want to make love to Apollo and flees. He runs after her. He almost gets her and grabs at her. In her anguish she prays to the gods, who change her into a laurel bush (bay leaf bush). Apollo is disappointed, but picks a laurel twig to make a laurel wreath and puts it on his head himself. So he got her after all and even makes himself the first Laureate.

Do I have to reconcile myself with Apollo? After all he IS a God! But an easily offended and sexist one.

It is an interesting synchronicity. The diverse veils of the Divine mix and lend each other's colours. I am not quite in harmony with God at the moment and therefore Apollo refuses me the access of this temple and the sight of his radiant shape.

As often the coast is fully built up, but usually I can find a little space to pitch my tent inconspicuously. Not today however. The sun sets in pink and red behind the islands just off the coast. The sea is indigo blue; the heavens are red. It is busy on the beach. There are dogs and people. It is getting dark. Ahead of me I see a small wooded peninsula, but having arrived there I find it fenced and watched over by armed guards, who send me on in the dusk. It is already dark; I have to pitch my tent in the garden - with empty swimming pool - of one of the deserted huge villas in the estate.

At 11.30 pm I wake up with a shock, for there is sniffing and growling at the tent door. A dog has found me. I am deadly quiet. Then he tries to pull a boot on its shoestring from under the flysheet. I clap my hands and bring my boots to safety. He is startled but then renews his research by hanging heavily over the tent, bending the poles; it is a large dog. I am glad he doesn't bark. In all manner of ways he tries to get his nose under the ground sheet. If he sees me I'll be in trouble. I am very quiet and after a while he goes away, but not far. Behind the house I hear him bark at another dog quite nearby.

I sleep until 05.00 am. Then I get up. It is better to get away from here as soon as possible. It is not very nice when some stranger pitches her tent in your private back garden. I do everything inside this morning. Even washing and packing. While busy something jumps on the tent. My God, there is the dog again. He has heard me! I get hit around the head, but only by a small paw. Relief; it is only a cat. At half past six I'm ready to go. The morning light is dawning. The *muezzin* chants the morning prayer. I leave the garden through the open gate and walk towards the main road. There are the dogs: two whoppers, two guardian dogs for this estate of villas.

This time there is no grace. They bark, they growl. I'm bitten; the first time softly, the second time sharper. The dog gets my trouser leg. Now, in my turn, I draw open my big mouth, shout and make a threatening gesture towards him. For a moment he withdraws. In this way I can keep them at bay until I'm on the main road.

The sun rises behind the mountains. I walk straight towards it. I sing the Japanese mantra of Masunaga. I feel how lovingly the first rays caress my face.

02.00 pm

The Summerland exists! I walk on the coastal road towards the east. There is little traffic. The sun burns on my arms; there is a warm breeze. Scents of Mediterranean herbs waft past my nostrils. From the high road I look deep down towards the sea. I can see the bottom through the blue, green and turquoise water. Hyper-green little pine trees grow from the rock face, standing out against the blue sea. Perhaps I will take a swim when I can get down to the beach. I have no idea where I am.

This morning I find an 'Evil Eye', or better, the talisman against it. I pick it up. I can use some protection. However, now I have an Evil Eye. And that is true. Since New Year's Eve and my kitchen window adventure I look at Turkey less positively. Especially I can't stand the general fiddling with prices. Not everybody does it, but many people do. This morning it hit me again: putting 80 cents on top of the price for a bowl of soup which is on the Turkish price list on the wall. The tourist won't understand it! I'm asking for the money back; I am angry. It is enough. The Turks are cheaters! But getting the money back is not enough. It hurts being cheated. I am not a walking wallet, I am a human being.

And now I have an Evil Eye. I expect to be cheated in every shop; I lost my trust in people and that is a great loss for all of us; mostly for the Turks, because I won't allow them into the European Common Market anymore; they are unreliable.

However, it works both ways. When I approach people with suspicion, they will respond to it accordingly. And I am actually infatuated with the Turks. They are funny and sweet and spontaneous and clever and I feel sad like having an unrequited love, and it is unjust towards the honest ones. I must find a balance between the euphoria of the beginning and the disappointment of today.

I don't want to look at Turkey with an Evil Eye. I'm sitting on a rocky boulder, looking at the sun; it warms my face so gently. I re-read the letter I'm writing; this one. Yesterday I wrote: 'Back from the Lover to the Father; they are almost two persons'. I wrote that in my innocence, but while re-reading I suddenly see it: God the Father, God the Son. It startles me, in a happy way; and there it is still stronger; the light of the Sun on my face and hands. These sun rays are especially for me, Johanna; they don't shine on anybody else. And suddenly there is the Great Lover again and takes me in his heart.

I leave the Evil Eye behind on the rock.

Thursday, January 11

Yesterday somebody gave me five tangerines; I am scrupulously given back my change at the greengrocer and two lovely wild dogs are following me. Everything is back into balance. And, how will I deal with the cheaters? I won't deal with them. I decide to let it go. I just pay, unless they are very large sums. The Cosmos will get even with them in its own time. Well, this feels so good! I won't give it any attention anymore.

After I have left the Evil Eye behind I find the temple of Apollo. His mighty torso and right leg are still standing there. Two delicate columns with capitals is all that remains of the temple; some floor pieces are still intact and there are lots of large fragments and pieces scattered around; fallen columns, the large toes of enormous sandaled feet; togas etc. In contrast with the Athena temples this sanctuary of Apollo - only second to Delphi - lies in a slight hollow in the landscape, which calls forth a very special atmosphere. Together with this Greek clarity (a special sort of daylight?) it gives an impression of a refined, pleasant and intimate nature. I am there at sunset, which is always a special moment.

After that I hurry off to find a place in the orange orchards nearby. You pick oranges from the ground and from the trees. I don't have any want of vitamin C. It feels strange to throw the peels on the ground; I can do it because they belong to this ecosystem, but I find it very difficult to just drop orange peel on the ground. I do it with a clumsy and guilty gesture. I must practise tossing it away and start to enjoy it.

Sunday, January 14

I sit now - I can't believe it - three metres from the grave of the apostle John, the gospel writer and perhaps the writer of 'Revelations'. Very near to this place he wrote:

'In the beginning was the Word
and the Word was with God
and the Word was God
This was in the beginning with God.'

Here he died at the age of 100 after his return from exile on the isle of Patmos just off the coast. John, the beloved pupil; his gospel is full of a deep mystical understanding and love for God and for Jesus, and full of resentment towards 'the Jews', priests and elders of Jerusalem and to Judas — Jehuda. Christians turned these into: 'the Jewish people' with all the well-known disastrous consequences for the Jewish nation in the two millennia afterwards.

I have come here with a very double feeling. The special mystic quality of St. John's Gospel has always appealed to me, but I find the way that Jesus associates with his contemporaries often loveless, arrogant and lacking in understanding. Of course it is not the real Jesus, but the one seen through St. John's eyes. And he gives me a strange 'double bind'. Is he the 'Apostle of love' or not? And I say aloud: "John, John! How could it come to this! There seeps through all your wisdom, so much hate!" And I think of Jerusalem, and of the return of the Jews to Israel/Palestine because of the European anti-Semitism - nourished by the gospel of St. John, and the painful grip of the tongs in which Israelis and Palestinians are held until this moment.

He is also St. John of the vision of the woman crowned with twelve stars, clothed by the sun and standing on the moon. And it was written in this land of Turkey, which carries the moon and a star as a national emblem.

At 200 metres from the grave of St. John there is the once famous temple of the Artemis of Ephesus, who carries twelve star signs around her neck. And John lived with Mary, his adopted mother, near Ephesus, where they both might have died. Tomorrow I will visit her supposed little house on the *Bülbüldag* (The Nightingale Mountain) close by.

Maria was declared 'Mother of God' in the Council of Ephesus in the 5th century; here in the very same spot where I am now. She was an older Jewish mother, who became mother of the world, greater than the Artemis of Ephesus ever was. Officially she is not a goddess. Of course not. She was a human being who was the mother of a very special human being, Jesus, who was later elevated to God/Man status. The

Roman Catholic Church jealously guards against Mary being worshipped as a divine being. It would be blasphemy. However the human need for connection to the divine feminine archetype is so strong that it grabs for every possibility to express it. So, in the male oriented Judaism/Christianity with its sometimes warlike God and the loving Father figure, the human being Mary emerges as a necessary compensation. She seems to combine in herself all the goddesses, who preceded her. She was honoured almost as goddess in this land of the Great Mother, land of the Star goddess, land of the Aya Sofia, the Holy Wisdom, of Cybele, of Aphrodite of Athena and Artemis. And her - unofficial - cult grew to great prominence in the Middle Ages in Europe until it was crushed by Protestantism, paradoxically to both its detriment AND enlightenment.

So Ephesus has two virgin 'goddesses'. I have seen the Great Artemis of Ephesus in the museum. She is like the date palms I saw in Izmir. She offers her fruits, her breasts to everyone in need of nourishment, giving abundantly. She is a virgin indeed, without any bodily curves from her waist, her body inaccessible by feet bound together by the narrow seam of her dress. She is a mermaid, a palm tree; her hands are broken off; her face with the damaged nose is of a strange well-known beauty. I know her; she is so familiar! Her headdress, her face between the earrings; I've seen her before. Of course, in pictures, but it isn't that! I know that woman! It is not a Greek statue; it isn't Egyptian either, neither is it Etruscan. The name Artemis was borrowed from the Greek. Here in Ephesus she was the wet nurse of humanity and the keeper of nature. Her image is covered with plant and animal patterns. She was Goddess of the hunt, forest walker with her two dogs, solitary in the nature where she belongs and which she animates, but her two missing hands make her unable to act today. I was in her temple. One column is erect. It used to be one of the Seven

Wonders of the World. What a sad place it is now. She has been forgotten. I stand at the spot where her statue once was and look between the remnants of the temple to the place where once her worshippers stood. There is nobody now who appreciates her gifts and thanks her for them. There is one place in that temple where she still lives in hiding: in the golden reed border growing in a damp place. There are animals here: geese, a puppy, songbirds, but people have forgotten the place of the Great Mother, of Cybele of Artemis.

Tuesday, January 16
Ephesus is the largest ruined city of the Greek/Roman world. It is a blessing that I am here in winter with its lovely temperature and hardly any tourists. I am most impressed with the Celsus library. Great antique wisdom written on book rolls was kept behind the columns of the facade. At the foot of one of the columns I find a roughly carved menorah. That means that close to here was a synagogue; likely the synagogue from where the apostle Paul founded one of his first Christian communities.

I wander along the antique remains, statues, colonnades, arcades, fountains, streets paved with large flat stones. I come to the large amphitheatre. I stand on the stage and hear how the masses chant for an hour: "Great is the Artemis of Ephesus!" (Acts 19 v.28). St. Paul hopes to preach the sermon of his life, but is kept from doing that by a wiser man.

I want to sing a song, but I don't dare and sit down on the lowest range of seats. In come a group of young Germans. One of the women takes a flute and twirls arabesques from it. Then other instruments appear. Two clarinets, a bügel, a fagot. I get a free concert in the winter sun, ending with a long and healing improvisation.

On the way back to the exit I hear a guide tell an interesting story. I had already seen that in this region wild fennel is growing everywhere and apparently has done so from antiquity. When Prometheus stole the fire of the gods and brought it to the people on earth, he used a dried fennel stem; it keeps its glow longest of all the plants.

Fire is warmth and light; with the use of fire a great change came about for humanity. Use of fire and development of consciousness go together. According to Rudolf Steiner in these - formerly Greek - regions the earliest 'day consciousness' was developed. It was the beginning of our rational way of thinking that today has begun to develop in technocracy and over rationalisation. The gods have punished Prometheus excessively. He is chained on an island, where an eagle eats away his constantly re-growing liver. The gods foresaw all the misery.

I am on my way to *Meryem Ana Evi*; the little house of Mother Mary on Nightingale Mountain. It is a climb of six kilometres through the pine forest. Tradition tells us that John the Evangelist built a little house for Mary here, where she lived with other women, died and was taken up to Heaven. She is supposed to have lived until an age of between 51 and 60 years.

In the beginning of the 19th century a German clairvoyant and mystic, Catharina Emmerich, received visions of the life of this first Christian community after the Resurrection of Jesus. She described in detail a place in the vicinity of Ephesus. She described the curves of the hills, the view of the sea, the town and the way you could come there. The work was published, but only at the end of the 19th century did it fall into the hands of the French Catholic Mission in Izmir. They went and had a look. They found the place and the ruins of an old chapel, which had been built on the foundations of a 1st century cottage. The people in the neighbourhood called it '*La Monastère*', the Monastery. Each year on the 15th of August,

Mary Assumption, people from an old Christian community nearby came to 'the Gate of Heaven' to celebrate this feast. There was no way to find out how old this tradition was.

The land was bought by the French mission in Izmir. The chapel was restored and reconsecrated and it is in Turkey and elsewhere a well-known place of pilgrimage. Also Muslims visit it to pray there. Meryem, Mary, is the only woman mentioned in the Qur'an by name and she carries great credit in Islam.

In nearby Ephesus she was pronounced: *'Theotokos',* Mother of God, in the 5th century Council. There Jesus received his final divine status and his mother took over the task of the great Artemis, whose temple had been more and more forgotten and destroyed by earthquakes and the rise of Christianity. Alas, her task as protector and animator of Nature was forgotten by the Church.

Perhaps Mary really lived here, on Nightingale Mountain, with a bunch of Jewish refugees, feeling relatively safe far from the city.

Large signs show the way to Meryemana. Three fat parking lots for coaches have been created among the trees. A wide tarmacked road leads past the turnstiles where you can buy your entrance ticket. But it is winter. There is nobody at the counter. I walk on and expect a lot of devotion and commerce. I pass a restaurant, a souvenir shop.

Then I spot the little chapel. In front of it, on a low wall, sits a fragile nun, dressed in a light blue habit with a dark blue woollen cloak wrapped around her shoulders. I take off my rucksack and place it against the wall and try to tune into this very old first century layer of existence, that layer where the real Mary, the human being, the woman, not the goddess, lived and worked.

Loud humming comes from the chapel and a moment later a man with a vacuum cleaner is coming out. The fragile nun says kindly with a heavy American accent:

"You now can enter the chapel if you want."

But I answer hesitatingly: "But I must..."

"Enter into the spirit, beautiful." she finishes my sentence. She understood. I leave my rucksack outside - the door is too small- and enter. It is a simple chapel of rough stones. On the altar sits, o shock, a statue of Mary with a damaged nose and without hands. She has the same wounds as Artemis of Ephesus! But where Artemis is a goddess without a pelvis, Mary has one, and a big one too, for she has given birth.

The fairy tale noted down by the brothers Grimm comes inevitably to mind: a girl is sold by her father (the Patriarchate?) to the devil, who cuts off her hands, for he can't get her soul; she is too innocent. After leaving her parent's home, since she cannot stay there, she marries the king, who has silver hands made for her. She bears a son whom she calls 'Sorrowful'. After a misunderstanding she has to flee and lives for long years in a little house in the forest, where an angel takes care of her and her hands are growing back.

There is a parallel with the woman from 'Revelations'. She bears a son as well and has to go in exile in the desert for long years until the time is ripe to return.

St John, who took care of Mary, perhaps saw her as a model when he wrote Revelations, but it is also possible that John meant the woman as 'Lady Israel.' The twelve star signs around her head symbolize the twelve tribes of Israel; the child she bore might not be Christ, but the Christian Church! It has ruled nations with its iron rod and was taken away from Lady - the people - of Israel. Israel was sent away into Dispersion and the child was led in front of God's throne.

On an even deeper level this Woman from Revelations is the Hagia Sophia, the Holy Wisdom, the forgotten feminine aspect of God. The moon she stands on is the mirror of the sun, symbol of the reflection of the Glory of God (Wisdom chapter 7 v. 25-26)

And she is also related to the Jewish Shekinah: God's Presence here on earth. In mystic Judaism the Shekinah is the people of Israel, forced into exile, roaming the earth in sorrow, searching the husband of her youth. The connection with Heaven seems to have been broken. The male God of Israel has forgotten his earthly spouse.

When I tune into the atmosphere of the chapel I first feel the devotional lightness which is characteristic of many convents. Everything is very well cared for, simple, attentive, clean, but beneath it I feel, different from other convents, a great tension and restlessness. The next moment I see an iron rod, which holds this place on Nightingale Mountain free of invasive powers, so that a bit of blue Heaven can exist here. The iron rod halts a power which wants to swallow this place.

The fragile nun enters together with another fragile nun. We pray the rosary in heavy American accent. I never have heard it like that before. Each Hail Mary - there are fifty of them - is pronounced with precise attention, each word spoken with consciousness and the first is as fresh as the last.

After that we have a chat outside. I am invited to stay in the convent for a night; have dinner and exchange experiences. First they have to ask permission of two young Turkish soldiers, who are guarding the complex; but they don't mind if I stay.

I see a notice board at the entrance of the chapel. The entrance fee plus parking money is going in its entirety (five Euros per person) to Selçuk council. The convent, which takes care of the complete maintenance of the place of pilgrimage doesn't get anything of it. They hope for the double generosity of the visitors. And I understand from what they tell me in not so many words, that the two nuns and the priest who live here are sometimes troubled by the Turkish authorities. They are not getting a permanent residence permit and have to make a trip to the nearest Greek island every three months to extend their tourist visa, and other unnecessary encumbrances.

Meryem, Mary, wasn't a Christian according to Islam. She was a good Muslim woman, but what's forgotten is that she was neither. She was a pious Jewish woman, living accordingly.

I think they look at this place as a Muslim place of pilgrimage instead of a Christian one. Many Muslims come here to pray as well.

And Muslims get converted here to Christianity. Only a short time ago two Turkish families were baptized and that is the worst thing of course. That makes this convent an instrument of the devil in orthodox Muslim eyes. A Muslim who converts to Christianity goes straight to Hell after his death.

Also the convent wants to build a larger church to welcome all pilgrims who come on hey days and they are not getting permission for that either. Secretly I don't mind the last. The way it is now, with the little chapel, it is small scale enough to be able to imagine those Jewish women in exile. A larger church would push away all that, together with nature, which is still very close here.

Sister Antonia asks whether the walk has changed something in me and I tell her something about my 'meetings with God' on the way. In return they tell me something about their own vocation. Sister Patricia tells me she was obese once before she realized her vocation. Now she is as slender as a lily. They are two angels in blue, caring for Mary until her hands have grown back again. They have another interpretation: "the Church has no hands in this place. They have to keep a very low profile to be able to stay here".

At seven o'clock in the morning it is light and matins are beginning. The forest has just woken up. The sun peers through the branches; birds are singing. In the distance I see the sea; it is there just like 2000 years ago. In my mind's ear and eye I hear Mary rise, draw water, make a fire in the fresh early morning. She is very close. I see her sitting at the fire.

She is embroidering something. She looks up and smiles at me. I see that she is embroidering a dragon, a Chinese lucky dragon. She laughs: "Not such a bad thing, isn't it?" Then she becomes serious. She holds up the material and it has changed into the suffering face of Christ. End of thought images.

I would like to stay here longer. Not now, but some time in the future. For six months, a year? And do what has to be done here. I would like to stay here longer with these women in present and past. I have the feeling that I can learn something here, but would I be able to cope with this invisible tension? And also, when we would get to know each other better, some of our ideas might clash and I don't look forward to the dimming of the lights which are now shining behind their transparent faces.

We say goodbye with a warm hug and I follow the path over Nightingale Mountain towards the south; away from the tension, away from the serenity. I can feel it wrestle in me for half a day and more.

Sunday, January 21, close to Milete
(the philosophers' Milete)

I'm almost afraid to write it down for fear it will start all over again, but since December 10, when I stopped worrying about it, I have had no new flea bites, and the fleas seem to have disappeared shortly after.

The days after Meryem Ana I find winding paths to err on through the mountains and on the plain. I encounter age-old hollow plane trees, which I immediately want to furnish with colourful carpets and curtains, because they are so large you can live in them.

In the olive orchards I am a guest of the workers. Habib and his wife, dressed in headscarf and harem trousers have a happy marriage; they are joking together and seem to be very good friends. A niece, a quiet withdrawn uncle and the woman next door have also come to harvest. The neighbour sits by herself in front of her tarpaulin with fallen olives, but the others are helping each other. First I am with Habib and his wife. He offers me a cigarette. I say that I don't smoke. He gives an appreciative nod and then lights one himself. His wife is carefully sorting out the olives, picks out the bad ones and throws the little twigs aside. She is merry; her hands work fast while she chats with husband and niece. I help for half an hour and then go to the neighbour. She is also wearing a headscarf and flowered trousers, but her eyes have a different way of looking at her surroundings; I feel somehow related. What sort of thoughts is she thinking? I don't think she likes this work. She is indifferent about the result and without cleaning them, shovels the olives in a rush in the open hessian bags. I have a meal together with them on the large carpet. Everybody has brought something. Habib's wife has fried eggs on a wood fire. There is salad, bread and fried potatoes. There are olives, figs and halva and they give me a good portion to take away for my evening meal. When everybody has eaten Habib lights another cigarette. The neighbour woman provocatively lights one too, but nobody pays her any attention.

I walk a while through a National Park and sleep in the mountains in a sea breeze, far away from all dogs. My mattress is punctured again and I fix it in a villa, which shall become the centre of a large villa estate on the green mountains around me. It worries me, all this frantic building in beautiful natural places.

Mehmet, Mustafa, Medin and Metten draw me inside among their seven barking dogs, help me repair my mattress and invite me for an evening meal and for an overnight. A young German couple is coming too and so do the wives and the daughters of the men. It is a real party and late at night the hashish filled water pipe is going round. 'Peace-pipe,' they

293

are all calling out to me, but I don't fancy getting high, however I do enjoy the hunky-dory atmosphere which accompanies the smoking. The people don't get dull, but very relaxed. Metten gives me a white rose and other attentions. We listen to Arab music, full of passion and desire. I dance in a corner on my heavy mountain boots; nobody sees it. Instead of on hashish I am getting high on this music. When all party guests have left I sleep on one sofa and Metten on the other.

We breakfast together in the morning and he shows me the way over all the small paths, over the looming mountain range, towards the south. I am in love with the Turks again. They really should get into the European Common Market.

For three days now I walk on soft roads; it is rather a detour, but I don't care anymore. I enjoy it! I go in a line as straight as possible and the rest will become clear. The Turks are very good at drawing maps in the sand.

I pray together with an imam in his mosque. He says a prayer for peace in Arabic. I hear several times the words Salaam and Jerusalem. Afterwards he thanks me for my request. And then he presumes that I am a vegetarian and left my husband because I wanted to be free. Is he a clairvoyant? He believes that I walked all the way from the Netherlands, but warns me, that not many people in Turkey will do so. "It is inconceivable for us. A Turkish woman of 53 cannot walk three steps." Yes what do you expect if by tradition they are supposed to stay inside their home all their life?

Saturday, January 27, between Akyol and Ören
I sit on the bank of a little mountain river on the most beautiful, wildest footpath imaginable. In the narrow valley there are small olive orchards and ruins of deserted houses. I see wild red tulips and white crocuses. Just now a young hunter has helped me down the mountain on which I had strayed by mistake. I hadn't actually lost my way; I knew where

I was, but I couldn't find any path. I'm not going very fast on the bottom of this high gorge, above which an eagle is circling and which cuts into the mountains with sharp bends. Where will I end up? According to the useless map I should have encountered a proper road long ago. I just ate my last bread-cheese-olive meal and will continue. I feel so safe in this valley. It has small fields crammed against the rock face; little woods in between; I walk the narrow path next to the bubbling brook. In this valley evil cannot come; it is also too narrow for a traffic road, perhaps that is why it gives such a secret and secure impression. I was discouraged from following it yesterday. It is 'zorba' there, wild, untamed. I have to wade through the river many times, that is true, but I enjoy it so much. Last night it was cold. Although it is only 25 kilometres from the warm coast, it is high. I estimate it about 800 - 1,000 metres. It was frosty, so I didn't sleep a lot. And I have to finish this writing session, leaning against the rocks, for I am getting cold; my feet are bothering me these days; I have painful toes and sore soles, my Achilles tendon is protesting.

Sunday, January 28

And this hidden path through the peaceful valley ends in a large plain; a loam filled salt lake between the woods, behind a high dam of sand. Is this developing land for a new housing estate? Are these white thermal salt lakes like in Pamukkale? I walk through the plain, searching for a path south-east. I taste a little water. Yes, it is salt. Shall I put some on the unsalted olives which were given to me a few hours ago? No, better remain on the safe side. The dried up and cracked salty loam-layers surround little turquoise, white rimmed lakes. I arrive at the dam. No pretty views meet me there but a conveyor belt, which throws loam and water over the dam into the plain. I cross a brown muddy stream and climb to the summit of the dam. Behind it is a wide valley with an enormous estate of factories and a few houses next to it. Behind it a road runs to the south. As far as the eye can see I see installations, conveyor belts, smoking chimneys. The transition from idyllic to the smoking womb of Mother Earth is too abrupt.

I reach the first factory complex and the end of one of the conveyor belts. I climb along the belt on a mud-covered ladder upwards to the factory building. Everything is covered in loam and mud, the steps, the railings, the platform and the next staircase which I have to descend to reach the road leading to the largest factory. It is late. I see a few men in the distance. They are busy hosing a mud-covered lorry. Great surprise shows on the faces when I seem to emerge from nowhere. One of the men is young and dressed in a posh grey overcoat, wearing spectacles under a well-cut hairdo, giving an intellectual impression. He is completely covered in mud spots including his neat hair and glasses. He speaks English very well and tells me that the salt lake is a dumping place for industrial refuse from the factory of electronics down there. My olives have been saved. So this place is not at all about thermal mineral baths in construction, but manifold environmental pollution. I can be such a dunce.

Just past the factory and bordering the road to the south I see another forest. After two cold, damp nights, in which I got myself a nasty cold, I sleep in a pine copse, warm, with my head and neck wrapped in a woollen scarf and I am woken up by the voice of the *muezzin* singing from the top of the factory mosque just behind me.

Monday, January 29
Only fifteen kilometres to Ören on the coast. Marmaris is coming closer.

I am hungry. Yesterday I ate my last meal at noon, apart from ten olives. And the next village I have only just reached at three o'clock this afternoon, but the shop is closed and the nearest village is eight kilometres on. I am getting really faint now. A fat village woman, who is sitting in the sun with her cat on her lap makes gestures: "Sit here!"

I obey and sit down. Ten minutes later she appears in her front door with a large tray carrying plates of seasoned bulgur, white beans in tomato-sauce, delicious yoghurt, even more delicious spinach pasties and hot tea. She puts that tray in front of me and commands:

"Eat!" and then sits down next to me to see with great satisfaction how I attack like a wolf and eat EVERYTHING! Never before I have been so hungry and never before have I eaten such delicacies. Four hours later, I am still relishing the memory of this regal meal.

In the morning I am invited inside a home to drink coffee. The whole family is still in pyjamas. We chat for a nice hour close to the fire. Gift: another bag of delicious home prepared olives.

After buying food in another village shop I sit next to it to eat it all. From every side people come to me to treat me with goodies! Salt on the tomatoes, olives, lemons, freshly baked pan bread and filled cabbage rolls. Every day I am presented with a new menu.

And again I don't know which path to take. This map is absolute rubbish! Not only has it the whole of Turkey on only two A4s, but it is full of mistakes as well.

I sit high on a rock with wonderful views over the sea and the peninsula of Marmaris. I want to go to Gökova, NOT to Jersekir! O, bloody hell, I have made a detour of FORTY kilometres and missed Ören, which I wanted to visit to see the monastery, and I am past it already ten kilometres too far east. Rubbish rubbish map!

Tuesday, January 30

There should be a path along the coast towards Gökova. I try to find it and choose the wrong road several times. Every time I have to retrace my steps. I struggle, try to tune in on 'what does your heart say?' But my heart is afraid to choose the wrong path and I don't hear anything. Angry I am with those crap maps in Turkey. Even the motorways are projected falsely, so that I made big mistakes there too. It is just not fair! I am doing my very best! Now just try to stick it out! However, deep in my heart I am afraid to be 'bad', not 'spiritual' enough! I hold on too much; I am too much attached to results and that's why I get punished. I am trying much too hard to be a good person. I let it be and walk on grumbling and murmuring inside. 'But I don't murmur Lord! Really I don't!' I know it doesn't work! However now I am on a very low spiritual level (I just chose another wrong path) Idiot! I can't let go anymore; I am stuck in my desires; I haven't got anything to offer anymore and failed completely. What did you think?! Ha! That you had something to offer there in Israel/Palestine? To the people in Jerusalem? Nothing but pure hubris! Better go home you. You got spiritually stuck and that is why you end up in dead ends and that is why you lost a good map: it is all tit for tat! You were asking for it!

I must stop this. This is not the right way to treat myself. I don't deserve punishment; I deserve a little more compassion. As soon as I have thought that I become more restful.

Alright: Then I just have to get lost! I've done all I could. I cannot do more. Slowly I return to my self-respect. I accept that I don't know; that I don't have an active intuition to find the right way. The right way is happening to me; I don't find it myself. More and more peaceful I become. And that low spiritual level? Suddenly I don't care about that anymore.

The process in me is as if a river meets a dam. It cannot flow on. It is a struggle, like a tiger walking up and down behind the bars of his cage. There is no way out, no way through. But I am not a captured tiger. I only have to wait until the water rises high enough to find the new water course which will continue to guide the stream. I just have to wait until good thoughts will rise in me, until I start to flow again. And I don't have to do this myself. It is done for me; it just happens and that is called Grace.

I turn away from the dead end of the quarry where my - wrong- path had led me. I walk back to the village. I don't know it anymore. Then, on the way back I find a carefully carved walking stick, lost by a shepherd! I take it with me and 50 metres on I find a very narrow, but well-trodden path in the right direction. That little path is only visible coming from the quarry, not going to it! Is this a better path? Or is it another loser? OK, I will get lost then. I don't mind.

It is right! I walk for long hours in the afternoon on this stony path. I do need the walking stick. Between the pink boulders I find one level place without stones under a pine tree. I sleep warm and soft. The crescent of the moon sheds an eerie light on the red rocks. In the morning a mosquito wakes me up just in time for me to watch the sunrise under a threatening black blanket of cloud. The cliffs and rocks are one and all fire!

I walk on until I stand on a vantage point where I can see the whole bay of Gökova. Opposite is the spit of land, which separates the Aegean Sea from the Mediterranean; islands in front of it. The sea is peaceful and wide. High above dark ships of clouds drift along the sky and transform the sun in a Majesty of Veils. Through the clouds it throws slowly moving sunny patches on the sea in long slanting bundles of light. Some sunspots are blazing like the focus of a magnifying glass. And I stand there, quietly leaning on my staff. It is too big for me; there is too much beauty.

Wednesday, January 31
And now I am here. Noon. I walked two kilometres in two hours, having to be careful on a steep path full of loose stones rolling off the mountain. Beneath me is a village on a small bay. It is still 35 kilometres to Gökova. I hope to buy a lot of provisions here.

3.00 pm
It was hardly a village and had no shop, but it did have a restaurant at a small marine harbour, although now there are only fishing boats. I have to walk two days over an earth road along an unspoilt coastline. It is too steep here to plunk down apartment buildings and hotels. I look forward to the walk like I would a plate full of profiteroles which I am going to consume and enjoy one by one.

But there is an uncertainty. As for real food I have only one more meal left plus two pints of drinking water. In ten kilometres there should be another restaurant and then nothing until Gökova. I couldn't buy food at the last restaurant, but I don't feel worried and I am very grateful, that after a day of enormous detours and a day in the rain, I am allowed now, after my conversion of yesterday, to walk along this beautiful coastline.

On the television in the restaurant I saw that Sharon - who was the firebrand of the intifada in Israel last autumn, has now been elected prime minister. Have the people lost their minds? Does Israel want peace or not?

My dreams are full of tenderness and physical love. I feel like St. Augustine of Hippo. During the day he was chastity itself, living in and with his God, but during the night lust had the upper hand in his dreams. During the day I tune in to the

Great Lover without a body. I feel his infinite tenderness, which fulfils me deeply, but doesn't touch the body. Lust and life, love and light; didn't they belong together? I chase away my play with the shadows. I don't want to dream about unattainable men. But at a certain moment I know: 'I married You, in Bulgaria, near the big stones. You wanted it and I didn't want it otherwise. You said: 'I want you completely for myself!' And I bowed my head and surrendered, but now I also know that You never can get my complete body and soul, even though I would want it. Because the lust is missing and that is part of my body. And also because You are too safe, safer than a human being. If it is Your will that I surrender body and soul to You, then You must find a way how that can be, beca   I do want to do your Will, but I don't know how!'

And then comes, with great peace and power   is knowledge in me: 'I want to find the love of my life. It is time to find the love of my life. Amen.'

The way along the coast is exactly as I hoped. Quiet, beautifully yellow with ochre-coloured sand, seamed with pine trees. The right hand verge drops steeply away into the sea, and the left hand verge climbs steeply up into the forest on the mountain. 'The Majesty of Veils' shows itself only sparingly. To be honest; I've walked for three hours already through thunder and lightning and pouring rain and am quite wet even under my poncho. The heavy waterproof trousers, which I bought in Izmir serve me very well; at least I haven't been lugging them along for nothing. The sun peeks through between the showers and I use the dry spells to write this letter. The promised restaurant was closed, but I could breakfast and buy food at an ordinary home. So all is well.

The coast is stunning here. "How beautiful!" I say when I see a twisted pine tree in radiant green in contrast against the turquoise waves below. "How beautiful!" as I see the sea foaming up against an ochre-coloured rocky pinnacle. "How beautiful," that clear blue anemone between the grasses. After all that rain the grass is juicy and almost luminescent. I look down on levelled horizontal rocky plateaus. They have neat terraced little fields with neat little houses next to them. Sometimes I see plastic houses; they are made of a wooden frame covered with transparent plastic; a smoking iron chimney pipe sticking through it; household items around it, washing up bowls, drying lines, rubbish bins, toppled vegetable crates and chairs. I should find it awful poverty, but actually it is very efficient and feasible in this temperate climate. I am almost a little jealous of the simplicity of their life.

Gökova is a kind tourist village on the coast. I see many little villas powered by solar panels, where B&B guests are welcome. Because I have to go to Mugla tomorrow to collect my mail, I rent a room for two nights. The 'lord of the manor' lights the old wood burner in my room. Outside it is still raining and inside I have hung up my wet tent and poncho from one wall to the other. While they dry out, pine needles and straws are falling on the ground, the bed and the table. I am as pleased as Punch with the purring wood burner and I forget the inclement weather outside.

Tomorrow I will decide whether I will walk eastwards on to Kash, to join my straight line from The Hague to Jerusalem before it runs into the Mediterranean.

There are definitely no passenger boats from the south coast of Turkey to Israel; I don't know why, perhaps there is a political reason. After arriving at Kash I will have to take the bus back to Marmaris; take the ferry to Rhodos and then take a boat from Rhodos to Haifa. Another thing I could do is to walk straight to Marmaris and diverge from my beloved 'straight line'. Looking at kilometres: if I hadn't had to take a detour along this meandering coast line because of the winter season, I could have covered the distance to Antalya, if not Gaziantep.

I have mixed feelings. Actually, I don't want this walk to end. I am so happy with this simple and pious life. I have no great expectations about my walk through Israel/Palestine as far as natural beauty is concerned. I will have to walk through the coastal region from Haifa and I remember from 1987, when I passed through it by bus, that the landscape was as corrupted and defaced as it is in the west of the Netherlands.

But also: I've had enough; it is true too. I long for my children, my family, my friends (not my house, not the Netherlands, oh no...).

Slowly the ceremony for Jerusalem is growing in me. Last week I realized: 'I will build a medicine wheel round Jerusalem.' Of course, why didn't I think of that before!

The family who own the B&B are not very harmonious. Over my head I regularly hear ranting and raving: the low voice of the father, the accusing voice of the mother. They rant and rave against their teenage daughter. She resists and defends herself; throws herself in tantrums. When I listen to the tone of her voice I can hear that she is constantly manipulating and using psychological warfare. I get very curious as for the reason of the conflict, but the last thing I'm allowed to do is to ask. When I see the parents pass my window the father gives a sad and helpless impression; the mother an angry and helpless one. On the balcony above my window I see the leaning arm of a young girl and a face which is at the same time unhappy and enjoying its secret power.

When I leave the room and meet the family in the corridor or the garden, they show cheerful faces and nothing seems wrong.

Sunday, February 4

It pours and pours and pours before, during and after Mugla, four days long. People tell me that it is normal at this time of the year and that I can expect it to rain for at least eight more days. Of course I can walk a day in the rain and then another day, but not very much longer. Wet, wet, wet, everything is wet. I am in my tent during the night while the rain goes on and on and on. I am in a meadow at sea level. The sea is 500 metres away and I have seen the growing puddles the night before. I might end up lying in one.

I don't want to walk in the rain anymore! Perhaps I should just go to Marmaris and then I will have arrived at Turkey's South Coast as well! I prefer to go to Kash, but *tamam* (OK) I will have to adapt to the facts.

That decision taken I can sleep more peacefully under the squalls. The next day I take the bull by the horns and turn into the main road to Marmaris. But halfway through the morning the rain stops, the sun comes out and I find a side path southeast in the direction of Kash. Great! I'm walking to Kash after all! For two days I walk on this rarely walked path next to a mountain river; away from the loathed traffic roads and I can sleep in my little golden tent during a last moonlit night. The river often crosses the mountain path and time and time again I have to walk barefoot through the streams. The stones on the bottom of the passing places are often sharp and slippery and the soles of my feet are starting to hurt. Also the stream is often very strong and reaches over my knees. With my heavy pack I tend to lose my balance, but with a stick in each hand I manage to cross any river and it takes the weight of my feet as well. At some point the car tracks disappear. I haven't seen shoe prints since yesterday; just the dips of raindrops in the sand and for a while the light spoors of a donkey. When I look at my own deeper footprints I know that it didn't have a load, or a person riding it. It meandered happily from one side of the road to the other. Where are all the people? I haven't met anyone since yesterday morning. My only companion is the foaming river left of me with its countless mountain tributaries flowing over my path into it. The last person I met yesterday sat between his beehives with his beekeeper costume on. He was a vague old man with staring blue eyes behind his beekeepers veil, bees buzzing around his head. He looked at me in a daze and asked where I was going to. I said:

"Direction Kash/Dalyan."

"On your own?"

"Yes," I said.

He was silent for a long time and then with a sigh he pointed towards the east.

And now? This is so clearly a road, and also very clearly it is never used. I start to worry a little. Where is it going to? Direction sou-south-east. Fortunately I still have plenty of food.

When I finally arrive at the end of the road, where it comes together with another road from the right, I see between two mountain tops at last the shining Mediterranean, but I also see a sentry box with two tiny soldiers in front of it and an iron bar shutting off the rest of the road.

I pretend not to understand and walk up to the soldiers to ask if I may pass.

No, I may not. The soldiers ask how I got here, for civilian cars are prohibited here.

I haven't driven, but I walked.

And where did I sleep, for there aren't any houses here for miles.

I point at the tent.

I'm not supposed to be here for this is secret military terrain.

Well how could I have known? I have not seen any prohibiting sign apart from the one in front of me on the fence.

They quite enjoy this unusual situation but don't know what to do. I have to give them my passport and they call Headquarters. I sit comfortably in the sunshine against the adobe wall and wait. A minibus approaches. Two officers jump out of it and two soldiers in the semi-darkness of the back are stretching their necks behind the back rests to see what will happen. I am treated courteously and kindly. Is this the army which is massacring Kurdish villages? Yes, it is the same army. With drawn rifles pointing in my direction I have to get into the minibus and am driven to Headquarters. I get a cup of tea and this incident is reported in the log. Then they explain what the possibilities are for me to walk on. The first is a detour of 40 kilometres over the motor way towards Dalyan, although the real distance between Headquarters and Dalyan is only fifteen kilometres. The second possibility is being brought under armed escort to Marmaris with the minibus of the military base on the military road. I choose the last with a heavy heart; I'm not going to walk 40 kilometres on a main road. And it has a certain charm, having a personal armed escort like a spy or a criminal!

I am happy with it now. I needed those last sunny, enjoyable days on the mountain road to be able to say goodbye to that long road through Europe and Asia. I am homesick already for my long walk. This part has really come to an end. I feel melancholy, but I am also thrilled. The most exciting part of the journey will start soon: my walk through Israel. I hardly sleep at night.

Monday, February 5, Marmaris
I am completely absorbed in getting information about Israel's present day situation. Today I have been reading my favourite Dutch newspaper *Trouw* online. It is publishing many interviews with inhabitants of Israel/Palestine at the moment. All opinions are very much blocking each other out and

contradicting each other. I should not try to discuss who is right or who is wrong; there is no end to it.

Also today I made a first draft of the letter to the Authorities in Jerusalem to ask permission for my little central ceremony. I have about 70 prayer slips. That is much less than I hoped for, but many invisible prayers accompany me. I had the idea of binding these prayer slips to white gas filled balloons, and to send them in this way 'to God'; to bring them in this symbolical way 'before His Countenance', a beautiful energetic movement. First I will do my clockwise circumambulation around the walls of the Old City, that is horizontal; then enter through one of the gates, North, East, South or West with my balloons to go to the *Haram al-Sharif*, the Temple Mount. And then let them go up in front of the Dome of the Rock. That is vertical; they go up there to descend in some unknown place and then the circular cycle will be completed. 'My word doesn't return to me without having borne fruit.'

It is a beautiful, simple and silly ceremony; exactly what is needed with all that serious misery.

And tomorrow the ferry leaves for Rhodos, if the weather is good, and it is! And then tomorrow evening I will embark on the boat to Haifa. I am look forward enormously to this boat trip of three days and want to tune in well into the Holy Land's atmosphere. Perhaps I will see dolphins too!

Wednesday, February 7

Just let go again Johanna. To go to Jerusalem means: letting go of everything unessential.

Yesterday the ferry would have gone to Rhodos, I had been assured, but it didn't. I was confused and disappointed. The weather was just brilliant! Why weren't we going? There weren't enough passengers. I was angry about the lack of clarity and tried to explain this to the person at the counter. But he didn't understand. He did understand I was angry and tried to make it up with offering me cups of tea; a torment both for him and me, because now I wanted him to relax with all his good intentions. Something was his fault, but he didn't understand what.

I'll have to wait until Friday now.

04.00 pm

I sit here in this patch of wood close to the sea, with high grass and lots of puddles in between and I paint pictures and write. The sun shines; it is warm. It didn't continue to rain for another eight days! We have been promised temperatures of 25ºC today. I have brought my bikini, but I don't want to go into the water so close to a large marina.

I'm thinking about the 'Our Father' and how it has gained extra significance for me during the last months.

'Hallowed be Thy Name.'

And then I think of the open space within the six-pointed star in my pendant which unites the symbols of the three Abrahamic religions; the space where God can write His/Her name in every language. I also think of the Turkish soldiers, on whose fighting caps is written: *'Allah Akbar'*, God is Great. In the Great War they fought against the English who had written on their weapons: 'In God we trust' and we Dutch, who are writing on the side of our silver guilders: 'God be with us' and more of that sort of blasphemy.

'Give us today our daily bread.'

This has become very relevant. In the morning, when I have hauled on my rucksack and I stand with my staff in my hand at the place which has given me hospitality for the night, then I pray this when I don't know yet whether I will meet a shop with bread or people who will want to share it with me. And every day I am grateful, because I always had it until now and everything else I needed. Also I am not worried about money. I think I will have just enough to finish with.

'And forgive us our trespasses, as we forgive those who trespass against us.'

I think of my own anger, sourness and irritation when a small inconvenience happens to me. I think of the hot and cold anger of the Palestinians and the Jews against each other, which does so much harm. And that I tend to lose my self-control quite often.

'And deliver us from my own angered evil' Amen, amen, amen.

'Because Yours is the kingdom, the power and the glory for ever and ever.'

Also my daily morning prayer, taken from a Jewish morning prayer, has been given extra significance:

'Blessed are You, O Eternal One, that You have returned my soul to me in mercy; that you - by Your great love - constantly sustain the work of Creation. Great is your love.'

Yes, every morning you return my soul to me; after a vulnerable night in a thin canvassed tent, under the stars, under the moon, against the rock face. No bears, wolves and murderers have harmed me. I wasn't struck by lightning, neither by too heavy rains, neither did I drown in flooding rivers or tsunamis or get blown away by hurricanes.

'During the day the sun doesn't harm me and during the night the moon shall not strike me.' (Psalm 121). And I wake up in the pure morning, a new gift every day. And I thank You, that by your great love day by day sustain the stars, the moon, the rock face, the bears, the wolves and the murderers. I thank you God. Existence is a mystery. I look at it with open mouth. I understand nothing whatsoever of it.

Thursday, February 8

I sit full of melancholy on the terrace of a Turkish teahouse for men. They are chatting with each other around me and I feel utterly safe. I must take my leave of Turkey. I will miss the happy extravert Turks. A little girl just passed. She is about eight years old.

"Hello!" she radiates towards me: "What is your name?"

"My name is Johanna. What is yours?"

"My name is Ovgu. How are you?"

"I am fine thank you. How are you?"

She is as proud as a peacock that she has been able to have a real conversation and that the honoured *misafir* (guest) has understood what she said and that she has understood the answer.

Children - well cared for, well dressed, clean children - play outside until late in the darkness without the parents being afraid that evil men will kidnap them. The Turks in the hostel however tell me other stories: about the cheating of foreign people by trades folk in the holiday centres; about the slyly ripped off tourists. Yes, those are the things which I find nasty in Turkey, the vagueness of prices and conditions. And also, the men in the hostel say:

"You are getting pampered and extra protection BECAUSE you are a woman!"

And the whole perspective with which I have come to Turkey turns upside down. It is not more DANGEROUS here because I am a woman and traditional Muslim values about women are different from those in the Netherlands. No, it is SAFER here because of that.

But what about the careful and sometimes bold efforts at flirtation? Apart from one or two exceptions, which could have happened everywhere, men have showed me a lot of respect. Greying hair? Ladylike appearance? You wouldn't say so from all the shy glances and lascivious ogling in my direction.

Yes, I have been pampered here; it is true. I enjoyed it enormously. I have been allowed to cream off Turkey, to experience the very best of it. Turkey is not treating everybody so kindly. I heard stories about the uncertainty of existence without social security; about the 'operations' of the Turkish army. An ex-soldier with whom I had a chat spoke about bombing a Kurdish hospital and the dead and dying he found there. He is still having nightmares about it; about alcoholism and the many men who cannot marry, because they haven't got enough money. According to the men the other side of women's repression is this: the woman doesn't care about the man, but about safeguarding her existence. She wants a furnished house and a man with a proper job. Only after that will she play her trump card: sexuality. That is the way men experience it here. They don't feel loved because of themselves, but because of their property. You can only get sex/love by paying up, either by marrying or by whoring. For some the European tourists, who fall in love with Turkish men, are a real solution. They have the idea that they are loved because of themselves.

I didn't mention Kemal Atatürk. His sharp head is as omnipresent here as Saint Nepomuc in the Czech Republic. In every little shop or office you see his portrait in many variations. On every little square, in front of every police station there is his bust; grim, piqued, grumpy and bossy. Only very seldom is he depicted as a hero. It is compulsory to have his portrait in your business, just like we have a portrait of Her Majesty the Queen in government buildings, but I don't have the feeling that the Turks are very impressed by his personality. The Kurds don't like him. Kurds fought on the side of the Turks in the wars. He promised them cows with golden horns and that was it. Atatürk was no man for minorities. His task was to keep the remains of the Ottoman Empire together.

Turkey; it deserves a song of praise! Or perhaps I should say, the coastal region does, for Turkey is of course much larger than the regions I walked through and I don't know much about the rest. I think of the palm trees. They are trees from comic books that grow on desert islands and in desert oases in faraway countries. And I just walked there: to a country where palm trees are growing. They are waving at me from the boulevards. I think of the courteous and graceful gesture with which even peasant women incline their head while greeting you.

Have I told enough about the animals? About the stray thin dogs and cats which are trying to scratch their daily food together? Some dogs do have masters. In Thracia the bosses were strict and the dogs fearfully obedient. Here in West Anatolia it is more like at home. The dogs that have masters are just as petted and loved and are just as disobedient as in the Netherlands, but the stray ones are kicked around quite a lot. The cats are subtly insolent. There are very beautiful ones, most with a thick Persian fleece. Yesterday I saw on the quay two cats which were entangled in an insolvable tragic conflict. The white one has initiative, she begs, hunts, contacts people, grabs and snatches. She is constantly followed by a large tabby filled with hatred and envy towards her. Every time the white falls back into spontaneous innocence and plays. Somebody gives her a piece of chicken. The tabby cat is also given a piece of chicken, at a distance, but he doesn't want it. He wants the chicken of the white one. Oi, how he hits and beats her every time she tries to have a bite. Tormented she rolls mewing on her back to defend herself, but she is never left in peace. She has to leave the chicken and walk on. The other cat now ignores the chicken to follow and torment her. You can send people into therapy, but what can you do about cats? How can they abandon this pattern? These are two innocent animals suffering at each other's paws.

In the two darkest months of the year Turkey and the Turks have given me light, have enlightened my journey. Chapeau!

Friday, February 9, 08.00 am, Marmaris

I'm at the harbour. In one and a half hour the ferry will depart for Rhodos. There is a mist over the bay. The sun has just risen from behind a mountain and gleams on the tops of the masts of the countless yachts which are moored here. I even see three-masters. Such a shame that they have all been unrigged. I asked at the harbour offices this week whether there were yachts sailing to Israel, but it is winter; the boats don't sail. Now the castle on top of the hill and some more white houses, start to catch the sunlight, but the hulls of the boats moored beneath are still in shade of night. Even at 08.00 am, when the alleys of the bazaar are still empty, a man steps from his moped and asks whether I go to Rhodos.

"Yes," I say.

"But you are very early!" he says concerned (or meddlesome).

Round the next corner two men are sitting already outside and drink their tulip-shaped glass of tea. One of them sees I want to go in the wrong alley and calls loudly:

"This way!"

And, when I pass them:

"Where are you from?"

"Holanda!"

He wants to have a chat, but I don't. When I pass them quickly he calls after me in unadulterated Dutch:

"Doeiiiiii!"

I feel strange this morning: hard, indifferent. What am I going to do in Israel? They've got plenty of problems there already. Do I have to bring hardness and indifference there?

03.00 pm, Rhodos Island

I crossed the blue sea on the ferry and now I sit on Rhodos beach in the warm sunshine. I just had a swim in the tepid waters of the bay, but I am fed up to the back teeth.

There are no more boats sailing from Rhodos to Haifa. Not for the last two months.

Well, they should have told me at the travel agency and they should have updated their websites with new information about departures and arrivals and dates!

I am so angry and disappointed!

I either have to wait three more weeks, until the first boat will sail, or take the airplane to Tel Aviv tonight. What shall I do? When I fly all the environmental gain of walking will have disappeared. I won't even start to think about having to fly back from Israel.

I decide to take the ferry back to Marmaris, Turkey. According to the timetable it goes back at 04.30 pm. Then I will start walking to Kash tomorrow after all and I will have done exactly what I intended to do in the first place.

I walk back to the harbour, but I don't see the ferry anymore. Now what has happened?!

Today it went back earlier. Everybody who had booked was already on board. In the winter the ferry is only used by foreigners who have to renew their Turkish tourist visa on Rhodos, says the official in the office. The next ferry will go in another week.

What a bloody mess is this! You can't depend on any information you're given! It drives me bonkers! What am I going to do for a week on Rhodos? I was so glad I could stop hanging around in Marmaris. How will I come to peace with this!

This is the work, Johanna! Everything you would have liked and thought sensible, you must let go of! That is what it means going to Jerusalem! Everything you were still hanging on to, and that is a lot: that is your beautiful three day boat trip to Haifa. Go ahead, book the airplane, just swallow your environmental gain, swallow your foot pilgrimage, go ahead, you don't know why, you don't know how. This is just bad luck;

down-to-earth bad luck and signifying nothing. It just means you have to bow your sanctimonious head for the plain facts. Go ahead and book your flight to Tel Aviv. For that amount of money you can get a return to Miami. Go ahead, bow your head: say you don't understand and that you don't know what the next moment will bring.

10.45 pm, Airport Rhodos
(I sit in the airplane waiting for take-off. I am already more at peace with it.)

I first have to pull some money from the wall before booking. The money machines in the old city don't work and I have to walk two kilometres to the new city for the next one. Everything is against me and this time I know it is not my stubbornness or my lack of surrender. The old fortified city is very impressive. Three rings of thick walls with deep ditches in between them; many narrow streets with old houses built of large stones. Also here most shops are closed. It is rather beautiful; I see high crenellated gates with statues of saintly crusaders over them. Palm trees grow here too and the sky is deep blue. I look for a little chapel to be able to sit for a moment to find consolation for my disappointment; a little mosque is OK too. There are many of them and all of them are locked. Is there no place for me where I can sit and let things sink in? In a backstreet I see a small orthodox chapel. The doors are open and a soft lamp is shining inside; an old *pope* with a long grey beard and soft face sits praying on his stool. I relax at the idea of sitting here for a while. But then the light is turned off; the *pope* stands up and before I can come inside the door is being locked.

"Please may I pray here for five minutes?"

He looks sweetly at me: "Tomorrow," he says and gives me a piece of cake: "Old tradition!" he says and walks on.

315

I must go to the travel agency to book tonight's flight to Tel Aviv. It is getting dark already.

(*We're in the air; I have just taken off my seatbelt.*)

After that I sit on a terrace for a cup of coffee; I am exhausted, but from what? An old gypsy, Michael, with a Greek guitar comes over to me to ask whether I need a roof and a bed. I don't. I tell him something about my journey. He is interested.

"Are you telling people about the Bible?"

"No, I ask them to pray for peace."

He knows where the synagogue is; it is close to his home. It is Shabbat's eve; I would like to see the synagogue, but the windows of the place are dark. Over the front door of Michael's house a large clumsy cross is painted. Inside it is chaos. An old blue scooter stands next to his bed full of rags. A table covered in sawdust, iron tools and the remains of a meal stands against the wall. Greek flags on the wall, a broken mirror, rickety wooden chairs and dirty cushions on the floor; a gas cooker covered in old grease, on which he makes a very reasonable cup of tea; several guitars in different stages of disrepair; a workbench; torn commercial posters on the wall: 'Amstel beer', 'Greece, the holiday country'. A washing line hangs through the room with a tablecloth hanging from it; ashtrays overflowing with cigarette ends; empty beer cans on the floor and everywhere, everywhere, on the wall, on the ceiling, on the doors, wherever you look: Christian crosses. Painted crosses; crosses laid in with seashells, crosses of mirror-glass, wood, stone and between the crosses countless nice and ugly icons of Christ, his mother and the archangel Michael. So, here is my little chapel in which I needed to pray and find consolation.

"I love Jesus very much," says Michael.

We drink tea. I ask him to play a Greek song on his Greek instrument.

He plays *Hava Nageela* for me.

I say that I know a beautiful Jewish song, which was written and composed on Rhodos about a girl, who was locked up in a tower by her father. Shall I sing it for him?

"But that is not really true; that is a fairy tale," he says.

I ask him if he knows a Greek song to play and sing.

He plays 'My Bonnie is over the ocean!'

I give up.

He tells me about his life. He has worked in America but had to return. In the winter he has no work and no company and he gets bored stiff. He is happy with my visit and soon wants to caress my hands and put his arm over my shoulders. I ask him how he got such a strong bond with Jesus.

"I was raised as an orthodox Christian."

He feels very lonely and says he longs to be touched by me. His face becomes very soft while he speaks about that, and I am moved, straightforward desire, honestly expressed, but I don't feel called upon to do that.

He insists on bringing me to the airport on his scooter, but I find the little motorcycle looking quite rickety; it has a small saddle and a narrow luggage rack for my wide rucksack and no helmet for me. I tell him I'm too afraid to sit on the passenger saddle behind him and I have already booked and paid for the airport shuttle bus from the centre. He keeps urging and urging me and I can't get through to him that I really mean it. OK, he will take me to the bus stop in the centre on his scooter, but it is only a seven minute walk and I don't want it and I tell him. I shake his hands warmly to thank him for the tea and his company and to say goodbye. He keeps trying to persuade me, puts his helmet on his head and starts pushing his scooter outside. He tells me where to wait for him at the foot of the hill. I need to disappear into the darkness without him saying goodbye to me. I hear his scooter start to drive to the 'agreed' meeting place. He might still be standing there.

The bus to the airport has arrived already. It stands in front of an old building. Between its windows I see little architectural ornaments; they are all different. Right in front of me I see a six-pointed star and within this the 'Flower of Life', a six-leafed flower, which is a symbol for the Christ. It gives me consolation. At the airport the alarm beeps at the checkpoint for weapons and explosives: it is my cruel-looking Bulgarian pocket knife! I can't take it with me in the passengers' cabin. It will be returned to me in Tel Aviv.

ISRAEL

Saturday, February 10, 09.15 am

Haifa Beach. I have just woken up after having snatched a few hours of sleep. This morning I saw from the plane the approaching coastline of Israel dressed in lights. I was very moved when the plane touched ground. Eretz Israel/Palestine Holy Land.

But how do I find myself in Haifa all of a sudden? After arriving at 03.30 am at Tel Aviv Airport I was faced with a new dilemma. Should I walk straightaway to Jerusalem in a few days? That would be another anti-climax after the disappointment of yesterday. I would prefer to follow my original plan to walk from Haifa to Tiberias and from there to Jerusalem. And, how stupid to arrive in Israel on Shabbat; there is no public transport! A taxi driver who stands in the deserted arrival hall offers me a cheap ride to Haifa. He lives there; this way he has a passenger to take home and he would like to hear more of my story too. I automatically think he is Jewish, but he is an Arab Catholic. I ask him who has become prime minister in the end.

"Sharon," he says. "Perhaps it will be better now."

I can't believe my two ears. Does he really think it will be better with Sharon? Being an Arab? When I prod him with questions a little more he doesn't really believe it either. He sighs:

"Sometimes you don't feel welcome in your own country."

He drops me off in Haifa at the beach, so that I can find a place to sleep there. It is almost six o'clock and dawn is arriving. I'm not pitching the tent, but lie down in my sleeping bag under the full moon. There are parked cars just behind me on the boulevard. A few languishing palm trees are trying to cheer up this boulevard. Two people are still, or already, walking over the beach. I collapse into sleep.

Now I have woken up next to my rucksack I feel like I have been washed ashore from the sea. It is just like the beach at Scheveningen; the same angle of light, the same sand, the same kind of people in jogging costumes with dogs which are running along the salty brim in large numbers. It is too cold to swim. I'm going to pack up and look for a breakfast, which turns out to be a large glass of freshly pressed kiwi-banana-orange juice. There are lots of fruit and vegetable juice stalls on the beach. I have to get used to prices at Dutch levels or higher. Walking north along the beach I hear Israeli dancing music. Coming closer I see at least a hundred people dancing in a circle. Every Shabbat you can come and dance free here on the beach. I dispose of my rucksack and stumble with them on my heavy walking boots. The terraces around it are black with onlookers. I find something of the idealistic, hopeful Israel. People are singing along and I am immediately helped by joining hands and counting of steps for me.

One hour later it is hot. The sun burns on my head. I walk to the temple of the Baha'i, which lies on the slopes of Mount Carmel among minutely cared-for gardens. If there wasn't such a tropical abundance of palms, cacti and other sorts of exuberant greenery I would find it pernickety, but now the care compensates the bursting jungle. The way the temple lays above Haifa it emanates a beneficial energy, supporting the city and making it light.

The African guard sees my monogram pendant. He is a Baha'i from Cameroon.

"If everybody will do his bit, peace will come soon. If not, it will be postponed, but come it will!" It also draws positive comments from his two Jewish colleagues.

I follow my path to the domed sanctuary in which the founder of the order has his grave. Like in a mosque I take off my shoes. Inside an African woman sits meditating on thick carpets. Baha'i wants to integrate existing religions and let them express themselves with all respect. They are truly broad-minded and spiritual, but somehow the atmosphere doesn't fit me. It is too refined here. On one hand I get the impression of perfect harmony, balance and integrity, on the other hand all this refinement is suffocating me. It is too beautiful, and, like in the mosques, a door seems to be closed. That is strange; I cannot accuse the Baha'i of narrow-mindedness. I think I'm not up to it yet. It is too noble for me here.

Having come outside I ask for the Carmelite convent. They don't know where that is. The African guard says that I should ask that old holy man yonder; he is sure to know. The old holy man is a fragile Hasid with silver white beard and side locks showing from under his black hat. With his whole family he takes a walk in the Baha'i park. I'm not asking him, but I find the convent *Stella Maris* on my own. The church has been built over the 'Cave of Eliah, the prophet'. According to tradition he lived here on the Carmel as a hermit. A beautiful image of the *Stella Maris*, Mary as the Star of the Sea, is sitting on the rock where he used to pray. Many local Christians come here to pray and light a candle. It is a very good place to be.

The shop where I buy food is run by Arab Christians. When talk turns to the political situation in Israel I feel they become wary. Carefully they say nothing evil about both parties. However they say that for peace to come it takes too long. They're not exactly wearing their heart on their sleeve.

The guesthouse of the convent sends me on to Beth-El-hostel. Bibles are strewn around here like manna from Heaven. It is a very Christian hostel. But it is nice and clean and is run by kind young people. They have that strange mixture of being pro-Israel and wanting to convert the Jews to Christianity. There is a German woman in my dormitory who is travelling around for three months and wants to visit the Jesus places. We have a lovely chat about chakras, auras and past lives.

There is a Dutchman too, Paul, who tells me something about his conversion to Jesus via the Bible. He is deeply moved when he speaks about it. Also the way he treats the Holy Scripture tells of an authentic love for the holy Word. What a pity that he accepts the language of the Bible in only one interpretation - his own - and he becomes judgmental when I want to tell him something about my way with God. I feel I am 'deluded' in his eyes. He thinks I am working with something of the devil. His judgement is painful for me, especially because actually he is a nice bloke and I tell him so. The German woman passionately tries to persuade him to open up to the Holy Spirit to receive new knowledge. But he doesn't want new knowledge. He asks me to ask Christ whether it is good what I'm doing. I don't need to ask Christ. I know it is good! Paula is so excited that she has met somebody with whom she can talk about her adventures with God that she can't stop anymore. She tells me that once she hasn't eaten for four months by completely tuning in to the love of God. She followed an Australian woman who is teaching this everywhere in the world. She started to eat again because she just liked it and then fell into a gluttony from which she is just emerging. She looks young for her age. She is 63, has a face without wrinkles and long black hair (dyed, she confesses).

Sunday, February 11, Haifa
Today I bought the best map of Israel I could find, scale 1: 250,000. Since I walked on at least a scale of 1:500,000 ever since Romania, this is for me a luxuriously detailed map.

The most direct way from Tiberias or Nazareth to Jerusalem goes via Nablus/Sichem on the West Bank. How I would love to go through and talk to the Palestinians. The first Jew I tell about my plan starts to pull his hairs out of his head.

"I don't want to read about you in the newspapers," he says in despair. The last two months fifteen people have been killed there for nothing at all!"

"But perhaps they were illegal colonists?"

"No, they were ordinary people who wanted to buy something or have their car repaired in a garage along the road. You are white and you look like us and they shoot before they ask. Don't put your head in a hornet's nest!"

And then I am in the middle of it: the hornet's nest of the question about my route.

To walk along the beach from Haifa to Tel Aviv seems a lovely thing. And to walk from Lake Tiberias/Lake Genesareth to Jericho and then to Jerusalem seems fantastic as well. West Bank under tension. The Israeli soldiers might not even let me through. Are the Israelis too scared or am I too naive? It is a fact that I have been warned through the whole of Europe against evil kinds of people, and that they never harmed me at all, on the contrary. I find myself a coward when I'm not going over the West Bank; I let it simmer for a while.

It is nice to talk to the people here. My golden monogram elicits many conversations. I get many positive reactions both from Jews and from Arabs. Here in Haifa there are hardly any Muslim Arabs; they all fled in 1948. The Christian Arab community has lived here since mid-nineteenth century. They were Lebanese converts whose families were encouraged by the Franciscans to move more south into what was then still part of the Ottoman Empire. The name Palestine was later given to that region by the British invaders in World War I.

The Jewish woman from the tourist information is satisfied with the election of Sharon as PM and she asks me what the Dutch think of him. I tell her what I think of him.

"Somebody had to do it," she says. "Somebody - a Jew - had to go in openness to Temple Mount, so that we can come there!"

But I know that everybody can go there! I know of many Israeli Jews who have visited the mosques without any trouble. People are so badly informed and there is too much fear.

In the Netherlands Sharon's move has been interpreted as aggressive wanton provocation and display of power. His move has nourished the Palestinian fear, that the *Haram al-Sharif* would become Jewish to build the Third Jewish temple!

Tuesday, February 13
Today I left for Nazareth and now, finally at 04.00 pm I start to approach the outskirts of Haifa. I wanted so much to walk. I haven't walked or camped for more than nine days.

Thursday, February 15
Nazareth is still a long way off. I have been walking from Haifa since the day before yesterday, and it is only now possible to drop off from the main road, where the traffic rushes on endlessly just like in my own over-cultivated country. My new Lonely Planet map doesn't show the built-up areas sufficiently well. According to the map I should have been walking through green areas since yesterday, but up till now I am still plodding through the city or little towns. It is raining; during the violent showers I usually take shelter beneath the little roofs at the bus stops. Then, when after a while the rain stops, I can walk another kilometre or two until the next shower. I am making slow progress. Also this land Israel/Palestine fills me with mixed feelings. In many ways it is just like the Netherlands; very densely populated and full of traffic roads. I haven't found a place yet where I cannot hear the traffic. Also the noise of airplanes is ever present. I cannot imagine that Jesus walked through this same land. On the other hand; it is very green. Green plants, weeds and flowers burst into bloom in exuberance; juicy grass and fragrant herbs; many unknown flowers. 'The winter is already past. *Nitsanim niru niru*

b'aaretz.' Red anemones, yellow rape seed, purple cyclamen of which carpets and carpets of light to dark purple; marigolds, Bougainvillea. Trees blossom and burst their buds. New leaves are showing. I pitch my tent in the evening and the next morning the grass seems to have grown ten centimetres. And the ground is sopping and I sop through it. The clay is everywhere. Even when I walk on a reasonable path it sticks thickly to my soles. I think: Eretz Israel earth. After three steps the clay rolls itself up on the noses and heels of my boots and drops off again.

In the morning I eat grapefruits (grapefruit orchard) or avocado (avocado orchard). Sometimes I feel like the White Witch from Narnia, overeating with forbidden fruit in the garden of Paradise. But it is not really forbidden. During the night I hear the avocados fall - plop - from the tree, and that little tree from which I ate grapefruits, gave dark brown fruit on the verge of over ripeness, impossible to sell, however the juice was sweet and warm.

The temperature is lovely and sometimes I even get a moment of sun. I sit near an Arab village and for the first time in two weeks I see a shepherd with his herd again. How I missed that! I realize I miss the domestic animals, the animals on and beside the road. The only things I see are gleaming holy cows rushing by on the main road. While I write this I feel a tickle at my feet and see them covered with countless little caterpillars, and over there a tiny shrew escapes under a stone. The little river I walk along with is the *Kishon*. Indeed the biblical *Kishon*, where the prophet Eliah massacred the Baal prophets. There are signs with warnings: 'Danger, very polluted water!'

Arik from the nearby Kibbutz Yagur says that it is because of the factory. I receive kind assistance from both Jews and Arabs. I'm glad I cannot really see the difference. Yesterday I got a bun and a kiss from an Iraqi woman. We were waiting together for the rain to stop in a bus shelter.

Lifts are offered profusely, just like in Turkey, and just like in Turkey people find my walking venture something strange. When I say I come walking from Haifa, they like it and find me wonderful, but when I continue and say that I came the same way from the Netherlands they don't respond. Somehow it doesn't register. And how will I raise the matter of my peace walk? To knock on the doors of churches, mosques and synagogues to ask for prayer for peace, must surely be superfluous in this country; I'm sure they are already doing that. I even might be an interfering nosy parker dealing with things none of my business. I do feel here a kind of: 'all shall be well'. No, even an 'everything is well'. And that is true and also not true; everybody knows that. I begin to wonder whether my 'all shall be well with Jerusalem' has something to do with this. It apparently is an Israeli slogan: 'All is well'.

I continue towards Giv'at Ela. From there I want to continue towards Illut and Nazareth. How strange. On the map there is no road between Giv'at Ela and Illut! And it is so obvious that there should be! A jeep is stopping and a nice young man asks if I want coffee and/or a ride. No, thanks, no coffee and no ride, but does he know the way to Giv'at Ela. Yes he knows, And to Illut? His eyes become grave. Illut is an Arab village, he says. He shows the way: "Be careful there!" and writes down his telephone number in case I might need it.

Giv'at Ela is a very clean and well-tended little village with well-dressed kind Jewish inhabitants. At the next bus stop, some Arab women are waiting; I get involved in an amiable talk, just like in Turkey.

In the small kosher supermarket I look for my usual hummus, oranges, cottage cheese and - if possible - bread without sugar. When it is my turn to pay, the checkout operator, a young man of about 30 years old, seeing that I am a tourist, greets me with a bitter: "Welcome to the state of Palestine!" He tells me that an uncle of his, only a few months ago, has been killed by a stone thrown through his car window, for no reason at all. "Only beasts do that sort of thing!" Discussion follows, the orthodox Jewish women, with their lovely hats on, waiting behind me with their baskets, are listening with interest.

Later I ask a jogging gentleman, dressed in impeccable white, the way to Illut. "You sure you want to go there?"

"Yes," I say.

"Be careful," he says. "They don't like us over there."

A narrow, almost invisible path is winding from Giv'at Ela to Illut. I greet a shepherd on the way. He greets me back. A little further I hear shooting. Sometimes a single shot, sometimes many rattling shots. Is it a machine gun? Suddenly the landscape has changed from modern Israel into the Holy Land; stony hills, olive trees, herds of sheep, villages with white square box-like houses in the distance. Sometime later I enter Illut. It is not a village, it is a little town. Two boys show me the way to Nazareth. They fill my water bottle and point interestedly to the compass dangling from my neck. A young girl speaks a little English. I walk on. Four young women are waving at me and asking me to come closer. I say that the sun is already low and I want to get to Nazareth before sunset. They understand. Two young girls want to shake hands with me. They are giggling very much. On the street a young man with a bald head and sunglasses greets me with the same wry greeting as his Jewish colleague of this morning, with only this difference: he says: "welcome to the State of Israel". In his face anger, despair and sorrow are fighting for precedence. Then a boy of about twelve years shouts at me. I nod in a friendly way to him, but his posture becomes threatening, as if he wants to hit me. He says something aggressive, which I don't understand, and the only thing I know to say is: "How do I go to Nazareth?" A large car is approaching with three young lads in it. Sharply and closely, with screaming tyres it passes me, turns around and races back to me the same way, cutting off my path if not my toes. Suddenly the mood has changed. I ask a few women, who are standing together, if this is the right way to Nazareth. They surly and icily show me the right way. Then between all the animosities suddenly a little girl detaches herself from this group of women and comes running towards me. It is a girl with Down's syndrome. Her face radiates upwards with a smile while she looks into my eyes and grabs my hand for a moment. She is a little star of love and hope in the darkness of antipathy.

I walk in the right direction now. The children in the square in front of the school shout at me: "shalom, shalom," and they throw dirty sweet wrappers and hands full of gravel. I walk out of the village. I have become afraid.

When I get so afraid so soon it would be better not to have any illusions about my courage in walking over the West Bank to Jerusalem. Nothing is 'well' here yet, nothing at all!

I walk on to Nazareth which lies in an unexpected valley behind the mountain which apparently I have been climbing. Down there are the spires of countless churches and mosques. I am touched by it. I am sure I have walked in the footsteps of Jesus today and I am sure he must have stood here and looked out over this white town. I descend via a large number of small staircases and through many twisting alleyways such as there must have been 2.000 years ago. Mary might have walked here as a young girl, as a pregnant women. In Meryem Ana I saw her last days; here were her first. Tradition tells us she was born close by in Zippori.

I get a bed in the convent of the Sisters of Nazareth. I am the only pilgrim at this moment and have a three-person bedroom to myself. The convent cloisters are of white stone.

Two large date palms are showing off at the sides of the white stairs leading up to the chapel. This is a very good place. For a while I sit in the dark chapel and slowly open up. I feel the love of God for me, Johanna, as if he knows me and waits for me, always. I am grateful that it is still there. But also there is restlessness in me about something I read in the Bible today. I am rereading the Acts and am surprised about the power of the new faith, described here almost tangibly, but I am sad about the intolerance of the apostles, especially Paul, towards people who didn't believe in what he had to say. He had no respect for the ways of others, not before and not after his conversion to Christianity. Through all of the Acts and also through the Gospels there is a combination of great power and great intolerance. No wonder the first Christians were persecuted when they were kicking everybody's shins. I already felt it in Meryem Ana. Not everything was hunky-dory. There was a lot of struggle, discord, no respect for people of other paths, unrealistic expectations, and bitter disappointments towards their own people. The apostles, even Jesus, are falling from their holy pedestals. They were just enthusiastic people with a thick skin and blinkers on. Just like Paul from Haifa is Paul from Tarsus. It is natural that not every Jew immediately falls for the new faith — just discovered by Paul. I'm sure I wouldn't. Especially when I look at the way Paul is choosing arguments. He sticks prophesies, which are multi-interpretational on Jesus. That is beautiful and sensible, but they are not proof; they are just ideas with which to resonate or not. The same prophesies are later interpreted for the prophet Mohammed, and that is beautiful and sensible too.

Friday, February 16

The sisters of the convent tell me this morning that there has been an assault yesterday in Tel Aviv; many people have died and been injured and I sit here, in front of the open window in the convent and look at the little shop over the road. Absurdity; red plastic blown up Santa Clauses are hanging outside in the shop window. Existence is incomprehensible.

The basilica of the Annunciation has been built on what is seen as the traditional place of the Annunciation. Under the convent of the Sisters of Nazareth on the opposite side of the road, remains have been found of a 1st century Jewish house with a Byzantine-style church on top of it. Oral tradition says that this was the home of Joseph the Tzaddik (The Just); husband of Mary and Jesus' foster-father, and home of Jesus as a boy.

In those days you could travel in three days from Nazareth through the mountains to Jerusalem. Shall I walk through this holy land? I never thought that my appearance might be taken as wanton provocation. I meant to pledge my solidarity also with the Palestinian view on the situation in Israel/Palestine.

I walk around with a knot in my soul. I should be glad that the coexistence of Christians and Muslims is reasonably good here in Nazareth, but I feel more the antagonism between them. That is also because of the news of the assault this morning. I am not happy to be here. Al those beautiful places have no impact on me now. In social habits these Nazarene Arabs are very different from the gentle Turks. They are used to masses of pilgrims and can be a bit harsh. Not that they are impolite; far from it, but I am nothing special here. Aha, the truth is coming out! Johanna wants to be special! But even so: that Jewish village with no connecting road to that little Arab town. Israel and Palestine only see each other's shadow, not each other's real shape.

I take the knot in my stomach to visit the old Greek Orthodox chapel of Mary's Annunciation. It is built over the Well of Mary, which springs up in and flows through the church itself. The building is full of the sound of water. For a long time I sit at the emerging source. Candles are burning in a side niche. A painting of Mary with a radiating baby Jesus in her belly hangs over it. It is here, close to the flowing water, under the mystic dark vaults, that my knot loosens up. Words arise in me: 'Deliver us Lord, deliver us from all distorted truths, hurt, brooding resentment, cold provocation and abuse of power. Deliver us from the miserable knot in which we all are caught. We don't know it anymore, really not, how we can go on. Deliver us.'

Well I can't make beautiful prose of it, but that's not the point. For a long half hour I've prayed nothing else but 'deliver us' as passionately as never before on this trip and it at least delivered me from my sorrowful mood.

I come to Israel because I think that the Jews have to be cheered up, but it becomes more and more clear that the Christians and the Muslims are more sorrowful here than the Jews, and no wonder, for they are always pulling the shortest straw until now. It is very difficult to retain my positive attitude, my connection with Jerusalem's light and compassion.

While I sit outside in a seat on a little square three Palestinian school kids come walking up to me. They put sweets in my hands and run away quickly after that. "Hello, bye, bye." That was consolation.

In the Arab bakery I get into a nice chat with a man from Ramallah. He bakes the biscuits and is Muslim. He tells me that he has a brother, who was shot in the leg by the Israeli army and sits now begging in the streets of Amman. He is quite laconic about it. I tell him about my peace walk and that yesterday in Illut, I did not meet with kindness only.

"Perhaps they thought you were Jewish."

"That doesn't make me less human!"

"No, but that boy has perhaps lost a brother or a father in the intifada."

Since the second intifada started last September 32 Jews have lost their lives against 500 Palestinians. He seems reasonably tolerant until we start to talk about the Three Holy Scriptures: Tenach, Gospel and Qur'an. According to him Muslims also expect the Second Coming of Jesus the Messiah.

"But the Jews are also expecting the Messiah," I say.

"No, in the Qur'an it says that they expect the Liar (someone like the Antichrist?). If it is in the Qur'an it is proof of Truth."

I won't wait for his arguments why the Qur'an is the Truth. I know them from former talks with Muslims. I know them from Paul in Haifa ("read Gospel instead of Qur'an").

So, the Jews are waiting for the Liar. I know that in the Qur'an, just like in the New Testament, little good is said about them. They refuse to accept Jesus/Mohammed and are therefore obstinate and evil. They keep going their own path and this is not tolerated by the grand messengers of the New Life.

When I take my leave I don't need to pay for the biscuits and I am invited to visit him in Ramallah to continue our conversation. He advises against walking through the occupied territories to Jerusalem. The intifada is too strong there. No, I can't go to Sjechem, to Nablus, I can't step in the footprints of Mary, who walked three days through the mountains to visit her cousin Elisabeth; I can't sit at the well of Jacob, where Jesus met the Samaritan woman, and where he was so happy with her response that he couldn't eat for joy. On that occasion Jesus was very tolerant and his heart was wide open. He had a soft spot for women, Samaritans and other second rate citizens.

In the souk I buy a tape with songs about Al Quds/Jerusalem by Fairouz, a Lebanese Arab singer. So, now I have also an Arab song about Jerusalem and not just European and Jewish songs. I have ascertained in the Netherlands that the songs of Fairouz are not politically charged. I listen to the first two tracks. It is so beautiful that I'm moved to tears in that little shop. Bollocks,

I am really getting too weepy these days, but the salesman is touched and hands over paper tissues.

I ask Mohammed near the convent, if he has a tape recorder, so that I can listen to the complete tape. On his table I see books by Yukio Mishima and Oliver Sachs. He speaks perfect English and French. There is no tape recorder here, but he knows the music well and doesn't mind to give a concise translation of the songs. They are beautiful and he loves them, but NO, they are not politically neutral. The song which brought tears to my eyes speaks about the return of the refugees to Jerusalem; about how the singer walks around the Old City and greets the people and encourages them with her music. Two songs are about war and they are very painful for the Jews.

He asks me how we feel in Europe about the election of Sharon as prime minister. I can only give my own opinion. What is new for me is that Sharon on his provoking visit to Temple Mount took 200 armed soldiers with him and he must have had permission of the Knesset to do that. Barak has come here in Nazareth before the election and offered his apologies (to get his votes back). Nazareth has said NO en masse against the Labour of Barak this time. Peres would have been a different story, but Barak, no! They feel used, abused and abandoned.

And then follows the story, told by this gentle young man. The story of the violation and the double standards with which the government is measuring: e.g. six months social work for the slaying of a stone thrower, but lifelong for the killing of a Jewish boy, and more and more. Numbers, ciphers, anecdotes. Humiliations; second hand citizens they feel themselves; being treated constantly with suspicion and contempt.

"Do you think I don't feel that? Being called adders, subhumans, half beasts, inferiors, by a rabbi in a radio broadcast. I have heard it with my own ears. What do you think

333

that does with my tolerance and good will? In 1948 things have been decided about us, without us, over our heads. Our land has been confiscated; our villages have been and are being bulldozered. In our houses in Jerusalem live Jews now, and then they are surprised we don't want peace, that we are rebellious? And now, these last months, I have felt the hate growing in me. It is not right; I know it. I won't act according to it; we must keep looking for peaceful solutions, but I notice that I am happy, happy with the assault of yesterday. Exactly the right people have been killed: the soldiers. I don't care whether all of Tel Aviv shall be bombed even if I was victim too. They are arrogant, they despise us, they are certain of their power, their money, their American support. They love to humiliate us. How can they, after having been through the Holocaust? They don't want peace, otherwise 65% wouldn't have chosen for Sharon. This is the man aiming for 'Greater Israel' and he wants to extend the illegal Jewish settlements on our land. Rings of houses they build around our towns to stop us developing ourselves. Do you know about the situation in Gaza? There are no proper sewers, no good schools etc."

When he has to take another breath I throw in between:

"Can you acknowledge that they are afraid of you Arabs? And that that is an inheritance of 2.000 years of Christian persecution in Europe? And that that fear has armed them to the teeth because they will never ever tolerate a Holocaust again. Can you imagine that that is the most important cause of the repression against you? That it is a collective neurosis taken from Europe, which you are now falling victim to? And that if they would feel safe, there would be a great relaxation? Look what Sadat of Egypt has achieved with his golden gesture, long ago, at Christmas!"

But he doesn't believe that. It is just a pretext to throw sand in the eyes of the Europeans.

"You know, I live here! They are not afraid. Why should they be? They are strong. They could wipe the whole of Syria from the map in one blow. No, they like power. They want to control the Middle East. They want a Greater Israel. Sharon's old dream about the land where we have been living for centuries."

And then the communication stops. In a few months he will fly to The Netherlands. He will visit a Jewish friend in Amsterdam.

"So you have Jewish friends!"

"On a personal basis friendship is always possible. The point is that I am opposed to the general inclination in Israel. When 65% elects Sharon, the provoker, the shedder of blood, then I don't believe that Israel wants peace."

He tells me he is glad to tell me all and then he asks me if I know good Dutch writers in translation. He wants to get to know Dutch literature before he comes to the Netherlands. I mention two book titles, which I know have been translated into English. *Rituals* by Cees Nooteboom and *The Discovery of Heaven* by Harry Mulisch. Both are Jewish, Oliver Sachs is too. But he can find that out for himself.

For a long time this conversation remains with me. Hopeless, hopeless; this is quite enough for me. How do I hold on to my light and my hope? I see the little book with the New Testament on my bed stand and everything in me turns away from the intolerance I find in there. There must be another way.

In my dreams I am under the Nazgul (a satanic black air creature from *Lord of the Rings)*. An impenetrable dark blanket of threat, malevolence and despair is hanging around me. I have a baby in my arms. It is like the Christ child in the belly of Mary. It is naked and cold and I cuddle and caress it and press it against my warm skin and I do it with great surrender. But, the child remains too cold; I cannot warm it sufficiently; it needs clothes.

Saturday, February 17
I want to go to Mass in the morning, but there is no Mass in the large basilica. Somehow that coincidence makes sense. I am too angry with Paul and Jesus. Angry about their intolerance, lack of understanding and their inability to let people go their own way in love and trust; angry about the texts with verbal abuse in the New Testament, which had such horrible consequences for Jews all over Europe. I sit here in a Christian church which holds those texts as sacred. What can I pray? I can pray the Our Father, the personal prayer which Jesus taught us. At *'and forgive us our trespasses as we forgive those who trespass against us'* I feel how I can forgive Jesus and Paul and the first Christians. Then I know that they did their best and apparently more wasn't possible. It should be good enough; I will let go again. Almost as a reward at that moment a father comes to me to tell me there is a mass in a neighbouring church. We walk towards it arm in arm under his umbrella.

Sunday, February 18, Monastery on Mount Tabor
This first unnerving week in Israel/Palestine seems to be very long. My own little problems have withdrawn into the background and the problems of the country seem to overwhelm me. I keep meeting Palestinians who tell me about their land, here in Galilee, which has been stolen by and built on by Jews. Sometimes the hatred oozes from every pore and although that hatred is not meant for me it still enters me as a bad feeling and I feel poisoned. I am dredging through the mud. Deep red mud, like blood. It sticks to my boots and taints my trouser legs, the tent and my backpack.

Adamah = earth/red
Adam = human/earth/red
Dam = blood
My walk here in Israel seems to be one great metaphor.

Tonight I slept in a place in the woods (planted by Norway 25 years ago). Everywhere were flowers and peace and only now could I feel that the land itself is so light and friendly, but above all powerful. It is a blessing, all that flowering innocence around me. There are already blossoming trees.

From the ridge of Mount Tabor I look at the views. In the distance I can see the plain of Megiddo (or Armageddon), a corner of Nazareth and countless other little towns. It is a densely populated area. On sopping clay roads I have walked here. Narrow roads where I don't meet any Jew; they pass hastily in their car on the main road, but I do meet Palestinians here. Every time I feel tense. Do I get grumpiness, surprise or cordiality?

This morning I buy breakfast in a little shop. It has Hebrew and Arab lettering on the porch. Three men are in the shop. They stop talking, look surly and ignore me. The girl behind the counter asks with turned away face in Hebrew what I want. Then comes the slow thawing when I don't speak Hebrew but English and she would love to practise that. Her little face turns into a flower. I get a chair and tea; she asks questions. All this free, because I just gave her an unintentional declaration of being Aryan.

I walk along the street when the school finishes. The children's curiosity triumphs over their aversion. A little girl passes me and whispers softly "Shalom".

Monday, February 19, Kfar Tabor

Yet again synchronicity has led me to Mount Tabor exactly on Transfiguration Sunday; the scene in the Gospel where Jesus and his three favourite apostles climb Mount Tabor.

This night I sleep in a small room in the monastery on this mountain, which pops up in such a special way from the surrounding landscape. The panoramas are breath-taking. Light everywhere. I can imagine it very well: the enlightenment of a human body, which has completely surrendered to God.

A charming French Franciscan monk sees that I am Dutch and carries courteously and elegantly my backpack to my small room. I am not allowed to camp; he finds it too cold for me. I have a nice conversation with him. Of course they pray for peace every day here in the monastery. I join the vespers, the Lauden and Mass. Two Indian nuns and three monks are here. The vespers are a bit clumsily put together. They are trying to sing but they can't. Then they just pray the rosary in Italian. I can easily join in Dutch. I feel how the prayer starts to rotate, centre and gain power, becomes passionate. The small chapel vibrates with it. It feels like an ascending helicopter. I feel how the poisonous hatred, which I took in this day, dissolves and now flows like a purifying stream through my body. A little also drops from my eyes.

Suddenly I seem to understand and speak Italian. The French Franciscan is continuing his charm offensive, opens doors for me, shows me where to go, feels responsible for my wellbeing. Later he celebrates Mass. Like a real Frenchman he doesn't water down the wine a lot. How could a bon-vivant like him bear to drink diluted wine even if it is the blood of Christ! In the morning he and a colleague drive me in a car to Kfar Tabor. Before they start the car they say a prayer together for protection and blessing while travelling.

In Kfar Tabor I can draw money from the wall and walk on to Tiberias. I sit on a bench near the bank. I have just painted

338

my red muddy boots on my picture. For the first time in Israel the sun shines on a picture. The black cloud of hatred becomes fertile rain for the land.

Tuesday, February 20, Tiberias

Lovely weather today. The roads have dried up a little. I can see little cracks appear in the clay, so I don't need to walk on the main road. The area from Kfar Tabor to Tiberias is mainly populated by Jews. Immediately here is the feeling again that 'all shall be well'. And I do believe that too, but I also feel that there is not the slightest problem. And I know that is not true.

At Porya, south of Tiberias I come over the last mountain ridge and I see deep down beneath me and far away to the north, the Sea of Galilee; green hillsides covered in flowers; cloud ships drifting past the sun and two little boats in the distance on the lake. The lake is blue and the weather is clear and I can see Capernaum in the north and still further away Mount Hermon and the Golan Heights. On the opposite side of the Sea of Galilee is the Land of the Gadarenes. In the south I see the beginning of the Jordan River valley; on the east side the high mountains of Jordan. I sit down to let everything sink in properly and enjoy the view.

I was in Galilee in 1987 and visited all the Jesus-places plus the mystical Jewish town of Safed. I had no time to visit the graves of the Tzaddikim in Tiberias and I have especially returned to Tiberias to do that.

Many Jewish teachers are buried here; also those very important ones from the 1st and 2nd centuries. Rabbi Yochanan ben Zakkai, who, after the sacking and firing of the Temple in 70 CE, kept up the courage of the Jews, structured Judaism in a form fit for celebration without Temple rituals and Rabbi Akiva, the inspirator of Bar Kochba (star-son) and the wars of rebellion against the Romans (132 CE). After the ultimate traumatic Jewish defeat the Jewish people went into

339

Dispersion. In the centuries afterwards they spread over the whole of Europe, North Africa and Middle East. In 132 CE the Roman emperor changed the name of the land Israel and gave it the name of their most hated enemies: the Philistines, calling it Palestina. There were Jews who stayed in Palestine, a shattered rest, but Rabbi Akiva founded clandestine education centres for pharisaic rabbis and so safeguarded the Jewish spiritual tradition, and like Rabbi Jochanan Ben Zakkai earlier, trained groups of people who would build up the new Talmudic Judaism as a follow up to the old Jewish Temple religion of the Sadducees - the official priests, which had disappeared with the destruction of the Second Temple. In this way he held together the 'crooked reeds' of the people of Israel. He introduced a new dynamic Judaism, that could function without the Temple and that would fulfil the prophesy of Jeremiah: 'Behold, the days come, saith the Lord, that I will make a new covenant with the house of Israel and with the house of Judah... After those days, saith the Lord, I will put my law in their inward parts, and write it in their hearts, and I will be their God and they shall be my people... They shall all know me from the least of them to the greatest of them...' (Jeremiah 31:31-34)

They are the rabbis to whom I want to pay my respect and pray at their tombs and thank them for the light that by their work has shone into my heart.

The first tomb is of Rabbi Meir ('Light') a student of Akiva. Round the tomb there is a small old synagogue plus a large complex of schools, rooms, offices, kitchens where all sorts of Jewish activities take place. At the entrance there is a sign which tells us to behave properly, dress decently with a covered head AND: 'Women are not allowed to dance here' What!? At the tomb the men and women pray separately. I sit - a little uneasy - on a plastic chair and listen to the women, who pray aloud from prayer books.

I try to concentrate and pray; but it is difficult. It is so different from a church. First I'll walk around and look. When I come back I see a woman leaning against the tomb and then I know: that's the way! When she and another woman have finished it is my turn to stand against the tomb. Then I feel how the prayer in me jumps upwards like a foal, straight into the soft strong light which connects Rabbi Meir with the Lord of the Universe.

Coming back from the temple I am called by an elderly, quite sizeable gentleman from one of the offices. He asks whether I want to light candles in memory of Rabbi Meir. Yes, I would like that. In the back of his little office he gives me a burning candle in my hand and while he pronounces a *beracha*, a blessing, I light three oil lights.

He is a handsome man, slightly overweight, with shining brown eyes, a short grey beard and an embroidered skull cap. He looks at me shyly, nervous and touched, takes both of my hands in his and says that he has seen me walking around and very much wanted to speak with me. He speaks a fast French, which I am not always able to follow.

"There are not many women like you, I respect you very much; I am so happy to meet you. You have a large good heart and are honest and sincere and a pious woman. *Vous êtes femme sainte.* (Oi oi oi, this way I will never be able to become a humble person.) *Je l'ai vu aussitôt.* I do respect you. Where are you from and how long will you stay in Israel? Do sit down!"

He embraces me and presses me to his heart. Surprised, amused and touched I let him. Then he invites me to sit on his knee, but that is going too far; that cannot be part of the candle ritual.

"*Bien sûr, madame*, don't understand me wrong. I think highly of you."

I sit down on the sofa and he sits down behind his desk. I tell my story, he asks questions; he listens. Two tears appear in the corner of his eyes.

"Peace for Jerusalem. Amèn amèn amèn! And also for you *madame*, what is your name? "

He writes my name in Hebrew on a piece of paper.

"I shall say a prayer for you that God may give you everything that you want. Do you have special wishes? "

"That there shall be peace in Israel."

"Amen amen amen, but, I mean, for yourself?"

And he speaks with great power a long prayer over the piece of paper with my name and those of my parents.

"No, don't offend me; I don't want any money for that! *Je suis tres heureux de vous avoir rencontré*, and I wish you all the best, and, please forgive me, but would you like to make love with me?"

And I immediately forgive him. This is just part of the whole thing. I say that many men have asked me this on the way.

"*Mais vous avez refusée.* You are right. Not just the physical attraction should be there, but also the attraction of souls. Do come to my heart!" and wants to embrace me another time.

But it is time for me to go; he entreats me to accept a 50 shekel note.

"You mustn't sleep in your tent tonight. It is cold; it rains, the wind blows. Perhaps it will even snow. Please grant me this pleasure."

At the far end of the square I turn around for a moment. He still stands in the door of his office looking at me as I walk away and I wave. The rest of the day I carry this heart-warming encounter with me as a comforting hot water bottle.

The sun shines again. What is going to be true of the forecast that the coming three days will be the wettest, the coldest and the stormiest days of this winter?

I am on my way to the grave of Rabbi Yochanan ben Zakkai and the grave of Maimonides, famous medical doctor and teacher from the 12th century. Like at Rabbi Meir's grave at the cylinder formed tomb of Maimonides men and women have to pray separated by a high white screen, but there are no people here. How do I know which side I should go? Just to be sure I put my headscarf on.

I put my hands on the round tomb; the sun shines in the puddles around me. I say my prayer and thank Maimonides for his wisdom. Perhaps it is the sun, the white tomb, the spontaneity and compliments of the gentleman near Rabbi Meir's sanctuary, but it seems as if I am wrapped in a huge golden warmth. I just can't leave here. Every time I think I should make a move to go to the other grave I know: 'Just a sec, just a sec longer here!' My hands are stuck to his tomb. Then I see that I am being watched by two men near the stall with prayer books and I do go on. Before entering the place where the grave of Rabbi Yochanan is, there is a tap and sink with a plastic jug with two ears which is used for the ritual washing of hands. Do I have to pour water over my wrists here too? I don't want to do anything which could desecrate this holy place. Clumsily I wash my hands and wrists, but I don't want to touch that dirty towel hanging next to it.

Rabbi Yochanan's grave is rectangular. It seems that he is much further away. I feel something cool and querulous. The sun has gone. I thank the Rabbi for his courage and ask for blessings over Israel/Palestine.

I also want to visit the supposed tombs of important ancient Hebrew matriarchs: Bilha and Zilpah, the two minor wives of Jacob the patriarch. Then there is Yochevet, the mother of Moses, and Myriam, her famous daughter and to finish with, her two daughters-in-law Zipporah (wife of Moses) and Elisjeva (wife of Aaron).

The tombs are very far away, high on a hillside and I have to climb a long way. The map is unclear about it. It has started to rain again. There are no signposts to the Tombs of the Matriarchs. At a bus stop I ask two giggling Hasidic girls dressed in black. They are the same beautiful Snow Whites as their Turkish sisters only they have spectacles on their noses. They speak English but at first don't understand me.

"O yes, Zipporah, Yochevet! You have to cross the main road and it is close to those green signboards." They wave at me while I cross three busy traffic lanes. After half an hour I arrive at the green signboards. There is nothing! Then I ask a passer-by.

"You are completely wrong here." He points exactly the way back towards the bus stop and there I go again. Why have these daughters of the mothers of Israel lied to me? Am I not allowed to visit their graves? I find my way near flat buildings and through building sites. The wind has risen, and when I finally find a signpost, it has increased to storm force. My poncho flutters and blows up in the wind. Contrary wind; I can hardly move forward. Don't they want me to come? On the way I picked a posy of flowers for them: purple bougainvillea and orange marigolds. But do they want it, my respect and acknowledgements? It is such an effort to find them. Where have the three benevolent matrons gone? Finally their mausoleum comes into sight. I am shocked. It is a half-finished construction; the roof hasn't been placed yet, but in the scorched niches in the walls around it many candles must have been lit already. It is dirty, there is rubbish lying around. The place is situated between grubby flat buildings, building debris, garbage around it. Is this how the Mothers of Israel are honoured? The mausoleum is a good start, but it seems to be broken down by wind and weather before it is even finished. I find a rain and wind free place to pray. So far away they are, the mothers, and they seem to reject me. And I would so much love to give them flowers! I stay there for a long time until the atmosphere softens (the wind dies down). They are not very friendly and they don't come close. It is already 3,400 years ago that they were buried here, if at all, but they don't have anything against my flowers anymore. I lay the little posy against the headstone, away from the wind and sing in Yiddish: "Let us be reconciled." As far as I knew we weren't quarrelling, but it seemed a bit like they didn't like me.

I bow deeply and then I am on my way to Rabbi Akiva's tomb. Just before sunset I arrive there. I am alone here too. I don't feel anything here, but I see a star disappearing into the universe. In its wide wavering tail it takes with it countless little stars into eternity.

So, enough piety for today. In the pilgrim's hostel where I stay there is a Mass at 06.00 pm, but I don't want to go there today. I am still full of the golden warmth of Meir and Maimonides, of the starry light of Akiva; I'm going to enjoy that a little longer.

Wednesday, February 21, Tiberias - Haifa

In front of the supermarket stands a small man of about 70 years old. He must have been about ten years old at the start of the Second World War. He searches the bags of entering people for weapons and bombs. I have to leave my rucksack under his supervision. When I leave the shop and he sees that I walk around with all sorts of fruit in my hands he gets me a plastic bag, which I refuse because it is environmentally polluting. In Israel the struggle to be able to refuse plastic bags hasn't stopped yet. Before you know it you are walking around with a backpack full of plastic. He remarks that apparently I am sensitive to the problem of environmental pollution. I tell him that in the Netherlands we are up to our necks in plastic bags and cars, that's why. He has seen the monogram on my rucksack and wants to talk to me about it. He starts a passionate plea for the abolition of all official religions, because they encourage intolerance. For the personal life religion can be a blessing, but for society it is a curse. Look at Israel. And although he has a point I don't agree with him.

"But then it isn't real religion," I say. "Religion, spirituality should have social relevance and it should be a blessing, otherwise what's the point? Spirituality just to please yourself, like a hobby, like an irrelevant toy?"

I explain what I mean with the monogram, but he finds it an impossibility. Peace talks can never have any results, but still Israel needs peace.

"We need to live in peace," he says slightly agitated.

"Amen amen amen," I say.

"But it isn't possible because of the Muslims. You cannot make peace with them. If somebody trusts them then..."

I don't want to listen anymore. It is enough. I don't want to hear anything bad about either Muslims or Jews or whoever else. Say something good about them. Through the whole of Europe I have heard stories from people to vilify other people. Of course, there is an enormous problem in Israel and in all those stories there must be a truth, but they don't help. They are harmful. Of all these vilified people I have experienced 99.9% goodness. Almost everybody has helped me and cared for me. It hurts me when good people are slandered.

This is actually a nice, gentle and sensible man, who has thought a lot about it. He is going back to his work. I have said the truth and the connection is broken. I am sad about that. I want to be good with people, but the first Palestinian who comes with shit about the Jews will get the same story. For the past week I have listened and learned and now I have to start resisting.

A lady has listened to our conversation and says that I am right. In the bus back to Haifa I sit in the seat next to a nineteen- year- old girl: a bespectacled Eastern beauty straight from the Song of Songs. She asks many questions about the sign on my rucksack and tells about her own spiritual Jewish path. So young she is, and so wise. That gives hope. Also the Palestinian couple, whom I had a conversation with in Tiberias had a very balanced view about the situation.

On the email I find a message of Inez P. a journalist of my favourite Dutch newspaper *Trouw*. She wants an interview. Oi oi oi, be careful, stay close to yourself and don't mention too much New Age and too much religion and Bible texts; just the essential. Otherwise the message gets spoilt by mystic stuff of minor importance. Inez P. appears from her articles as a neutral but involved and sincere person. She lives in Tel Aviv. I trust her, but she is interested in the social and political side of things and not really into religion or spirituality.

Friday, February 23 , Nasholim seaside resort
The beach is beautiful; the south-westerly storm powerful. I can hardly walk against it. Two kilometres per hour is my maximum today. The showers are splashing abundantly through the whole day, but always the sun comes out afterwards. Yesterday I had in mind to walk an easy 35 kilometres over an even and very walkable wet beach, but thirteen kilometres was the most I could do with lots of resting and sheltering in between. It took me from 10.00 am to 05.00 pm to walk thirteen kilometres!

I notice that I am anxious about the interview and that I am looking for ways to get the real message across without being ridiculed by the newspaper because of my 'spiritual' interests. *Trouw* has been expressing its contempt for anything to do with new spirituality quite often lately. I know I only have to be myself, but knowing isn't the same as feeling. Also I don't like to be so tired and exhausted from the wind and the conversations on the way. This way I am not giving the proper impression. At night, in the darkness, while I lie in my tent looking outside before falling asleep, suddenly a silent owl perches in the pine tree opposite the tent. It looks at me, turns his head the wrong way round every now and again, but stays put and looks at me, and I look back. Then I remember that today already twice the image of an owl has popped up. One time on a box of matches and the next time a large wooden owl standing in a garden; and now a live one, just in front of me; which doesn't fly away. That is a message. The owl is a symbol of wisdom and lying there in the tent the knowledge that I only have to be myself and trust my own wisdom, becomes suddenly integrated in my body. The anxiousness dissolves completely, and that tiredness? That will help me not to blabber too much and just to say the most important things. The owl flies away; I feel reassured and fall asleep.

With this speed I can arrive in Tel Aviv only in four days. In the rocky 'dunes' along the beach red tulips and purple hyacinths are flowering. This beach really reminds me of the Netherlands! Today I met someone who had never heard of the Netherlands; quite refreshing! I temporarily took the monogram off my rucksack. I am too tired to have intensive conversations about 'the Situation.' My heart starts to protest even when I climb a little hill and I have to rest all the time. This whole question of Israel/Palestine really goes to my heart and the strong crosswind doesn't do any good either. Even if Jerusalem has a heart condition, I don't need to get one! Take it easy!

The bread in Israel is disgusting! They put sugar in the bread! And most of it is white! And when finally I can lay my hands on a wholemeal loaf, then there is even more sugar in it. In bread! It is as sweet as cake and much too soft, baked with too much extra gluten. Yuk.

Monday morning, February 26, Netanya

Shooting stars galore last night. I sleep without the tent. The sleeping bag is wet with dew. On one side I lie under a high rock face with a signboard warning: 'Falling rocks!' On the other side the sea is only a few metres away. I have to sleep under the rock face not to lie in the water. Perhaps it will rain and the water will rise. No, that is nonsense. The Mediterranean is big. I am next to a few rocky boulders; I leave my rucksack packed. In case of a high tide I can climb on the rocky boulders. I lie here being afraid of Water, Earth, sea and rock. In the middle of the night I see a naked man at a distance of 75 metres dancing insanely in the water and on the beach. Is it a junkie? There are many needles and condoms on the beach. Thank God he doesn't see me. I didn't have a moment of shut-eye this night.

Wednesday, February 28, Givat Shmuel near Tel Aviv

The talks, the invitations, the interview; my head is swimming. Still I have this strange tiredness to describe it all. I do want to; lots of things are happening; I remember it, enjoy it and have a mind to write it down, but now already, after six sentences I feel exhausted. So I only write down a few notes:

Beautiful but dirty beaches.

Doctor on the beach, philosopher, but wants Great Israel and all Arabs out. Hates Arabs. My resistance remains without result.

In Netanya I am invited to a luxury hotel suite for shower, dinner and story. She is a Canadian psychotherapist with a son of 20 years old and they listen with eye, ear and heart wide open. What a love they give me and how we encourage each other.

Close to Tel Aviv I put my tent on the beach for the last time. After office closing time a lot of jogging people start moving along the rim of the sea. They smell of soap, aftershave, deodorant and perfume; I feel repelled like a mosquito. I can't smell myself, but probably it is of honest sweat. Towards sunset two fishermen – Arabs, come to the beach. They fish during the whole night 50 metres from my tent. They make a little fire, which they keep burning all the time. I feel so safe, so safe because they are here. How strange everything is.

Proprietor of a cafe in Tel Aviv. He is pessimistic. He is sorrowful; he had to dismiss two employees, Palestinians from Gaza today.

Old man in bus, speaks German. Is paranoid; has been in concentration camp.

Ordinary life in Tel Aviv. Shop assistant. Quick, efficient, harsh. Receptivity is 'not done'. Yet, when I take space and time out and will not be rushed, there is interest, openness and intelligence.

Conversations are at very high level. Three quarters of the population seems to be intellectual.

Interview. I am still nervous. I'm impressed by the status of *Trouw* in the Netherlands. Inez P. is interested and honest. She is even hospitable and offers a bed. Later I find the interview on email. It is really nice!

A relation (Ganesha) in Austria has given me the address of a Jewish family in Givat Shmuel. When I call them and mention his name, they immediately invite me around for dinner and a bed for the night. I am impressed by their kindness and their knowledge about 'the Situation'. All these people are troubled and sad, because it didn't work out, the peace. I don't feel any hate, but much sorrow. They feel that the role of oppressor is forced on them. They feel isolated. They don't believe anymore that the Palestinians want peace. They are tired, exhausted. According to them the Palestinians want all the land back and kill every Jew. The religious Jews are saying: "God must give a solution. We don't know it anymore. We have tried everything.

Israel is the only land we ever had and ever will have. We feel deeply at home here. Where must we go?"

Here, in the area of Tel Aviv, I don't feel at all that 'all shall be well'.

I have to stop writing. Palpitations.

Thursday, March 1, eight kilometres east of Lod

Walking through the woods I am beckoned by a lunching family at a picnic spot. They want me to join their meal. They are Palestinians from Bethlehem. The woman translates what the man says. He says that he is fed up with the mess of 'the Situation' and wishes all of Israel/Palestine could have clean and healthy minds like many Americans and Europeans. Their toddler son Isa (Jesus) sits on the ground. Carefully he picks all twigs, pebbles, papers and other iniquities from the forest soil.

"He is always doing that," the mother says. "He says he is cleaning the world."

The last three days it was hot and also today it will be hot. I am advised to take five litres of water on my pack, but my bones are already protesting with two. I can't carry 20 kilos, especially not with this heat. This morning I ventured to throw away my one and a half kilo heavy waterproof trousers from Izmir. The forecasts for the weekend are good: dry hot weather and I hope to have arrived in Jerusalem on Monday.

My host from Givat Shmuel found on his map for me a long distance walking path through Israel from north to south (Eilat) which is also visiting Jerusalem. Ideal! But when I arrive on the spot to link to the path nobody knows anything about it. So I will just continue walking randomly south-east on a quiet road. Down there I see another army camp. Would I be allowed to pass there? I ignore steadfastly the yellow signboards with the Hebrew letters and a large exclamation mark. I don't know what it means, neither do I want to. Then I pass along rifle ranges where humanlike shooting targets, reasonably riddled with bullets stand at the side of the road. Am I in any danger? I don't feel worried.

I started to walk very early this morning at 07.15 am. It is 10.30 am now and blazingly hot already. I rest beneath some eucalyptus trees. Go on, take a few swigs and walk down, to that camp. Just try if you can pass.

01.10 pm. No, I couldn't but they did show me the way to the Israel path. It was very close and signed with blue and white signs. It is a luxury to walk on a long distance path after seven months of navigation on your own. Every corner and fork in the path is signposted. The silence is lovely. I am alone and slowly adjusting to that sudden shift to 30ºC. In a grapefruit orchard the grapefruits are on the ground just for the gathering. I eat five. And, what a relief, no difficult conversations.

Friday, March 2

I camp between cacti and flowers. Around my little tent I count more than fifteen different kinds and colours. Yesterday evening I spent half an hour cutting all the thistles and thorns away before I could pitch the tent. This is the valley of Ayalon, close to the West Bank. On the other side I see - very close - the little Arab towns. Over my head airplanes coming from Ben Gurion Airport are taking flight.

It is Friday afternoon and I am still walking on the Israel path and I am really enjoying it very much. I still have 30 more kilometres to savour before arriving in Jerusalem. A little before closing time, towards the end of the afternoon, I leave the path and walk into a village to buy food for two days. It is an orthodox-Jewish village and I zip my lower trouser legs back on because I don't want to offend anybody with my naked legs; because of the heat I walk today in shorts and sun top, for the first time for months. After I have done the shopping I sit down on a bench and eat. On the next bench two boys are 'learning' Talmud-Torah; in an American dialect. I can't understand a word. They wear white shirts, black trousers and skullcaps. When I ask them for directions I get an answer in excellent English. They ask me if I know any Hebrew and I answer them with:

"Bereshit bara Elohim et hasjamajim wa et ha aretz" (In the beginning God created the heavens and the earth).

They look at me with serious faces and say with some respect: "Very good!"

When I leave the village a car overtakes me and stops at my left hand. The window is turned down. I see two small children in the back and a young woman wearing an elegant hat addresses me: would I have time to take a cup of tea with them? And of course I have time.

At home the Shabbat shopping is unloaded and I am given tea and, when she hears my story, an invitation to celebrate Shabbat with them. I am delighted and accept. Her husband Avi comes to say hello. He speaks some Dutch because his grandfather was Dutch. They are jovial and cordial people and I am made to feel very welcome and very much at home.

They will get more guests for Shabbat: an orthodox-Jewish woman who is a childhood friend and is married to a secular Jew. He is deeply involved with Sufism and speaks Arabic very well. Both women have babies to breastfeed. When I tell them that I have been doing Talmud-Torah in a Dutch yeshiva for *gojim*, (non-Jews) they are happily surprised. Avi teases me and says that tonight he will test me on my knowledge. The house, a single family home in a new part of the village, is in great disorder. Rachelli takes off her hat, swirls around a shawl and starts making the dessert. Avi manages the vacuum cleaner, the floor cloth and the mop. He is tidying away the toys which are lying about everywhere, but the children immediately bring them out again. There is a boy of five,

Amittai, of two and a half, Naftali and a girl of one year, Laila. She is still a baby, who goes on all fours through and under the furniture. All three are now dressed in clean Shabbat clothes. Naftali - in an unguarded moment - has found a piece of chocolate that immediately leaves its traces on his round little face and clean shirt. The skullcaps are falling off from time to time and mother has to remedy that and put them straight with a little pin. Beautiful toys lie around the whole house. Rachelli and Avi tease each other. Rachelli explains, that they fit very well together. She always makes the mess and Avi tidies it up. The baby cries. In the middle of the chaos she sits down to nurse her. A little more than an hour before the beginning of Shabbat and there doesn't seem to be an end to what has to be done. Peaceful and shining she sits there, Laila happy at her breast. She asks me about my connection to Israel. Avi hurries past with bucket and floor cloth and a pile of clean clothes from the washing machine which has to be ironed. When he makes a remark about the time left before sunset, Rachelli looks at him in a teasing provocative way and doesn't give a 'shuge'. He shrugs his shoulders in hopelessness, winks at me and walks away. Half way through he comes back to tell me, that later, when the Shabbat has begun, they will sing a song in honour of the woman, who worked so hard to have everything spic and span before Friday evening.

The four guests have arrived. Rachelli quickly puts my dirty washing in the washing machine and chases me into the little office, where I can make phone calls at ease and read my emails. All my offers to help have been rejected.

One hour later: the table has been laid with a pure white tablecloth, silver cutlery, white china, silver Shabbat candlesticks, the *Kiddush* cup to bless the wine (from this *Kiddush* cup the ritual Christian mass cup or Last Supper cup has been derived). Two *challah*, sweet white braided loaves are waiting under a white embroidered cloth. Everybody stands behind his chair and looks dressed up to the nines. Apart from me. The only thing I could do was putting on a clean T-shirt and clean socks. The ladies are wearing very beautiful hats and even the children (two toddlers, one five year old and two babies) are quiet for a moment. They give me, as special guest, an extra welcome. Then the Shabbat's candles are lighted with some ceremonial. Rachelli, as the mother of the house, reads a long prayer. The wine is blessed, the bread is broken. Avi now reads a prayer and the children begin to get a little restless. The little boy of the guests is waving his little silver cup and shouts impatiently: "Jajin, jajin, jajin!" (Wine!) The food is being served. Rachelli is also a vegetarian. Yes, they already guessed that I would be a vegetarian too. Her friend has brought a mushroom pie. There is a choice of salads, soup, warm vegetables, 'schnitzels' and chicken legs. In between the courses Shabbat songs are sung. When the children have eaten they can go to play and while the pandemonium breaks loose the adults at the table have a thorough and profound talk about the differences between Judaism and Christianity and spirituality in general. The male guest recites a poem in Arabic. He translates and something really touches me: "I (God) was a hidden treasure and I loved it to be found." They are very interested when they hear about the Jewish-Christian dialogue which has taken place in the Netherlands in the past few years; in the new religion lessons in schools, where Judaism gets the place which it is entitled to and where the old 'replacement theology' is forsworn.

Laila now is in danger of falling off the plastic garage, which she has been climbing with her plump little legs. The other three children amuse themselves thoroughly by climbing over each other and crawling under each other in an endless movement, but when I tell the adult guests about my visit to the grave of Maimonides in Tiberias and how I prayed there, Amittai comes to me with a picture of this teacher, which he puts shyly into my hand. Between the primal screams he has apparently listened to the talk at the table. With another long prayer the meal is finished. The remains return to the kitchen. All goes to the right sink (meat side) and not to the left sink (milk side).

The next morning Rachelli lends me a skirt and I come with them to the synagogue. It is completely white. Behind the white curtain that is in front of the women, I see vaguely the silhouettes of the men in spotless prayer shawls over their black suits. The women are also dressed mostly in black, anthracite or grey, with white silk blouses to lighten up the darkness. The hats are of the latest fashion and *'cloche'* model, but apart from that vary from extravagant with silk roses on top to a stiff cup, with the same sort of women beneath them. Also here the children walk and play freely and happily between the grown-ups during the service, but no noise is made.

I sit at the table where the prayer books are. The elderly woman next to me uses a prayer book with the Dutch translation of *Onderwijzer*. She turns out to be Dutch and invites me after the service for breakfast. Her husband is Dutch too. When I enter their home I arrive in a very Dutch environment. It is a little old fashioned. Of course it is. They came here shortly after having survived the horrors of the war. I hear stories about going into hiding, about parents who never returned, about a parson who offered them hiding and wanted to convert them to Christianity, about the time in the Resistance (my hostess was sixteen then). I can listen and speak Dutch to my heart's desire. At home I would have found my host very Jewish, but here I recognize him as truly Dutch. He doesn't want a new temple on Temple Mount. God wanted to live in unity with his people, but his people weren't up to it yet. They wanted a temple and ritual sacrifices. Then he translates a Bible periscope in the following way: "God said: now, if you have to, build your temple, BUT I SHALL LIVE BETWEEN YOU IN SPITE OF IT'."

According to him 'the Jewish people are often sorely tried because they have agreed to live close to God. Each little mistake you get on your plate in this way. All unholy attachments have to be dissolved. Perhaps with others God will close an eye every now and then, but not here in Israel. He wants perfect people, and we are not!'

Only yesterday I was thinking that here in Israel you have to be even more precise in your living and thinking than elsewhere, because there will be an immediate repercussion. All your attachments must go on the stake and the karmic bow is short. My hostess thinks that the difficulties of Israel are originating from the fact that not enough Jews are living according to *Halacha (Jewish Law)*. Hmm, I doubt that. According to the doctor whom I met on the beach, the difficulties of Israel were the outcome of demoralisation and corruption, but in another way. I asked what that demoralisation and corruption was and to my great dismay he answered the following: "Israel should have kept that bit of Egypt, should have taken Jordan and thrown all Arabs out. It didn't do this and now we are left with the bad results."

I am happy with my host's story of: 'Close - live in unity with God!' It is almost the same that Jesus taught: 'I and the Father are ONE.'

Although it is Shabbat I leave in the afternoon. Can a *goy* walk as much as she wants on Shabbat? Or can't she? 'Shouldn't the stranger within your walls respect the Shabbat as well?' Rachelli and Avi walk with me a Shabbat's distance to wave me goodbye. They give me a 1:50,000 map as a present. I can use it during the last days of my walk to Jerusalem. The weather is still warm. I have been fed and rested and energized. I feel a deep gratitude to these wonderful, modern, up- to-date, spiritual people. The atmosphere was light, warm, noisy, authentic, graceful. I was grateful for not having to have difficult political talks. I give myself dispensation of not knowing my hosts' political views. My days have been filled too much with that of late. Lovely hats too.

I sleep in Neve Shalom, the famous village where Jews and Palestinians try to live together in peace. The intifada has done its work here too and people have grown wary of each other even here in spite of everybody's goodwill. Still I hear hopeful sounds from a visitor. She is often in Ramallah to do voluntary work. She has never met with any difficulties there for her being Jewish. She goes there without fear. Her family think she is bonkers. I also hear something about a Jewish-Arab network of women. On the West Bank there are addresses where you always can ask for help and who can either put you up or point you in the right direction. I wish I had known that before my decision not to walk along the West Bank.

Sunday, March 4
Today I walk on a wood-and-hill-path to Mevatseret Tsion, ten kilometres before Jerusalem. Yossi from Hungary, who invited me while in Budapest to stay with his family, lives here in Mevatseret Tsion. In the evening he picks me up at the agreed place and together we climb the hill of the same name. Over the hilltop there is a fence to separate Israel from the West Bank. "Behind that fence - I hope - will later be Palestine," he says.

It is the mountain from where, coming from the west, you can have your first view of Jerusalem and it is called: 'The Announcement of Zion.'.

There it lies at my feet in the descending dusk, the Holy City, spreading out to the horizon; illuminated with thousands of lights, the crescent moon drifting above it like a boat.

I have arrived!
I did it. I succeeded.

A slight waft of emotion passes through me. That is all. It is too big for me, too big to realize that I really walked here.

In Yossi's house in the white apartment castle I enter again into Middle Europe. On the wall I see large paintings of a notable 19th century grandfather and a young slim grandmother in wedding dress; in the large bookcases figures literature in many languages. When I enter the house a concerto of Franz Liszt plays on the CD player. The table is festively dressed with precious old china and there is a feast coming from the kitchen and Hungarian wine in the glasses. His impressive wife comes home and brings a young guest. Table talk is about women's emancipation, the Holy Grail, cathedrals, pilgrimages, love stories, the occupied territories; the manipulations of the government in not giving the medium-sized Arab towns the status of town. As long as they have a status as village they only receive financial support for a village.

Monday, March 5

Today I am going up to Jerusalem on a narrow track through a narrow green valley, beside rock caves which are old graves. It is quiet. There are no people around. Olive trees grow here. I pick a fresh olive branch. I walk slowly, meditatively. This morning I took a bath and put on clean clothes almost like a ceremony. Apart from my trousers I am completely dressed in white. I am going up to Jerusalem, olive branch in hand: 'How light on the mountains are the feet of the messenger of joy, who announces peace.' I feel joyful; I feel light.

The sun is warm. Here and there a bird is chirping. Wild cyclamens are flowering. I want to push through to Temple

Mount, the *Haram al-Sharif*, to lay this little olive twig together with the most beautiful of the prayer slips in front of The Dome of the Rock. 'May Jerusalem become a radiant centre of peace!' My mission will be almost complete when this prayer penetrates that sacred compound. And I will deal with all the rest later.

"I have come," I say. "You called me hither and I have come. I have done what You asked and I have done it with joy."

My heart is wide open and relaxed. I walk slowly, steady, enjoying, up, up to the east. Two girls dressed in white meet me on the path. They stand high above me on the path like two angels from the Bible.

"Where do you come from?"

I tell my story and that today is a day of great joy for me, because I have reached my destination. "Are you Jewish?" asks one angel.

"Why do you want to know that?" I ask.

"Have you come to do *Alyah* (to live here)"? asks the other, and:

"Congratulations, all respect!"

I continue through the narrow valley. On top of the gorge I can hear the ring road roaring.

I cross it. This is North-west Jerusalem. I walk through busy, wide streets, direction Old City, olive twig with prayer slip in my pocket, in my thoughts. One more hour I walk.

Now I am approaching the white walls of the Old City, the Jaffa gate. I am entering the Heart, straight on, straight on I rush, faster and faster, to the Temple Mount, to the *Haram al-Sharif*; through the narrow streets, dark and light. Most of the shop shutters are closed. There is no trade; there are no pilgrims, no tourists because of the intifada. A sign: 'to the mosques'. I know the mosques are closed, but to be on Temple Mount would be enough already.

There are the high green doors giving access to it. But in front of it I see a lot of green and blue soldiers and policemen. They stop me.

"But I can visit Temple Mount, can't I?"

"No, just Muslims. Are you Muslim?"

"But I have been here before!"

"Since six months only Muslims can enter. Are you Muslim?"

"Yes, I am Muslim in the deepest sense of the word, but not in the traditional sense."

"Then you can't enter."

I can't enter. The most joyful and holy place of Jerusalem is closed to me; the place on which I focused the long way to Israel.

The olive twig with the prayer slip sits quietly and subdued in a corner of my pocket. I sit quietly and subdued on a big yellow stone just outside the gate.

But not for long.

I shall write a flaming letter, that, on the place where God called the prophet Mohammed, blessings on his name, to speak with Jesus and Moses, it is forbidden for Christians and Jews to pray. I shall write that I understand that it is difficult for the Mufti to give access to Israeli Jews because of the political question and the provocative deed of Sharon. I shall write that I want to see the new gold on the roof of the Dome of the Rock, because I too contributed to its restoration. It will be a beautiful, respectful, honest, loving letter. I shall bring it and then I shall wait for an answer. But now, sitting next to my rucksack, I first must process my deep disappointment, that the most beautiful and most holy place of Jerusalem, the heart of the very city, has been armoured and locked away and is only accessible for Muslims and that from this holy place every

Friday after the noon prayer, despair and anger spread out over the old city.

I sit here, on the old stones, my own heart as heavy as lead.

I will visit the Western Wall, the Wailing Wall. That is a good place for me now. My rucksack must go through the X-ray checkpoint. I show my cruel-looking Bulgarian pocket knife and my metal glasses case. The knife is confiscated and an officer comes to talk with me.

"You cannot carry such a knife in Israel."

"But how am I going to cut my bread and cheese and peel my apple?"

"If you wish you can come and talk a few more hours at the police station."

I leave the knife behind. It looks dangerous, but it is as blunt as a bowl of porridge.

I drape my large pink flowery shawl around my trousers by way of a skirt. Each woman who prays at the Western Wall is wearing a skirt. I am here on a plastic chair again, getting adjusted. There is the Wall. I feel sadness and despair and that is not because I have just been refused access to Temple Mount. What is that, in the left side of the Wall where the men pray? A God who mourns with His people? A chained God without hope?

"You have called me and I have come. Here I am, Lord and I am glad! *Hineni,* 'Here I am."

I shall write a magnificent letter to the Mufti. And, those 70 prayer slips? No, I will not put them in the Wailing Wall; they will have to ascend, to go up in the air in a light, silly, happy ceremony.

The stones of the Wall are warm and polished by the sun and all hands and foreheads which have touched them through the last 2,000 years. Leaving the Wall I copy the other women, walking backwards, facing the Wall. I take off my shawl and haul up my rucksack. Now I will go to the Holy Sepulchre Church, through narrow streets with closed shutters. Are there snipers here? No, there are playing children.

I cannot pray in the church. I don't like it here; I feel a strange heavy and schizoid energy. This time I don't get a stomach ache, like fourteen years ago, but I am constantly belching. Yes, it is a place of strong energy, but in need of salvation.

On the outside of the church a small chapel is attached with access for about ten people. At five o'clock there will be an English mass there. It is an intimate event. The sermon is an informal chat in a small circle. During Communion I feel for a moment the Great Lover with his unconditional love. Everything is well.

One of the people there brings me to the convent of the Sisters of St. Claire on the road to Hebron (*Derech Hebron*) for lodgings.

Friday, March 9, Purim
I am really pleased with my bed in Convent St. Clara. Although it is half an hour's walk from the Old City, it is so peaceful and quiet within these high walls. There are thirteen French-speaking sisters here. I spoke to three of them. They have an enlightened vision of the relation between Christianity and Judaism and politics. They are not of the kind: 'Oh the Jews are so obstinate.' On the contrary, it seems there has been great spring cleaning as far as anti-Semitic prejudices and former Christian religious errors go.

At night the *Derech Hebron* is lighted with orange street lanterns and the traffic is busy, but when I close the door in the high wall behind me, these lights and traffic noises remain on the other side and the still convent garden is bathing in moonlight. The door to the chapel is open and I can always slip inside for a moment of quiet.

What happened after I arrived in Jerusalem? I worked hard and wrote to all my email contacts that I had arrived. I have sent postcards to all people who helped me on the way and who gave me their address. It was quite a pile. That was the first chore. Then I must think about my balloons, about the letter I want to write to the people of the Temple Mount. I got the balloons, 60 white, slightly grubby balloons. It was all I could get. Just let go of the idea it has to be perfect. I am searching for a portable helium balloon filler. I walk round for half a day, a whole day. Nothing. I did find in the party shop on Ben Yehuda avenue a possibility to fill the balloons there. But then I have to walk two kilometres through the new and the old city with 60 flying balloons - prayer slips attached - to the place where I shall let them go. That place is still undecided. Who was talking about a small inconspicuous ceremony? It will look like a testimony and I don't like that.

Perhaps a portable helium canister will pop up around the corner, so that I don't need to walk through the city with those balloons for I wouldn't be happy with that. But OK, God; I have promised to throw myself in your arms. You can have me hide and hair. So if I must I must.

I have heart-breaking conversations. Everybody is suffering under 'the Situation'. There is such sorrow, such incomprehension for either on either side. I cannot provoke any understanding for each other's point of view. People just don't hear it. I walk through the broken heart of Jerusalem. I can keep crying; it was always the effect of this city on me, but I have stopped. It doesn't do me any good.

Is it a territorial question, a religious question or both? There is no solution in sight, and still I know: I am here not for nothing, exactly now. Which of the two people bear the greatest blame? To blame each other doesn't work. Who is to blame? God I'm sure! God has brought them together here! I constantly forget that a paradox cannot be solved on the level that it is posed. No, I must wait, be patient, pray, hope and be with it; until new insight comes with people who have to take the decisions; insight, enlightenment, striking thunderbolts, nuclear bombs or earthquakes. Who knows?

I receive a lot of positive comments on my golden monogram. You can see people look, walk on and sometimes return for a talk.

Next to all these encounters in the city, there is a special kind of people milling around here: the pilgrims. The ordinary tourists and pilgrims aren't here because of the intifada. The tourist shops in the old city are closed, the alleyways deserted save some children and merchants who haven't given up hope. "Another two months and I cannot feed my family anymore!" Some are looking tormented and pale and have blue sagging lines under their eyes.

The pilgrims; about fifteen in total, have all come here on a special mission either on foot, by push-bike or in some other special way. There are many strange spiritual birds; half tramp half saint, like the boy I met in Regensburg. Many people are divorced or being in the process of having one. Most know each other and I get to know them as well: Fernando, who would give away the vest from his body if needed and who is very courteous; Elisabeth who takes care of the vestments in the small chapel on the side of the Holy Sepulchre. Most only meet Christians. I don't hear them talk about the Western Wall or the Dome of the Rock. They work as volunteers at the St Vincent de Paul Society or the hospital of St. Louis or elsewhere in the Christian part of the Old City. There they get some pocket money, a roof over their heads and a bed. They want to be here, where God lives between his people. They have new rosaries and we pray passionately for peace, for unity between the Christians here.

There is a lagging conflict between the Greek-Orthodox and the Roman Catholics about a renting contract. It was in the gossip columns in *Haaretz* and the *Jerusalem Post* how they fly at each other's throats. Jerusalem tests everybody on their qualities of fusion or fission. It is very light here and very dark. A cleaving axe hangs over it like the sword of Damocles. From here the people come whose scientists have discovered the nuclear bomb. From here the people come that carry wholeness in themselves. Jesus Christ the great healer. In modern times it was Sigmund Freud who started to bring together the parts of the soul which had been split off by culture and tradition. He was the great pioneer of holistic modern psychology. Looking at the first commandment from his point of view you could translate it as:

'Thou shalt not make a 'cut-off' or 'split off' of that which is above the earth, on the earth or under the earth. Hear Israel, the Lord your God is ONE, Undivided and Whole!'

Purim starts today: the feast of Queen Esther and Mordechai, about the saving of the Jewish people from the murderous hands of Haman. A special treat; Haman's ears, are being baked and in town many people walk around in fancy dress: young girls with sexy cat ears, whiskers, tight leggings and striped tails or long blond wigs. They have angel or fairy wings and haloes or plastic crowns on their heads. Boys are dressed like devils and adult men, talking business into mobile phones, wear wigs and fool's caps and shamelessly do their shopping in the supermarket.

I hear that ultra-orthodox Jews have thrown stones at Arabs according to the retaliation law which is mentioned at the end of the Biblical Book of Esther. This book, which is called the

Megillah ends in a massacre on the followers of Haman. What a pity to end such a nice story with.

Today I visited Myriam N. One of the people I met in Komarno, Slovakia, gave me her address. There was a wonderful 'click' and we talked the whole afternoon about all and sundry, art, spirituality, books, karma, including our comparable love lives. It is so nice to meet someone again who doesn't blame the Palestinians for everything. She lives close to me on the *Derech Hebron*. Exactly between Bethlehem and the Holy Sepulchre. She has measured it on the map.

Sunday, March 11

Soeur (Sister) Marie-Yeshua tells me: "There is a lot of prayer for peace in Jerusalem, here, everywhere. Many groups are praying. That is why something very bad hasn't happened yet."

According to sister Marie-Yeshua this prayer lifts Jerusalem above the destruction which threatens it. Also today I received an email from the parapsychological Society Bilyay in Istanbul. It is an answer to a letter I wrote a long time ago, in which I asked them to meditate for peace in Jerusalem. The email tells me, that all the prayer for Jerusalem is helping well and that there is no war until now. So; this signifies.

I prepare my ceremony and I have bought a skirt. My letter for the Mufti/Palestinian Authority is ready, neatly typed and printed at my fixed internet cafe in the Old City.

I want to fast for a day before I bring my letter.

Monday, March 12

A fig tree grows just outside the window of my little cell in the convent of St. Clara. When I came here it was still without leaves, but now its branches are getting soft and the buds are bursting. Summer is coming. I look into the high-walled garden of the convent. The little rosebush has become a fountain of pink roses. Many strange birds are sitting in the fig tree. A kind of woodpecker I don't know and a robin, a different sort of thrush and also a 'hop', a large bird with blue feathers and a special tuft on its head. It is the first bird to start singing in the morning with long elongated warbles.

My email inbox is full of friendly messages: a letter from the orthodox Jewish family where I celebrated Shabbat; and an enthusiastic message from an American writer asking for information about my walk; my daughter's boyfriend in The Hague suggesting photographing me at the Western Wall with the webcam standing on the roofs behind it. I have an appointment with Myriam, the painter, whom I met last week, for another lovely afternoon chat.

Standing at the Western Wall today I feel again as if there is a wild, rebellious and brooding being chained in fetters. It is incarcerated in the Wall. It is just as stuck as the peace process. What is it?

When I walk home my heart gives me cause for worry. I can hardly climb the hill, even without a heavy pack. This is not right. I must have it checked after I get home. This time I don't have emotional stuff, so it cannot be that.

Tuesday, March 13
Today I circumambulated round the old city and laid 'the Medicine Wheel'. At twelve places in the city wall, of which eight real gates, I washed, blessed and anointed a stone with the oil which was given to me by the Romanian sister Ambrosia: the oil against fear, blessed by many holy priests. Two bunches of smudging herbs sage/thuja I burned while walking round the walls. It was difficult not to get distracted. At certain places it was very busy and I couldn't sit inconspicuously near a stone; so concentrating and staying centred was not always possible. But I couldn't do it any better.

Also today I had a conversation with a Muslim sitting in his shop in the Old City. But was it a real conversation? As usual the other person tries to convince me of his truth and I cannot say so much. He didn't like my monogram at all, in contrast with most Muslims outside of Israel. He would like to break it in pieces. He is a very good speaker and can make his opinion very clear. He doesn't try to sell me something and finds the talk important instead. He says that the Old City is safe for tourists and pilgrims. Everybody here can see whether you are a foreigner or an Israeli. Jews from foreign countries without territorial claims have nothing to fear either. Six months ago, before the intifada, everybody was welcome to come and see the mosques. Jews as well. But not anymore. He explains that his heart says: 'Make peace!' But his head says: "No. It is not right. The Old City shouldn't be owned by the Jews. We have let our hearts speak too much."

I ask why children have been put forward to fight the battles of the adults.

"We don't find life so important. The children know where they go after they die. And even we, when we die in the intifada we know we will go to Paradise. That is why we are not afraid of Death. The Jews know they will go to hell when they die. That is why they cling to life. They are scared."

The expression in his eyes is contradicting his well-paced courteous way of speaking. His eyes are tired, heavy and hopeless.

The Palestinian, who hands me my fallafel-pittabun in a snack-bar on the big shopping street in West Jerusalem, looks so tired and sad, that I ask him: "What is the matter?" He has to continue serving his customers, but when he has a free moment he comes back to speak with me.

"Five", he says, while sticking up his fingers. "Five boys of my extended family, hurt and killed in the intifada, shot by the Israeli army". It is difficult for him to speak and he moves only with great effort. His body seems to be petrified in sorrow.

"I don't hate the Jews. I really don't. How could I work here if I did?" He points to the shopping public outside. A few laughing youngsters enter the shop and order kebabs.

"But they are so different, so hard, so without worries. They have no idea what is in my heart. Nobody who enters here has ever asked me. I don't know how to continue. How am I going to live with this despair?"

His boss waves his arm to him. He is not allowed to talk any longer. The customers are waiting.

Near the Western Wall a young orthodox Jewish woman addresses me. She is very pregnant and radiates enterprise. She is - in her way - trying to give me a good message. She tells me that if I will keep the Noahide Commandments (meaning no idolatry, sexual excesses, shedding blood and the eating of un-bled meat) that I will share in the Coming World with the Jews, and I don't need to become Jewish. I find the Noahide Commandments much too easy. I've been doing that for years.

She also says that the Palestinians have no right to the land, for the Bible says, that Israel belongs to the Jews and they have to disappear from here.

"But Tenach texts are allowed to be interpreted 70 times!" I say.

"But only one is the true one!" she says.

"But the true interpretation can only be known in the Coming World according to the most famous Jewish teachers."

"No, the true interpretation is already known." It is the one of her present rabbi.

"The Jewish Messiah shall come, not the Christian one, and he shall rebuild the temple, and as far as Jacob and Esau go, Esau has conned his father, not Jacob! Jacob was good and Esau evil."

I protest vehemently. It is very clear from the Bible that Jacob was the deceiver and not Esau.

She says that you have to read it with the eyes of faith, and then you feel it is true.

She takes her leave with her sweet face, her heavy belly and her disgusting ideas.

I look upwards. Behind the Western Wall I see the golden Dome of the Mosque on the Rock; the crown of Jerusalem with her powerful sacred halo. I can understand so well they keep the business closed up there!

Wednesday, March 14

This morning I dress carefully. I wear a long skirt and a headscarf and now I will bring my letter with my request to allow me to bring my collected prayers for peace into the *Haram al- Sharif*, the Temple Mount and to bring them 'before God's Countenance' tied to white balloons. I am on my way to the Mufti and the Palestinian Authority. I am wearing the monogram uniting the three Abrahamic religions. It sings in me. I walk as light as a feather along the *Derech Hebron*, along the Zion's Gate, the old city walls, The Tower of David and through the Jaffa Gate. I walk through the little streets straight to the Great Green Doors. First I am stopped again by all those uniformed Israelis standing in front of the gates. Then I am sent from one gate to the other. They think it strange. I have to show them my passport and then I am allowed to bring my request to the people of the *Haram*. My letter is accepted by a few men standing in the gate. They said the Mufti isn't there. He is here on Saturday between 10 am and noon and they ask me to come back then. This might be a test. A religious Jew would never come on Shabbat. I hope they really will give my letter to the Mufti.

When I walk back through the little alleyways I find myself deep in the Arab part of the city. There are plenty of shops which are open and it is busy with local people. I feel relieved and open. It is in God's hand.

Friday, March 16

Myriam the painter has found for me in the Hebrew newspaper an advert about an interreligious meditation group every Friday around the noon prayer near the Western Wall and this morning I joined it. It is on a little square looking out on to the Western Wall, the golden Dome of the Rock behind it and the *Al Aqsa* mosque. It started six months ago, after the start of the intifada. An unusual lot get together here: a German *sadhu* in white *dhoti* with faded blonde long hair, a Jesus face and a drum; a beautiful blonde meditation fairy, who speaks Hebrew with a strong American accent. She is dressed in white as well. Furthermore, two theosophical looking old ladies, a punk girl, a Rasta man, a white Jamaican, a few orthodox Jews, a young Palestinian with a face which I don't entirely like. It is clear that he doesn't feel at ease and it makes his face look strange. There are about twenty more men and women from Jerusalem, mostly Jewish.

The beautiful Dvorah leads the meditation:

"Breathe in all pain of the mothers of Israel, the mothers of Palestine who have lost their children. Breathe out love.

Breathe in Death,

Breathe out Life.

Breathe in fear,

Breathe out trust."

Some people have tears running down their face. It is twelve o'clock; the call for the noon prayer resounds over the Western Wall from the *Al Aqsa* Mosque.

"Breathe in the prayer of the Muezzin; breathe out the prayer of the Muezzin."

Just after that the bells of the churches begin to chime.

"Breathe in the ringing of the bells. Breathe out the ringing of the bells."

Then a voice meditation follows on the words *Shalom-Salaam-AUM*. Four young soldiers keep watch near us, strange freaks. They find us silly and act derisively and giggle. A Palestinian boy who is passing is caught by his collar and he has to show his passport. The ultra-orthodox Jews, some of whom write on their walls 'Arabs out' are left in peace.

We are praying, aloud, in Hebrew, in English. We pray to God, we pray to Mother Earth. A woman, another Myriam, sings a song based on Exodus: "Heal the *Knesseth* (Gathering) of Israel, heal the *Knesseth* of Ishmael." It touches me deeply.

The Muezzin announces the end of the noon prayer and five minutes later the mosque is emptying. Countless Muslims with their chequered headgear, women with spotless white short headscarves over their long coats are passing our square. We wave, please come and join us! But they look suspiciously in our direction. I'm not surprised given all our strange looking people. An elder Palestinian comes - with Arafat scarf and Qur'an straight from the *Al Aqsa* Mosque to strengthen our lines. He recites in the circle the text of today. This meditation circle has been started also on his initiative. The 'Peace' is getting hands and feet via small practical projects for which financial support and time is requested.

Myriam the Singer invites me to celebrate Shabbat with her. I tell her I have to be at the Green Gates tomorrow morning at 10.00 am and shall have to break the Shabbat. That was not a problem. First some of our group go and eat hummus in the Arab part of the Old City. I join them. In a little open shop with three small tables we enter the Israeli way; that is, suddenly and bluntly. Negotiations about the price of the hummus are on the way plus threats to walk out if the price isn't lowered to Arab level.

"Don't be such a Jew," one Jew shouts to another. He is ashamed. The beautiful Dvorah bursts out: "If we want good relationships we have to have fair prices too."

I want to tell her about the playing around with prices in Turkey and that you shouldn't take it too seriously, but in the group tumult it gets lost. The table talk is animated but the Arab owner and his helper don't look happy. I don't believe they are really content with our invasion. A forced little smile is all we get. The blunt and extravert Israeli ways are alien to them. I know there is little bad behind it and much good nature, but they experience it as cold and arrogant! A young, dark haired girl however sees his unhappiness. She makes careful contact via her beauty and smile. The man thaws a little. Later she dances in the alley in front of the shop with two satin, swaying cords with tassels. She is very adept at it. She dances focused but relaxed and gives her beauty without sexual emphasis to the young Arab boys standing around her. We come and stand there too, admiring her. Myriam sings:

"Empty vessels, holy vessels, empty dancing, holy dancing". The sadhu beats his little drum. When she finishes she thanks with a dark deep voice the spectators for their attention and then she goes her way, disappears, young Jewish girl in the maze of Arab alleys.

Our little procession goes on - under loud drumming - through the Jewish quarter. 'Please be quiet' request the small signboards on the walls. And again I see the graffiti with 'Arabs out!' We try to rub it away with spittle, but that doesn't work. Then Shaul adds with a felt pen somewhere between the letters a little *yod*, the smallest letter of the Hebrew alphabet. Myriam bursts out laughing.

"Do you know what it reads now? It means: 'Arabs out, but God shall thwart this plan'." Having come at her home I am given the vacuum cleaner and she prepares dinner. The table is dressed with the two Shabbat's candles and another two small ones, which I am allowed to light. Together we speak the *Beracha*, the blessing over the lighting of the Shabbat's lights. And I really feel it, even more than last time: she is here, the Shabbat's bride. Another energy is tangible, light and dark in one, warm, golden.

"God does that. I ask God for everything."

The guests are arriving, some of the people who were there this afternoon; Shaul and Elisa, her neighbour. They bring delicious macrobiotic food. There is the wine, the two *challah* under the embroidered cloth. We stand around the table behind the chairs. Myriam covers herself in the prayer shawl and then she asks if I want to speak a Christian prayer over the meal. That is an unexpected gift. I pray a Jewish prayer: Jesus' Our Father. They are pleasantly surprised.

Myriam and Shaul are blessing the wine in the Kiddush cup together. The candle light shines on the white table cloth. And then suddenly, I am in church. This is the consecration; this is the *mannah* falling from heaven, the wine of life. This is blessing, grace and light. We feel it, all four of us and hesitate before serving the soup. Myriam has the talent to open up the Gates of Heaven.

Also at this Shabbat table songs are sung and deep conversations are held. Elisa has made paintings of the visions of a Jewish seer about Jerusalem. He also was there at the meditation this afternoon. We go and have a look at it.

There is the Old City in its square form on the four directions and its eight gates, which shall be twelve in the future. Over it the Heavenly Jerusalem of Revelations hangs over the city, ready to merge with the Earthly city. And then I see on top of this Heavenly Jerusalem my own monogram: the cross, the star and the crescent moon. From there a pyramid of light showers over the Dome of the Rock deep into the mountain below. In the top of this pyramid there is a woman. She is the bride, the Shekinah, the presence of God on earth, the Holy Spirit, Sophia. I literally see in front of my eyes what I experienced fourteen years ago on Temple Mount as the presence of God, with feminine aspects. I suspect the Shekinah speaks Arabic.

But then what is the presence of that wild, captured being in the left side of the Western Wall, just in front of the Dome of the Rock? It has in energy so much in common with the Great Lover. Is it his shadow side? Sometimes I think, that the emotional image, which comes to me is the translation of a power in the earth's crust, co-vibrating with all the prayer. But what is it that I experienced on the Danube in Hungary and Bulgaria? There it linked to the Sun and this is linked to the Earth or with the Earth's crust? With the magma in the heart of the Earth, which comes from the Sun? With the beginning of the Great Ravine starting here in Israel and running into the Heart of Africa? I don't understand it.

Much later, after I have come back to the Netherlands, there is something which adds to the mystery. The place where I feel that strange presence is exactly on the straight line running from the pyramid of Gizeh to the Dome of the Rock, part of a terrestrial pattern called the Abraham Triangle running between Jerusalem, Mecca and Gizeh.

Saturday, March 17

At the agreed time I am again at the Green Gates. People send me to the office of the Mufti on the *Bab-al-Ghawani*. His personal assistant is called. Surlily she speaks to me. She has not received my letter. Then she reads part of the copy which I brought with me and says dismissively that it is not a case for the Mufti. Then she sends me away to the office of *Al Waqf*/the Palestinian Authority. After I've waited there for half an hour I am courteously received by an official. He hasn't received my letter either. He explains that - as a non-Muslim - I have no right to pray in Muslim places. I tell him about my experiences with mosques and imams in Europe and Turkey, who didn't have any problem with my praying in their mosques and asking for their prayers for peace. Also I tell him that in the Netherlands prayer groups of Muslims, Jews and Christians exist who visit each other in their holy houses. That is new for him and I should ask the Mufti after all. I leave on his desk the fresh olive twig with the prayer slip: 'May Jerusalem be a radiant centre of peace!' I ask him to lay this, in the name of the people in Europe and Turkey - in the Dome of The Rock. He didn't say no.

I didn't go back to the office of the Mufti. I couldn't face another encounter with his hostile personal assistant. Instead I wrote on that same day a new letter, stamped and posted this time, to the Mufti, where I don't mention the balloons anymore, but where I ask why non-Muslims who want to pray in Jerusalem are not admitted to the mosques and elsewhere they are. I never received an answer to that letter.

Many Palestinians who see me close to the Green Gates are reticent, surly, grumpy and just about polite. I have the feeling I shouldn't make a wrong move. I don't. In the rest of the Old City I don't feel hostility, but, just like in the Arab towns in Galilee, depression and great sorrow. The eyes of the people are filled with hopelessness.

In Convent St. Clara there are more guests at the moment. One of them is a passionate French preacher, who feels it his duty to preach his Gospel here in Israel.

Not so much the doctrine: that Jesus died for us on the cross, but the teachings of Jesus; that you can have direct contact with the Divine and that is real religion. Several times already I have clashed with him, because I don't want a sermon every morning as soon as I get up. He thinks he has to convert me too, but I am already converted. Actually I quite like him. He is alive, living without restraint, full of God's word.

Also there is a noble young Italian woman, solicitor by profession, who is searching for her real vocation. She is a little strict. When in the morning we sit in front of the altar during Mass, she sits opposite to me on the other side and it seems as if there is a rainbow of prayer between us. It reminds me of the two cherubs on the Mercy seat on the Arc of the Covenant.

Sister Marie-Yeshua is a tall young woman with glasses, who loves camping just as I do and before becoming a nun walked 500 kilometres from Nice to Rome with just a sleeping bag and without money.

Sister Marie de la Sainte Famille is small and old and asthmatic. Often she can't sleep at night for her being oppressed and coughing. She points at my monogram.

"Don't you have any trouble with that in town?"

"It draws out many conversations."

She points at her pendant cross.

"I love the Jews; they remind me of Jesus. He was like them. But one time one of the black Jews spat on my cross. I wiped it immediately and kissed it. Poor Jesus; it was not his fault that the Jews have suffered so much under the cross, but it was our fault, ours, the Christians, and that is why my poor Jesus must suffer again. And another time, in the bus, an ultra-orthodox father was behind me in the seats with three lovely cute little children. He pointed at me and started to say horrible things about Jesus and the Christians, so that those sweet children started to look with horror towards me. That did hurt me I must say, but I understand. They are traumatised and I want to suffer it because of my sweet Jesus. Happily there came another black Jew and told him to stop. And he did."

While descending from Mount Zion, coming from the Zions' Gate, a merry black Jew overtakes me. He has flashing black eyes, brown skin, neatly curled side locks under his black hat and wears a perfect black fitted suit. Invitingly he stretches out a hand and introduces himself. He is Eli from Israel and do I speak Hebrew? No. He offers his arm. If I want to I could get married to him under the *chupah*, the wedding baldachin this instant. Like a young dog he jumps up and down the stairs to the *Derech Hebron*. I have to come and sit next to him. He wants to talk with an arm around me. I don't want that. And with just Hebrew it will be difficult.

"Amsterdam," I say. "Holland, The Hague, Johanna". And there it stops. There he goes again, jumping up over the stairs back to the Zion's Gate.

In Jerusalem - as anywhere - I get a lot of invitations for 'Love'. The worst one and the nicest one was the following:

After some introductory chat: "I am a Roman Catholic. I studied with the Franciscans. I want to talk with you. Just talk."

I want to walk away, politely greeting. He shakes my hand, quasi to say goodbye to me. But then, in a last effort, holding my hand, he plays his trump card, almost begging me:

"I've got a very big one; I can do it seven times in a row. I can make you very happy. You are very beautiful; you have a beautiful body!"

I pull my hand back and run away laughing. Wonderful! So honest. So refreshing!

At my last visit fourteen years ago, when I was still juicy and young, no man was interested in me. And now they are? I don't understand it.

Tuesday, March 20
The balloons have gone up! Under the most beautiful circumstances you can imagine (second of course to the Temple Mount). Via the meditation group on Friday I received an invitation for the 'Spring Equinox, the planetary vision-festival 2001 on the World Day of Planetary Consciousness'. A whole mouthful. On Mount Scopus north-east of Jerusalem there is a whole night of meditation, prayer, games, singing, poetry, with a central theme: 'The Launching of the Heavenly Jerusalem' (from Revelations) during sunrise in the presence of the twelve tribes of Israel.

Standing on Mount Scopus you see at one side the Judean desert, the Dead Sea and Jordan far in the distance and the other side gives onto Jerusalem, the Old City and the Temple Mount with the Mosques. A group of about 60 people, some the same strange figures of the Friday meditation and more of my kind sit in the darkness with candles and guitars around a huge bonfire. The visionary, Yitzaq Hayutman, is present as the organiser of the launching of the heavenly Jerusalem. According to him the nine lost tribes of Israel are returning in this time. They don't need to be Jewish, sufficient is to feel connected to Jerusalem and he welcomes everybody who has come here from the Dispersion. Suddenly I feel part of the twelve Hebrew tribes. How nice is it to be an outsider no longer.

After his introduction he is busy again with the model of the City, which is a square net in which he has, according to the pattern of the Kabbalistic Tree of Life, fastened GAS FILLED BALLOONS. One large golden balloon sits as the Dome of the Rock in the middle, in the Tree of Life's place of 'Compassion'. I tell him about my story and my prayer slips and get a positive reaction immediately. I am allowed to blow up my own balloons with the helium appliance (Why did I slip the balloons and the paper prayers into my bag tonight, I ask myself...) I can attach the prayer slips, share them out to the people there and launch them together with the Heavenly Jerusalem at sunrise. It involves a lot of fiddling with them just before sunrise, but exactly the last prayer slip is attached, the balloons have been shared out and the blown up tapestry of balloons forming the Tree of Life are waiting as the first spark of the sun touches the ridge of mountains in Jordan on the far side of the Dead Sea. Everyone and everything becomes silent. A young wizard from England blows his 'conch'. Twelve people in all colours of the rainbow sit on a round carpet, six-pointed star in the middle. The sun rises higher. Aaron blows the ram's horn with long drawls and short hoots. The silence becomes deeper. We all stand with our faces to the light. There, the sun shines on the Dead Sea. The desert takes on colour. A wind starts to blow. Aaron stands on the wall which keeps us from falling down the mountain. He holds his prayer mantle like a flag; his side locks are blowing in the wind. Under his mantle the sun rises until it is complete in heaven, a severe, burning, stately disk. Myriam sings: "Oh, Lord of the Universe, heal our mother, heal our mother."

Three very happy dogs come to play in the circle, gambol between the twelve tribes of Israel, on top of the six pointed star, chase each other and tumble about each other. Slowly we turn to Jerusalem. The sunrays now touch the golden Dome of the Rock, the roofs of the Old City. Slowly the anchoring ropes of the balloon carpet are loosened and also my balloons with the prayer slips drift around 'the Heavenly Jerusalem' towards the Old City. The Heavenly Jerusalem with the golden giant balloon in the middle curls up and rolls together, while it disappears in the distance like a colourful crumple and also my balloons do not always make it upwards. That is how clumsy our ideas sometimes are realized. Still I feel great satisfaction. The work is done in a beautiful way; no, not on Temple Mount, not in the Old City, but here, together with my silly spiritual family, together with the sun and the New Jerusalem and the prayer slips which I carried through all of Europe, all going up into the new light of God.

Beating the drum and clapping our hands we return in the dawn to the campfire. The English wizard from Dorset, who looks like Robin Hood, has put a large cauldron on, in which he has brewed a magic potion. He tastes. No, not enough love yet. We have to imbibe the drink with love. When it is ready we all drink together his herbal love potion. Yitzaq gives me a lift home. He is interested in what I feel in and around Jerusalem. His wife invites me for Shabbat.

Monday, March 26

Today the Annunciation of Gabriel to Mary is celebrated. I put a freshly picked posy from the convent garden in front of the Mary statue in the Lady chapel. Today I did all the shopping, bought the last presents, booked my flight home and paid for it. I fly back on April 9.

I buy vegetables at the Palestinian market just outside the city walls near the Damascus Gate. From twenty metres distance the greengrocer comes and hands me a fallen penny which I hadn't seen. I eat a dish of hummus in the Old City. It costs six shekel. I only have a note of ten shekel and he doesn't have any change. He gives me back five shekel. On the way out I find a one shekel piece. I am bringing it back just like I got back the penny.

In the little internet cafe where I have my perch I feel always safe and welcome. The owner prays behind me on his prayer mat. He tells me later that he does breathing and karate exercises every morning. Outside noisy boys are passing. One of them wears his arm in a fresh bandage. Many soldiers patrol the alleys.

The brooch with the red star, the hammer and the sickle of my old friend Cestmir I brought to the Holy Sepulchre like he asked me. I want to light a candle for him, but all I can get at the moment is an old stump. I light that, but he isn't that old!

Also I sat down in the Holy Sepulchre to read out solemnly all names of the people I met on the way, gathered on my long list.

After the blessing of the gates of Jerusalem I am still searching for a central place to find and bless the Heart Stone, the central stone of the Medicine Wheel and connect all the stones and the gates in the geographical centre of the city. I come to a beautiful quiet place in the Jewish quarter. Excavations have revealed an old city wall beneath the old building levels. Little flowers are growing there among the debris, glass shards and Coca-Cola tins. It is here that I find 'the Stone', large, pink, in the shape of a heart. Without curious bystanders I can do my work. I sit next to it, wash, bless, anoint it, and connect in all peace and quiet every gate of Jerusalem and each place where I anointed a stone with this central one, while a gentle, nourishing and heavy peace starts to infuse my body, my limbs, my head and my heart.

And now the last link has to be attached to the first link. I must bring back the Grail to the place where it started its mythical wanderings through Europe.

The Coenaculum, 'The Upper Room' on Mount Zion, with its delicate mediaeval/crusader energy and strong astral image of the Last Supper, is closed today. I take it to be a sign that I am not to go there with the little Grail badge of my mother. Wandering through the city I chance upon another 'Upper Room' in the house, which is traditionally supposed to have been of the gospel writer Mark, where during the life of Jesus, he and all the apostles gathered when they were in Jerusalem and where, after his Ascension, they waited for the Holy Spirit. A Syrian Orthodox Church is built on the foundations of that house and a little Upper Room is on the first floor. The lady who gives access to it sings the Our Father in Aramaic. It resonates for a long time in the room. I sit there on the brim of an old stone bench. It doesn't feel mediaeval Christian here, like in the Coenaculum, but, oriental, rough, angular, more ancient. I leave my mother's little Grail badge in the hollow of a stone in the wall and if nobody has found it, it must be there still. The Grail has been brought back to Jerusalem. My Grail, the green grail of Glastonbury, I have brought her back to God. Oh, God, in your mercy, heal the heart of your City of Peace. O God in Your mercy, heal the people of Jerusalem.

In the Benedictine Abbey on Mount Zion I am in the vespers. In their circle-shaped church with all the signs of the Zodiac in mosaic on the floor, they sing a German hymn about the Annunciation. It is almost as if the Holy Spirit hovers like a white dove over my head and I sit in a ray of quickening Light. I am reassured to notice that from my feet seem to hang two white cords, connected to each other below by a heavy white, many-pointed star, so that I am kept quite grounded, and I feel how the Great Lover calls me to surrender.

In Convent St. Clara I have a cup of tea with the French preacher. He looks at me not quite at ease. He says he can see the Holy Spirit resting on me.

At night I have an appointment with Myriam. Three quarters of an hour I wait outside at the convent's gate. She doesn't come. Gone Holy Spirit, inner peace, open heart. This is not the first time appointments haven't been kept and this last one settles it. Angry I am and then sad. That is no way to treat a human being. Is all that cordiality, friendliness and generosity only an outside matter? It confuses me. Is this such a superficial society? I start to doubt everyone. That invitation for Shabbat, is it really intended? And the offer to come to Sinai for almost free at Pesach, was that a true invitation?

Tuesday, March 27
The night was unruly. From my safe place behind the convent walls I hear sirens all through the night. There has been a Palestinian attack in Talpiot very close to here with people maimed and killed and also one in the Jewish quarter in New Jerusalem. You see soldiers everywhere. I don't feel well, I am not in balance anymore. This isn't just me, but also the general atmosphere. So, just keep going and don't take any unnecessary risks. I cannot paint pictures now; I am not happy enough.

This afternoon I take the bus to the Hadassah hospital. In the hospital synagogue Marc Chagall made twelve stained glass windows depicting the twelve sons/tribes of Israel. They are in bright colours, blue, red, yellow and green.

While I am looking at the window of Ben Jamin, the same wild spiritual presence as in the corner of the Western Wall is emerging. It is not entirely pleasant, and it gets stronger at the windows of Simon and Levi. It is almost as if I can sense the energy of those sons. Rabble they were! That strange presence seems to be at one with the characters of SOME of Jacob's sons. Very different from for example the window of Judah which is much more serene.

What did God think? "If I can manage to turn around those three with their brothers, then I can manage with the whole world!"

The windows are magnificent, light, deep, colourful, melancholy, gentle and strong. I feel such a contrast with the 'inside' of some of them.

According to the Bible Simon and Levi murdered the men of a whole town because its prince had been too forward with their sister, although he desperately wanted to marry her later; and she probably would have liked to.

The Benjaminites had their way with a runaway concubine and gang raped and murdered her after she had been abandoned and cast out into the street by her husband, the revengeful coward! Because he was afraid the Benjaminites would grab him instead.

I stay there a long time, pondering and looking while visitors come, look around and go again. There is someone else who stays there longer, an elderly man taking notes.

Slowly I walk back to the bus stop. I get on the bus and sit down. Next to me a seat is empty, but half way through the ride somebody sits in it. It is the man from the synagogue. We recognize each other.

"There was a sort of connection between us in the synagogue," I say.

He nods and explains that taking notes opens up the way to meditation for him. He throws them away later. He is Austrian, a guide for pilgrims, but he is here now to please himself.

"You have the air of a priest," I say.

Again he nods. He gets off the bus at the Knesset; he wants to attend a meeting.

"So then you speak Hebrew?"

"No, I'm going to taste the atmosphere."

The day has a strange, messy unpleasant energy. All through the bus ride I am secretly praying my rosary. Israel/Palestine needs a lot of prayer today, says soeur Marie-Yeshua. We almost have a nasty difference of opinion on a religious matter. We were within a hair's breadth of the splitting power of Jerusalem, but we managed to remain connected.

Last Saturday I asked Yitzaq the meaning of the word 'Shaddai.' He told me that this name of God is much more ancient than the Tetragrammaton JHWH and that makes sense. The JHWH name is much lighter and more balanced.

'Shaddai' could mean 'breast' but has been derived from 'mountain' in that sense. There is also an affinity with 'Sjaded' which means 'evil spirit' or 'angel'. And later I hear that in Iranian Zoroastrianism the word 'Shad' means 'fire'. They honoured the spirit of fire. But it also is the word for 'happiness'. These days the contemporary Iranian followers of Zoroaster, a group of people who never became Muslim, are looked upon as 'devil worshippers' by Islam.

Today I find money in the street. Shekels, five cent pieces, even a Dutch coin of one cent and an American dollar cent. That means something, but what?

Thursday, March 29

That means, that Yitzaq offers me a job to work for his Academy of Jerusalem. My visa runs out on May 10, so I could work until then. How I would love to do that; stay a bit longer to be able to work for 'The Heavenly Jerusalem'. But when I enquire if I can change my flight back home it turns out that I would lose the complete travelling fare. I can compensate it with what I would earn with Yitzaq, but then I wouldn't have anything left to eat. If only I had waited three days before booking!

The city is full of soldiers and tense police people. Palestinians are held up in the middle of the street and searched. I can still see the upset face of one of them. I made a deep bow for him and looked him in the eyes. I hope he understood how I felt for him and that I didn't agree with it. I hope too that he had a thought for the soldiers. Those two tense, heavily armed little soldiers, who might not have liked it at all to be doing this and perhaps that is why they put on such stiff unfeeling faces. Not because they like to exercise their power. Children they are, eighteen, nineteen years old only!

At the checkpoints of the cordon which lies around the Old City you can cut slices of the high tension. There the Palestinians come because they find it their duty to be present and they silently provoke soldiers and police. All parties are as tense as cats just before the fight; pretending nothing is the matter.

In between I visit the Mount of Olives. The gardener gives me a twig of a 2,000 year old tree; I visit the Magdalene church, the place of the Ascension. There are more pilgrim groups now. They walk through the Garden of Olives, visit the cave of Gethsemane, and wear yellow caps with the Jerusalem cross on it, or pink shawls and big cameras on their bellies.

Friday, March 30

Today is Palestinian Land Day. The connection to the land is celebrated and it is remembered how many illegal land confiscations the Israeli government already has completed to put Jewish colonists on Palestinian land. And it is memorized how many people have been shot by the Israeli army while demonstrating against those confiscations. Many Palestinians today are beautifully dressed in long white robes.

I walk through the Jewish quarter to the meditation square opposite the Western Wall. I see people walk around with piles of human-shaped cardboards. They are targets full of bullet holes. They have practised. From the police stations more people come with more of those piles.

On the square there are only a few people. Not everybody is here. Some are demonstrating against the closing off of the West Bank by the Israeli army. But there are enough people here to have a meditation. It is not just Land Day today, but also it is exactly seven months ago that the second intifada began. Some people say it didn't begin because of the forcible visit of Sharon to Temple Mount, but it had been brewing a long time before already. Some people don't understand that it started, because peace talks were happening and they, in their goodwill, feel betrayed by that second intifada.

Everybody expects trouble. The Green Gates on the right side of the Wall, close to *Al Aqsa* Mosque, are completely congested by police and soldiers. The sharp sound of many helicopters drones constantly above our heads. Today we read the hundreds of names of the Palestinians, who have died by the acts of the army or others and the names of the Jewish people who have perished by suicide bombing, stones or snipers ever since the second intifada began. It is heavy duty work. The names have to be pronounced with respect and feeling without accusation to either side, in compassion. There are too many, much too many.

There the *muezzin* intones the 'God is Great'. He is hoarse today. At the end of the noon prayer, when the people are coming out of the mosque we hear shouting. Stones are thrown from the top of the wall at the people praying below. Then the shooting starts. We stand trembling in a circle, linked up with our hands. The *shalom/salaam* sticks in our throats until somebody succeeds in producing the first sonorous sound. Now our sound becomes stronger. Stay in the circle, keep your peace, 'the Peace', don't get distracted by the mistakes which are being made on the other side of the square. Pray for those who are wounded, are dying at this moment, pray for those who do the wounding. 'Salaam, Shalom, Aummmmm. God is Great, God is One, Pearl in the heart of the Lotus, Holy City.'

The prayer is more powerful than ever. Curious passers-by walk swiftly to the balustrade to look curiously at the place where perhaps blood is shed. After twenty minutes the shooting stops, as has the shouting. People resume their walks and some of us can cry now. This doesn't work; it isn't good. Children of God. The names haven't all been read yet. Ibrahim Abu el Hawa, the Palestinian who began this group, reads from his paper the Jewish names: a woman of 28, a baby of one year. He can't cope anymore. He can't go on reading and he cries with deep primitive sobs. The lady rabbi from America tries to give him consolation. Heavy it is today, heavy. Even the cool composed Deborah breaks down: "What is happening with our good earth, our land, too much blood has been shed, too much."

Ibrahim invites Naomi, the American rabbi and me to have dinner with him at his home on the Mount of Olives. We accept his invitation and drive to his home in a detour. The normal roads have been blocked. At home his wife and sister receive us warmly. His mother lies on the sofa and sleeps. She is a frail beauty of 110 years old with fine cheek bones and deep eye sockets. His father was 142 when he died. Trees and people can get ancient on the Mount of Olives.

We are served food. It is kosher, says Ibrahim. Every Friday his wife cooks a Shabbat meal for visiting Jewish people. On the wall are pictures of school classes and little hospitals. Ibrahim helps them financially. Naomi's heart brims over. She is in Jerusalem for the first time.

"We are together, a Muslim, a Jew and a Christian. So easy," sighs Naomi. "So easy."

On the sofa his mother sleeps serenely. From the roof of his house we see the Dead Sea and there is a wide view over the West Bank with all the little towns.

When he brings us back with his van he goes out to buy drinks for us in a little shop. The people in the street greet him with great respect. A group of boys asks us whether we are Jewish, but without any animosity.

In the evening there is 'Adoration' in the chapel of Convent St. Clara. The Sacrament is on display in the golden monstrance on the altar. It is dark in the chapel, but the monstrance is illuminated. I feel the pulsating energy coming from it, filling me with peace and sweetness. I sit down close to it on a meditation seat. Soeur Marie-Yeshua is a few metres from me, lying prostrate on her prayer mat, hands stretched out towards the altar. I know she is praying for Jerusalem.

In the night I dream that by mistake I have been locked in that part of the convent only accessible to the sisters. I am looking for a way out, because I don't want to disturb them. I pass a large room, where the whole community kneels in worship for the Sacrament. They are dressed in the most beautiful seductive nightgowns in all sorts of colours. Some have attired themselves with colourful feathers. There is a man with them, who teaches them to pray. He is young, thirty years or so and has dark, strict but not unfriendly eyes and looks like a cross between a Jewish person and an Indian one. I only see his head and shoulders. Then I find the way out and wake up.

When I tell the dream to sister Marie-Yeshua and wonder who that man was - definitely not Jesus - she says: "It probably was an angel."

Saturday, March 31

I have said goodbye to the Old City. I feel very much at home now. I know several people and they know me. I hardly ever get lost anymore. It is Shabbat. Is it because of that that I don't feel despair and grumpiness near that place in the Western Wall? I feel power and love now and I see an Ancient of Days with a clear face and sleek white hair and beard.

The Holy Sepulchre is full of tourists today. Many people pray, many people take snapshots. Some are striking poses while being photographed in the tomb or on Golgotha. I can't bear this and leave. In front of the rock of Golgotha an African Franciscan monk dances with rhythmic finger clacking for God. Thank you, this is real. Downstairs at the Tomb stands a large company of Eastern clerics in gold brocade robes. They sing and pray and are taking censers around; fragrant smoke fills the vaults. There are soldiers there in green uniform and red fezzes. The priests aren't very well-focused and chat in between.

I leave the church and enter the Coptic monastery in the corner. Here, dignified black priests dressed in red, much mended woollen robes, read peacefully to themselves. A bird sings.

Under Golgotha there is a deep cave with a large pool of clear water. You could have a boat ride on it. I walk down the steep, slippery stairs to reach the water, carrying a candle in my hand. That is the only light. This is called St. Helena's Well. It is quiet here, cool and damp. Drops fall from the rocky ceiling into the water. It sounds so melodious and fresh.

People are not as flighty as I thought. There are messages for me on email. I am so happy; I can really go with the group to Sinai. And that wait of three quarters of an hour last Monday? That was a mistake. Tonight we have another appointment.

Sunday, April 1, 2001

Today it is one year ago, that I took the first footsteps in the direction of Jerusalem, ten o'clock in the morning from the medicine wheel in the Don Bosco park behind my home in The Hague. Today, also at exactly ten o'clock, my bus is leaving Jerusalem towards Eilat for a last camping week in the Sinai desert at the foot of the Horeb.

My pilgrimage to Jerusalem is over. Next week I fly back to the Netherlands. How wonderful it will be to see my family and friends again.

Johanna van Fessem

Isaiah 25 6-8

And in this mountain shall the God of hosts make unto all people a feast of fat things, a feast of wines on the lees, of fat things full of marrow, of wines on the lees well refined. And God will destroy in this mountain the face of the covering cast over all people and the veil that is spread over all nations. God will swallow up death in victory and will wipe away tears from off all faces and the rebuke of God's people shall be taken away from off all the earth.

Revelations: 21, 1-4

And I saw a new heaven and a new earth: for the first heaven and the first earth were passed away and there was no more sea. And I, John, saw the holy city, the New Jerusalem, coming down from God out of heaven, prepared as a bride adorned for her husband. And I heard a great voice out of heaven saying: 'Behold, the tabernacle of God is with men and God will dwell with them, and they shall be her people and God herself shall be with them, and be their God. And God shall wipe away all tears from their eyes, and there shall be no more death, neither sorrow, nor crying, neither shall there be any more pain, for the former things are passed away.